Lord (Giles) Radice was Labour MP for Durham North and Chairman of the powerful Treasury Committee until he was appointed a Life Peer in 2001. His previous books include *Trio: Inside the Blair, Brown, Mandelson Project*; *Offshore: Britain and the European Idea* (both I.B.Tauris); *Friends and Rivals: Crosland, Jenkins and Healey* ('the best political book of the year' – *Independent on Sunday*); *Diaries: 1980–2001* (shortlisted for Channel 4 Political Book of the Year in 2004) and *The Tortoise and the Hares: Attlee, Bevin, Cripps, Dalton, Morrison*. *Southern Discomfort* (Fabian Society, 1992) is regarded as one of the most influential political analyses of recent years. He brings to his works the skills of a historian and the insights of a politician.

'Giles Radice has a quartet of special gifts. He is a skilful practising politician, a top-flight political historian who naturally blends his analysis with a sensitive feel for the biographical and an acute eye for revealing combinations that make the rest of us think again about what we thought we knew. That is why this book is a treat.'

Peter Hennessy, Attlee Professor of Contemporary History, Queen Mary University of London

'Giles Radice has had the original idea of pairing leading politicians who influenced their era. The result is not only a fascinating and enjoyable read but also a stimulating one, as he distinguishes between initiators and facilitators, both necessary and often complementary in successful governments.'

Peter Riddell, Director of the Institute for Government

ODD COUPLES

The Great Political Pairings
of Modern Britain

GILES RADICE

I.B. TAURIS

LONDON · NEW YORK

Published in 2015 by I.B.Tauris & Co. Ltd
www.ibtauris.com

Distributed worldwide by I.B.Tauris & Co Ltd
Registered office: 6 Salem Road, London W2 4BU

ISBN: 978 1 78076 280 7
eIBSN: 978 0 85773 907 0

A full CIP record for this book is available from the British Library
A full CIP record is available from the Library of Congress

Library of Congress Catalog Card Number: available

Typeset by JCS Publishing Services Ltd, www.jcs-publishing.co.uk

Printed by ScandBook AB, Sweden

CONTENTS

Once again, to Lisanne

ILLUSTRATIONS

1a Churchill, who in 1939 most Tories judged to be an unreliable adventurer, was by the end of 1940 thought to be a great war leader. Attlee described him as 'a beacon for his country's will to win'. (3799432a © REX/Ewing Galloway/UIG)

1b Clement Attlee was at the other end of the charisma scale from Churchill. However, the Labour leader's effective management was also crucial to the success of the wartime coalition. (80747714 © Bentley Archie/Popperfoto/Getty Images)

1c The new British prime minister, Winston Churchill, accompanied by his coalition partner, the leader of the Labour Party, Clement Attlee, makes a last visit to Paris in May 1940 in a vain attempt to keep France in the war. (3314655 © Keystone/Stringer/Getty images)

1d Winston Churchill returns to London in June 1942 after a meeting in Washington with his new ally President Roosevelt, and is met by his deputy Clement Attlee, in charge of the Cabinet during Churchill's frequent absences abroad. (79667329 © Popperfoto/Getty Images)

1e Two of the greatest twentieth-century prime ministers, Churchill and Attlee, walk together after the 1950 election, which Labour had narrowly won. In wartime they combined to form the exceptional partnership which helped save the country. (3063860 © IPC Magazines/Picture Post/Getty Images)

2a An unusual photograph of Bevin and Morrison together at a wartime meeting. The two Labour 'big beasts' had a notoriously difficult personal relationship: Bevin called Morrison a 'scheming little bastard', while Morrison said that Bevin was a 'strange mixture of genius and stupidity'. (50498087 © Ian Smith/Getty Images)

2b Attlee, with Bevin and Morrison, celebrate the party's landslide victory at the July 1945 general election. As in the picture, so in his cabinet: the Labour Prime Minister astutely kept the two men apart, with Bevin in charge of foreign affairs and Morrison running the domestic front. (79621904 © Popperfoto/Getty Images)

2c Ernest Bevin at his desk at the Foreign Office; Bevin was arguably the most imaginative Foreign Secretary of the twentieth century, helping create the Western alliance and implementing the Marshall Plan. (78978839 © Popperfoto/Getty Images)

2d As Lord President and leader of the Commons, Herbert Morrison ensured that Labour's programme was put speedily onto the statute book. In many ways, he was the linchpin of the postwar Labour government. (78957120 © Popperfoto/Getty Images)

3a Harold Macmillan as chancellor of the Exchequer, speaking to the 1956 Tory Party conference, with the Lord Privy Seal, R.A. Butler, beside him. A few months later, after the Suez debacle and the downfall of Anthony Eden, Macmillan ruthlessly outmanoeuvred Butler to become Conservative leader. (3353318 © Haywod Magee/Stringer/Getty Images)

3b However, the two men formed a highly effective partnership with Macmillan as the dynamic prime minister and Butler as his able lieutenant. (84079000 © Reg Speller/Springer/Getty Images)

3c Macmillan, with the support of Butler, won the 1959 election with the slogan: 'Life's better under the Conservatives. Don't let Labour ruin it.' He also set in train the decolonisation of Africa and forged a new, European direction for British foreign policy. (1327618a © REX/Associated Newspapers)

3d This Vicky cartoon illustrates the key role played by Butler during Macmillan's lengthy trips abroad, when Rab was left at home, as he said, 'holding the baby'. (from Lord Butler's *The Art of the Possible*, p. 197)

4a The Labour prime minister, Harold Wilson, and the Tory leader of the opposition, Edward Heath, at the state opening of Parliament. Wilson had just defeated Heath in a landslide victory. (1477901a © REX/Associated Newspapers)

4b As this Vicky cartoon implies, the relations between Heath and Wilson were strained. Heath disliked Wilson and Wilson despised Heath, whom he regularly outsmarted in debate. (Associated Newspapers Ltd/Solo Syndication)

4c Prime Minister Heath signs the Treaty of Accession in Brussels on 24 January 1972, when the UK joined the European Community. (Heath Collection)

4d Harold Wilson, with Helmut Schmidt the German chancellor, at the Labour Party Conference in 1974. Wilson was preparing the ground for successful renegotiation and a victory for the 'yes' campaign in the 1975 referendum. (Wilson Collection)

5a Margaret Thatcher emerges as the outspoken environment spokesman at a Tory Party press conference during the 1974 general election, while the party chairman, William Whitelaw, looks on apprehensively. (80751891 © Rolls Press/Popperfoto/Getty Images)

5b Thatcher with Whitelaw during the second ballot for the Tory leadership, following Heath's defeat. Mrs Thatcher comfortably beat Whitelaw but wisely appointed him her deputy. (HIP0046904 © Keystone Archives/HIP/TopFoto)

5c Mrs Thatcher in characteristically triumphant pose. Arguably the most dominant of the postwar premiers, she once said in a famous but unintentional double entendre, 'Every Prime Minister should have a Willie.' (81695b © REX)

5d Whitelaw advises Thatcher. He was her indispensible enabler, conciliator and sheet anchor. (11665a © REX/Peter Brooker)

5e Together Thatcher and Whitelaw launched the 1983 manifesto. When Whitelaw resigned in 1988 following a minor stroke, senior cabinet colleagues saw his departure as a severe blow to the government. (78951593 © Popperfoto/Getty Images)

6a This photograph shows Prime Minister Tony Blair appearing on the BBC's *Breakfast with Frost* programme. By far the best communicator in modern British politics, Blair was stylish and charismatic, with the ability to appeal beyond Labour's heartlands to the aspirational voters of the Midlands and the South. (466649643 © Jeff Overs/Getty Images)

6b Brown could make eloquent conference speeches but was less good on television. He was the policy expert of New Labour and also an outstanding chancellor of the Exchequer, at least until the end of the second term. (490707777 © Jeff Overs/Getty Images)

6c So long as they were working together, Blair and Brown were an unbeatable partnership. They created New Labour, helped bring it to power, and sustained it by winning three successive elections. (829844488 © Steve Eason/Stringer/Getty Images)

6d This photograph from the 2001 election shows how frosty the relations between the two men could become. In the end, the government was undermined by Brown's refusal to accept the number two position. (Sean Dempsey/PA Archive/Press Association Images)

7a The leader of the Tory party, David Cameron, and the leader of the Liberal Democrats, Nick Clegg, announce the first peacetime coalition in the rose garden of No 10 Downing Street. (1181836i © REX)

7b Good personal relations between the two men, as well as self interest, helped the coalition survive such controversial issues as tuition fees, the referendum on the alternative vote, the collapse of House of Lords reform and changes to the health service (which they are announcing here). (116028629 © Peter Macdiarmid/Getty Images)

7c Cameron and Clegg launch the so called midterm review. In practice, the coalition was increasingly dominated by the Conservatives. (159069821 © Getty Images)

7d Cameron mishandled the European issue by appearing to give more emphasis to appeasing his Eurosceptic critics and winning back votes from UKIP than from keeping Britain in the EU. His unwise commitment to hold an 'in/out' referendum, made in this Bloomberg speech, loomed like a dark cloud of uncertainty over British politics. (3542789a © REX/Murray Sanders/Daily Mail/Associated Newspapers)

PREFACE

Odd Couples is my fourth comparative biography of leading modern politicians, blending personalities, policies and politics. The first, *Friends and Rivals*, was a critique of my revisionist heroes, Tony Crosland, Roy Jenkins and Denis Healey; the second, *The Tortoise and the Hares*, was an assessment of the relationships between the giants of Clement Attlee's 1945–51 cabinets; the third, *Trio*, was a study of the three outstanding members of New Labour – Tony Blair, Gordon Brown and Peter Mandelson.

Odd Couples, which considers pairings of both Labour and Conservative leaders, is painted on a broader canvas. It describes how combinations of politicians, mostly with contrasting though complimentary talents, have, at key moments, helped shape modern British politics.

I have seen (looking down from the gallery of the House of Commons), met or worked with all the politicians discussed in this book, with the exception of Bevin, who, as foreign secretary, signed my first passport. I was also fortunate enough to be able to interview many former cabinet ministers, MPs, peers, civil servants, academics and journalists. I am extremely grateful to them all. I would like to thank Jane Williams and Sarah Price for their personal memories of Lord Butler.

My thanks to Penny Bochum, Andrew Blick, Charles Handy, Lord Hennessy, Lord Liddle, Simon Latham, Peter Riddell and Lisanne Radice for commenting on drafts of the book.

I am most grateful to Penny Bochum for her research work throughout the book, to Andrew Blick for his advice on the first three chapters and to Simon Latham and Richard Heller for their assistance on the policies of the coalition.

I am also grateful to my cousin, Mark Barrington-Ward, for allowing me to quote from the unpublished diaries of his father, R.M. Barrington-Ward.

Thanks to the House of Lords Library for their help.

I would like to thank Joanna Godfrey and Iradj Bagherzade for their editorial advice; Sophie Campbell for her production work; Jessica Cuthbert-Smith for her copy editing; Antonia Leslie for publicity; and, once again, Linda Silverman, for her invaluable assistance with the photographs.

Special thanks to Nicki Applewhite for making sense of my manuscript.

Finally, I take full responsibility for the opinions expressed in this book.

INTRODUCTION

The format of *Odd Couples* is a linked series of chapters which seeks to show how pairs of political leaders, Conservative and Labour, have made crucial contributions to key turning points in recent UK political history.

Why couples? Biographers and historians usually concentrate on a single outstanding personality – for example, Churchill, Attlee, Thatcher or Blair – to encapsulate a particular historical period. It is, however, striking how, in our parliamentary democracy, it is often not one person but the cooperation between a brace of leaders that have helped shape political events. Indeed, it is one of the main arguments of this book that modern postwar politics cannot be fully understood without grasping that at many key 'crossroad moments' it was the contribution made by a combination of politicians that helped make history. *Odd Couples* seeks to demonstrate the impact of outstanding pairs in such crucial periods and episodes as that of the wartime coalition, the 1945 Labour government, the Macmillan administrations, entry into the European Community, the Thatcher revolution and the New Labour era.

Most of the chapters feature big personalities. Indeed, some involve rivalry and conflict – think Bevin and Morrison, Macmillian and Butler, Blair and Brown. But *Odd Couples* shows how these leaders, despite their conflicting ambitions, worked together and how circumstance, such as war, electoral arithmetic, the search for party cohesion and success led to political partnership. In this sense, an underlying message of the book is that, contrary to conventional wisdom, cooperation often exists between leading politicians.

It is also striking how often successful political partnerships have required a combination of talents, with a persuasive and dynamic leader working in harmony with a skilful and efficient second figure. One might call the first an 'initiator' and the second a 'facilitator'.

Odd Couples describes a number of celebrated examples of such partnerships. By definition, coalitions involve cooperation between politicians of different parties. The opening chapter is about the wartime coalition of 1940–5. If one was writing solely about the conduct of the war, it might have been appropriate to confine oneself to Churchill, but the coalition government also helped reshape domestic life in Britain. Hence the first chapter brings together two unlikely bed fellows – Churchill and Attlee. The existential crisis of 1940 led Clement Attlee, the notably uncharismatic leader of the Labour opposition, into coalition under Churchill, who, until then, had been judged, especially by the majority of his own Tory party, to be an unreliable adventurer. Churchill, however, turned out to be the great war leader who saved Britain. Attlee described him as 'a beacon for his country's will to win'. He was a classic initiator. However, Attlee's role was also crucial. As deputy prime minister, he ran the home front, introducing key social improvements vital to civil morale. He was also a superb chairman, guiding the Cabinet highly effectively in Churchill's frequent absences and, with his Labour colleagues, dominating Cabinet committees – the very model of a facilitator. Churchill and Attlee may have been different in background, style and temperament, but the success of the great wartime coalition owed much to their contrasting yet complementary abilities.

The last chapter, which is about the first peacetime coalition since the 1930s (though there may be more in the future) explores the relationship between David Cameron and Nick Clegg. The dynamic of the government is clearly only understandable in terms of the partnership between these two young and inexperienced party leaders who came together to form a coalition between the Conservatives and the Liberal Democrats after the Tories had failed to win an overall majority at the 2010 election. Political arithmetic and the economic situation (but more the former than the latter) drove them to construct a coalition agreement, though, as time went on, pressure from their respective parties as well as their own weak leadership began to undermine the effectiveness of the coalition.

The two main political parties – the Tories and Labour – have often represented within themselves informal coalitions. The Conservatives have been a combination of dogmatic right and a more pragmatic left, while Labour has balanced the competing views of a moderate right with a more doctrinaire left. Governments of both colours have been most successful when they have been able to harness the energies of the different wings of their parties in common endeavour.

Contrasting views have sometimes been represented by two major figures. Thus, although Thatcher was the initiator, the Thatcher free-market revolution of the 1980s was not her achievement alone. Above all, she owed her success in part to the support and loyalty of a powerful ally, enforcer and drag anchor, William Whitelaw, former chief whip and leading 'One Nation' moderate, whom she had defeated for the Tory leadership. Whitelaw was very different to Thatcher (he was the facilitator) but she admitted that she needed his guidance and moderating influence.

Earlier, it was the partnership of two progressives, Harold Macmillan and R.A. Butler, which launched the postwar Conservative revival and helped the Tories establish an electorally rewarding reputation as the party of affluence. Although these men's relationship was partly one of rivalry – a contest which the more ruthless Macmillan almost always won – they were able to create a constructive working combination which enabled the Tories to dominate the politics of the 1950s and early 1960s and set a new direction for the country. Politically, they had much in common and their different temperaments and skills (Macmillan was the 'initiator' and Butler the 'facilitator') strengthened rather than weakened their partnership.

In the famous 1945 Labour government led by Attlee, two Cabinet ministers stood out as 'big beasts' or 'initiators' especially during the more creative earlier years – Ernest Bevin and Herbert Morrison. Bevin, a trade union leader who described himself as 'a turn-up in a million', was arguably the most outstanding foreign secretary of the century. Morrison, political fixer and former leader of the London County Council, was the supremo on the home front and a highly effective manager of government business. Their personal relations were exceptionally poor (in part because they were both 'initiators') but in the Labour Cabinet they worked together to the benefit of their party and their country. The key was Attlee's astute management, which succeeded in keeping the two men operationally apart: Bevin in charge of foreign affairs with Morrison running domestic affairs. It was this organisational device – a typical 'facilitator's' move – which ensured that the two men's combined efforts were available to assist the government in creating the welfare state and in helping shape the postwar world.

Much has been written about the rows between Blair and Brown, the two leaders of the New Labour governments (1997–2010) who both wanted to be initiators, though Blair was the more credible in that role than Brown. From 2005 onwards these rows seriously weakened the government, and in 2007 Blair was forced to resign as prime minister. However, the partnership between the two men from 1997 to 2005, when Brown was acting as a facilitator, was highly successful. It not only created and sustained the New Labour project, but also gave the party the longest period of power in its history, as well as enabling their government to introduce significant economic and social reforms.

The chapter on entry to the European Community (EC) shows how crucial historical events can also be influenced by party leaders acting not in partnership but in competition, but with both contributing to a successful result. British membership of the EC, probably the most far-reaching development in postwar foreign policy, was shaped both by the Tories and the Labour Party. It was the Conservative prime minister, Edward Heath, who took Britain into the EC. In opposition, the pragmatic Labour leader,

Harold Wilson, who was ambivalent over Europe, rejected what he called 'Tory terms'. But, in government, Wilson renegotiated the terms (though critics argued that the renegotiation was a cosmetic exercise), won the subsequent referendum (initially opposed by Heath) and thus ensured that Britain remained in the European Community.

There are a number of ways to approach the history of modern politics. It can be described in terms of broad themes, such as, for example, the rise of welfare and affluence, the decline of deference, the waning of British power. Another way is more biographical, bringing together personality, policy and politics either in the form of individual biography or, as in this book, of pairings or groupings of politicians.

Odd Couples, which is about pairings, seeks to show how often politicians, working together, have helped to shape key moments of recent political history. It describes the often contrasting personalities involved in such pairings and how necessity brought them together in constructive partnership. The following chapters analyse the background, upbringing and development of the different pairs of leaders; to what extent they were 'initiators' or 'facilitators'; the formation and working of partnerships; and how these have contributed to key historical moments.

1

FINEST HOURS
Churchill and Attlee

Winston Churchill and Clement Attlee formed one of the most famous partnerships in British political history. Two of the country's greatest twentieth-century politicians, they came together to form the historic wartime coalition which in 1940 saved the country from catastrophic defeat and then stayed in office until the war in Europe was eventually won.

Only Churchill, the prime minister, and Attlee, leader of the Labour Party, deputy prime minister from 1942 (and later prime minister of the 1945–51 Labour governments) served in the War Cabinet throughout the coalition government's life. Churchill was the war supremo, the towering figure, and the inspiring national talisman and initiator. Attlee described him as 'the greatest leader in war this country has ever known', who in 1940 stood 'like a beacon for his country's will to win'.[1]

Attlee was at the other end of the charisma scale from Churchill, so much so that one of his most fervent admirers, Peter Hennessy, has written that he had 'all the presence of a gerbil'.[2] However, the Labour leader was also crucial to the success of the coalition. In many ways, he was the linchpin of the administration. As well as being a member of the War Cabinet, and deputy prime minister, he was also a member of the two other key wartime committees, the Defence Committee and the Lord President's Committee; and, during Churchill's long absences abroad, he proved to be a highly competent acting prime minister. Equally important was his role as political fixer. One of his biographers wrote that 'He had to conciliate Conservative backbenchers, reassure Labour, mediate between Labour and Conservative ministers and even between quarrelling Labour ministers, and manage Churchill's political and personal idiosyncrasies.'[3] Like all great facilitators, Attlee was, above all, adept at keeping all the balls in the air at once.

Churchill's reputation rightly rests on his superb war leadership, Attlee's on his role as the prime minister of the postwar Labour governments.[4] By 1945, Churchill's name had become synonymous with British pride in standing alone against Hitler's Germany. Attlee, the 'sheep in sheep's clothing', emerged from Churchill's shadow after the war as the leader who founded Britain's welfare state and National Health Service.

The two men, both brought up in Victoria's reign, were very different in background, experience, temperament and style. Churchill came from a famous aristocratic family. He was born on 30 November 1874 at the ducal seat, Blenheim Palace, the Vanbrugh pile named after one of the great continental victories of Churchill's soldier statesman ancestor, John, Duke of Marlborough.

Churchill's upbringing was not a happy one. He was virtually ignored by his father, the celebrated but erratic Conservative politician, Lord Randolph Churchill, and often neglected by his mother, the striking American socialite, Jennie Jerome. His education at prep school and at Harrow was patchy. Apparently not considered bright enough for university and the law, he only got into the Royal Military College at Sandhurst at the third attempt, though he passed out in eighth place.

However, from the first, Churchill saw himself as 'a man of destiny'. His escapades in Cuba, on the fringes of empire on the Indian North-West Frontier and in the Sudan, where, as a cavalry officer, he took part in a celebrated charge at the Battle of Omdurman, and in the South Africa war where he escaped after being taken prisoner by the Boers, satisfied both his restless desire for adventure and glory and provided raw material for his numerous articles and books.[5] They also made him into a national celebrity by the age of 25 and marked him out as an outstanding candidate for Parliament, to which he was duly returned as Conservative MP for Oldham at the general election of 1900.

It was almost inevitable that the son of Randolph Churchill should want to go into politics. It was not so certain that it would be as a Conservative. In April 1897 Churchill wrote confidently to his mother from India; 'I am a Liberal in all but name [...] were it not for Home Rule – to which I will never consent – I would enter Parliament as a Liberal.'[6] His Liberal inclinations, especially his support for free trade and for action to reduce poverty, were strengthened during the life of the 1900 parliament. There may also have been an element of opportunism. For a rising young politician it is usually preferable to belong to a party on the way up (the Liberals won an overwhelming victory at the 1906 election) rather than a party on the way down (after resigning from office in 1905, the Tories spent a decade in opposition). Whatever the motive, in 1904 Churchill dramatically crossed the floor of the House and took his seat on the Liberal benches, next to the radical star David Lloyd George, later prime minister, who would become a close ally.

Churchill's conversion to the Liberal cause marked the start of a glittering ministerial career. Over the next decade, he rose rapidly, serving as a reforming president of the Board of Trade, the youngest ever home secretary and a notably energetic First Lord of the Admiralty. However, despite his fascination with all things military, World War I put a temporary halt to his upward political trajectory, when the failure of the Dardanelles campaign which he had advocated and the formation of the first wartime coalition led to his resignation (in November 1915) from the government. Two years later, Churchill was rescued by Lloyd George, premier of the second coalition and Britain's wartime leader, who made him minister of munitions. After the war, he served first as minister of war and then secretary of state for the colonies.

In the early 1920s the collapse of the Lloyd George coalition, the split in the Liberal Party and the rise of the Labour Party created a major problem for Churchill, which he resolved by rejoining the Conservative Party – 'reratting' as he once described it. At the October 1924 election, which the Conservatives won, Churchill stood for Epping, as a 'Constitutionalist' candidate with the backing of the local Conservative Association and was returned to Parliament with a comfortable margin. To his surprise, the new Tory prime minister, Stanley Baldwin, rewarded him for his switch of allegiance with the mouth-watering prize of the Treasury. Churchill proved to be a cautious and orthodox chancellor of the Exchequer, for which he was criticised by the celebrated economist John Maynard Keynes, especially for his decision to realign the pound with the gold standard.

If Churchill had skilfully navigated the hazards of the 1920s, he was less successful in the 1930s, during which he acquired a reputation for being reckless and erratic. His brilliance as both a speaker and a writer was acknowledged across the political spectrum, but his judgement was often considered faulty. In the early 1930s his diehard position on India (aptly described by Roy Jenkins as 'the dead end of trying to preserve the Raj of 1896'[7]) put him outside the mainstream of the Conservative Party, while his ultra-royalist stance during the 1936 abdication crisis isolated him from most MPs. As a consequence, his percipient warnings about the menace of Hitler, his courageous opposition to Prime Minister Neville Chamberlain's policy of appeasement and his eloquent and well-informed speeches on the need to build up British defences, especially of aircraft, were not heeded. Indeed, if Churchill had retired (he was 66 in 1940) or had died before the war, his reputation would have been that of a highly gifted maverick who had failed to fulfil his promise.[8]

Clement Attlee was born eight years later than Churchill, on 3 January 1883 in the London suburb of Putney, the seventh child and fourth son in a family of eight. Clement described the Attlees 'as a typical family of the professional class brought up in the atmosphere of Victorian England'.[9] His father was a leading City solicitor and his mother came from a family of doctors. They provided their children with a comfortable and loving home, buttressed by the familiar routines, games and seaside and country holidays of the southern middle class.

Until he was nine, Clement, painfully shy and small for his age, was taught at home by his cultured mother, learning poetry by heart and reading books from his father's library. After prep school and Haileybury School (where, like Churchill, he enjoyed English and History and was also an outstanding cadet in the school corps), he went up to University College, Oxford in October 1901. He loved his time at Oxford, read widely around his special historical subject, the Italian Renaissance, and achieved a good second-class degree. One of his tutors wrote about him, 'He is level headed, industrious, dependable with no brilliance of style or literary gifts but with excellent sound judgment.'[10] These were qualities which he was to deploy so effectively as Churchill's deputy and later as Labour's prime minister.

Attlee's path into politics was far slower and his experience of ministerial office far less varied or exalted than that of Churchill. He came down from Oxford in 1904 with little idea of what he wanted to do. He was called to the Bar in 1906 but his interest in the law was, as he later admitted, 'very tepid'.[11] However, in the autumn of 1907, he took over the running of Haileybury House, a boys' club in Stepney. By bringing him face to face with the poverty, slum housing and precarious employment of London's East End, this decision transformed his life. Some time during the later part of 1907, Attlee began to call himself a socialist, a dramatic step for someone of his background and temperament. In many ways, he was and remained throughout his life a conventional member of the professional classes. As his earliest biographer put it, 'it was a desire, not to destroy his social background, but to extend to all the benefits that he himself had enjoyed which impelled him.'[12]

Before the 1914–18 war, Attlee saw himself as not much more than a committed social worker and a rank-and-file member of the Independent Labour Party (ILP), with no greater ambition than perhaps one day being elected to the local council. However, his years in Stepney had given him a close knowledge of working-class life and the prospect, should he wish it, of a firm political base in the East End.

The war was a turning point in Attlee's life. Serving in the army at Gallipoli in 1915, in Mesopotamia (now Iraq) in 1916 and in the last stages of the war on the Western Front, Major Attlee proved himself a reliable and courageous officer, capable of leading his men in action without panache but effectively and humanely. Despite his innate shyness, he had become a far more self-confident person. With the new prominence of the Labour Party as a result of the war and with the internal party reforms introduced by Arthur Henderson, opportunities were opening up for middle-class supporters like Attlee. At the end of 1919, he became mayor of Stepney and in November 1922 he was elected as MP for Limehouse.

During the 1920s, Labour replaced the Liberals as the main opposition party and, under the charismatic leadership of Ramsey MacDonald, twice formed a minority government. Attlee's ministerial progress was steady rather than spectacular. In the 1924 government he became under secretary at the War Office, an appointment which was welcomed by the Conservative-supporting newspaper, the *Morning Post:* 'For the War Office, Major Attlee has the recommendation of excellent war service. He was not a conscientious objector.'[13] In MacDonald's second minority government, Attlee was first appointed chancellor of the Duchy of Lancaster in May 1930 and in March 1931, as the economic situation deteriorated, was moved sideways to become postmaster general.

Crucially, in the political crisis of 1931, despite having been MacDonald's parliamentary private secretary (PPS), he did not follow MacDonald into coalition with the Tories and Liberals. Paradoxically, it was Labour's disastrous defeat at the October 1931 election that propelled Attlee, until then a relatively junior figure, into the leadership of the party. While all his potential rivals, except George Lansbury and Stafford Cripps, lost their seats, Clement Attlee, reaping the reward of his close relationship with his constituency, managed to hold on by 551 votes. Lansbury, Attlee and Cripps formed a curious triumvirate, with Lansbury as Labour leader. This lasted until the 1935 party conference, when, following a fierce attack for his pacifism by the trade union leader, Ernest Bevin, Lansbury was forced to resign. Attlee led the party into the 1935 election on a temporary basis: Labour won 154 seats, a big improvement on 1931 but still far behind the National Government's total of 432. In the leadership election which followed, Attlee comfortably defeated Herbert Morrison and Arthur Greenwood (who became deputy leader). The key to his victory was that, after MacDonald, Labour MPs did not want a charismatic leader but rather somebody who would act more as a competent and loyal chairman of a committee.

However, as the international situation worsened, some MPs and activists began to argue for a less passive, more inspiring leader. It was not Attlee, but Bevin, as chairman of the Trades Union Congress (TUC), and Hugh Dalton, as chairman of the Labour Party, who together took the initiative in moving the party away from pacifism and towards re-armament and resistance to dictators. By 1939, there was still a widespread feeling that Attlee was a stop-gap figure who survived only because the party could not agree on a replacement.

It was the coming of the war which not only transformed the prospects of both Churchill and Attlee but also brought the two men together. The weeks immediately following the Munich crisis were arguably the most difficult for Churchill of any time during the 1930s. Yet, within 18 months, he had become prime minister. Following his powerful attack in the Commons debate (3–6 October 1938) on Chamberlain's Munich settlement with Hitler, which Churchill denounced as a total and unmitigated defeat, and his decision to abstain at the end of the debate, he faced serious opposition within his constituency party, with hostile resolutions being passed by several branches. It needed a general meeting of party members – at which a resolution in support of the sitting MP was carried with 100 votes in favour but with a significant minority of 44 against – to shore up his political base.

However, in March 1939, Hitler's annexation of the rump of Czechoslovakia vindicated Churchill's warnings about Nazi aggression and greatly strengthened his position not only with his constituents but also with parliamentary and public opinion. When Hitler invaded Poland on

1 September 1939, Chamberlain, after some equivocation, declared war on Germany. Now that war had come, it was inevitable that the Prime Minister would have to invite Churchill to join the government. He offered him his old job as First Lord of the Admiralty, with a seat in the War Cabinet. In the words of the signal flashed to the Fleet, 'Winston is back'.

If the coming of the war transformed Churchill's prospects, it could also be said to have saved Attlee's leadership of the Labour Party. Had a peacetime general election been held in late 1939 or in 1940, Labour would almost certainly have been defeated again and Attlee would probably have been replaced as party leader. As it was, at the parliamentary party meeting of 15 November 1939, he had to face the indignity of having three of his colleagues (Greenwood, Morrison and Dalton) nominated to succeed him. Although all three declined to stand (Greenwood on the grounds that 'a contest would encourage Hitler', Morrison that, given Attlee's recent prostate operation, a contest would not be 'kindly or generous', and Dalton that he did not wish to be a candidate), there was clearly no great enthusiasm for Attlee.[14] Typically, when Attlee was asked about a contest for the leadership, he replied that he would never regard as disloyal the nomination of a colleague to replace him. A beneficial effect of his modest, collegiate style of leadership was that it allowed other politicians, arguably in some respects more able than him, to flourish and prosper while also leaving him in place as leader.

At the start of the war, Labour refused to participate in a Chamberlain government. This was no longer for pacifist reasons but because the party distrusted Chamberlain and did not think he would make an effective war leader. Under Attlee, Labour, with the support of most of the parliamentary party and of the unions, had gradually become an anti-appeasement, patriotic party, ready to ally with dissident Tories, such as Churchill and Anthony Eden, and with the small Liberal Party to replace Chamberlain and to provide effective resistance to Hitler. Indeed, the relationship which Attlee and Greenwood had built up with Churchill in the years leading up to the war was to prove an important factor in the formation of the wartime coalition.

Following Hitler's rapid conquest of Poland and the sharing of the spoils with the Soviet Union, the first six months of the conflict was the period of the 'phoney war', with the British and the French standing on the defensive in the west. Then events suddenly speeded up. On 4 April 1940, Chamberlain foolishly told the Conservative Party that Hitler had 'missed the bus'. Four days later Hitler replied by invading two neutral countries, Denmark and Norway. The bungled and ill-coordinated Allied attempt by sea and land to check the German invasion of Norway ended in failure and retreat. Despite Churchill's responsibility as First Lord of the Admiralty and also as acting chairman of the so-called Military Co-ordination Committee, the Norwegian fiasco led in the end not to Churchill's resignation but to the fall of the Chamberlain government and the replacement of Chamberlain by Churchill.

At the beginning of May, it had been Attlee who, as leader of the opposition, took the initiative by calling a two-day debate on the conduct of the war. The Liberal MP, and later leader, Clement Davies, tried to persuade him to put down a motion of no-confidence, which, if carried, would lead to the fall of the government. But Attlee's view was that rebel Tories would be more likely to revolt if the debate took place on the more innocuous-sounding motion 'for the adjournment of the House', which allowed a debate without necessarily requiring a vote. On the back of such a procedural device was launched the most dramatic and far-reaching in its political consequences of any parliamentary debate in the twentieth century.

On Tuesday 7 May 1940 at 3.48 p.m., Chamberlain opened the debate with an unconvincing defence of his government's handling of the Norwegian operations. Attlee followed Chamberlain. He made two crucial points. First, his criticism of the government included its overall direction of policy:

The people find these men, who have been consistently wrong in their judgment of events, the same people who thought that Hitler would not attack Czechoslovakia, who thought Hitler could be appeased, seem not to have realized that Hitler would attack Norway. They see everywhere a failure of grip, a failure of drive, not only in the field of defence and foreign policy but in industry.[15]

He then turned to the Tory MPs whose votes would decide the outcome and bluntly reminded them of their patriotic duty:

They have been content, week after week with ministers whom they knew were failures. They have allowed their loyalty to the chief whip to overcome their loyalty to the real needs of the country. I say that the House of Commons must take its full responsibility. I say that there is a widespread feeling in this country not that we shall lose the war [...] but that to win the war, we want different people at the helm from those who have led us into it.[16]

As Attlee had foreseen, the debate then led to damaging criticism on Chamberlain from his own side while the Conservative MP for Birmingham Sparkbrook, Leo Amery, quoted Oliver Cromwell's famous injunction to the Long Parliament: 'You have sat here too long for any good you have been doing. Depart, I say, and let us have done with you. In the name of God, go.'[17]

That evening and the next morning, the lobbies and corridors of Westminster were abuzz with gossip, rumour and plots. The question facing the Labour Party was whether or not to press the debate to a vote. If a substantial number of Tories could be persuaded either to vote with Labour and the Liberals or to abstain, Chamberlain's position would become untenable. However, if only a handful came out in revolt (as had happened after the Munich debate), the Prime Minister's hand would actually be strengthened.

The second day continued to go against the government. For Labour, Morrison concluded a powerful speech by revealing that Labour intended to divide the House of Commons at the end of the debate, in effect turning the adjournment motion into a vote of censure. Replying to the debate on behalf of the government, Churchill had an exceptionally difficult task. As Harold Nicolson, an enthusiastic Churchill supporter, noted:

> on the one hand he has to defend the services; on the other, he has to be loyal to the Prime Minister [...] He manages with extraordinary force of personality to do both those things with absolute loyalty and apparent sincerity, while demonstrating by his brilliance that he really has nothing to do with this confused and timid gang.[18]

The result of the division was a devastating blow to Chamberlain's administration. On the face of it, it still had a comfortable majority. But the government's normal majority was slashed from a possible 213 to 81. Forty-one government supporters had voted in the Labour lobby and there were about 60 deliberate abstentions. At a time of grave national crisis and with Hitler about to attack in the west, the Tory revolt had gone far beyond the usual anti-appeasement rebels. Hugh Dalton wrote in his memoirs: 'When I went into our lobby it seemed to be full of young Conservatives in uniform – Khaki, Navy blue and Air Force blue all intermingled.'[19] Chamberlain left the chamber ashen faced; his first reaction was that, in view of the strong feelings in the House against him, he would have to resign.[20]

Two meetings at 10 Downing Street the following day (9 May) were crucial to the fall of Chamberlain and the accession of Churchill to the premiership. At the first meeting, which was composed of Chamberlain, Churchill, Lord Halifax and the Conservative chief whip, David Margesson, Chamberlain made it clear that he believed that it was essential to bring Labour in and that, if the Labour leaders maintained their refusal to serve under him, he would have to resign. He added that Churchill (with his anti-union reputation going back to the General Strike) might find it more difficult to get Labour support than Halifax.

According to an account by the Foreign Office permanent under secretary who saw Halifax immediately upon his return from 10 Downing Street, Halifax replied that, as a prime minister in the Lords he would neither be in charge of the war nor the leader of the Commons. He would be a cipher with all the responsibility and none of the power. Churchill would, therefore, be the better choice.[21]

In the late afternoon, it was the Labour Party's turn. At this second meeting, Chamberlain, Churchill and Halifax sat on one side of the cabinet table, while Attlee and his deputy, Arthur Greenwood, were on the other. Attlee's version of the meeting was that Chamberlain 'was hardly worried and seemed to think he could carry on'. Attlee was brutally frank: 'Mr. Prime Minister, the fact is our party won't come in under you. Our party won't have you and I think I am right in saying that the country won't have you either.' When asked whether Labour would serve under any other Conservative, he replied that he thought 'yes' but, on both issues, he would consult the Labour National Executive which was meeting at Bournemouth before the opening of the Labour Party conference and would telephone through the answers the following day (10 May).[22]

At dawn on 10 May, the outside world intervened on the closed world of Westminster. The news came through that Hitler had invaded Belgium and the Netherlands. Chamberlain was tempted to use the German attack as an excuse to delay his resignation, but the Lord Privy Seal, Sir Kingsley Wood, Churchill's new supporter, told him that, on the contrary, it made it all the more essential that he should resign and that there should be a coalition government. The Labour Party held firm. Before leaving by train for Bournemouth for the executive meeting, Attlee and Greenwood issued a statement calling for an urgent and drastic reconstruction of the government. The Bournemouth meeting, which took place in a smoke-filled hotel basement room, reaffirmed its refusal to serve under Chamberlain but unanimously agreed that it should join a national government under a new prime minister.

Before leaving for London to negotiate his party's way into government, Attlee telephoned Chamberlain's private secretary at No 10 from the hotel call box and read out Labour's resolution to him. Attlee's message was given to Chamberlain, who was presiding over a meeting of the War Cabinet. He repeated Labour's reply to his Cabinet colleagues and announced that, 'in light of this answer, he had reached the conclusion that the right course was that he should at once tender his resignation to the King.'[23] Chamberlain then went to the Palace, handed in his resignation and advised the King to send for Churchill. Just after six o'clock on the evening of 10 May 1940, the King asked Churchill to form a government.

Churchill told the King that he would immediately send for the leaders of the opposition parties to try and form a national administration. Thus it was that, when Attlee and Greenwood arrived at Waterloo Station from Bournemouth, they were met by a naval officer who immediately drove the two men to see the new Prime Minister at the Admiralty. Churchill formally asked Labour to join his government and offered Attlee two seats in the War Cabinet (which were obviously meant for Attlee and Greenwood) and more than a third of the overall places in the administration. Churchill also mentioned Bevin (to become minister of labour) Alexander (First Lord of the Admiralty) Morrison (minister of supply) and Dalton (minister of economic warfare) as men 'whose services in high office were immediately required'.[24] Churchill's offer was both generous and far sighted.

The initial coalition-building meeting between Churchill and Attlee and Greenwood went smoothly. One reason was given by the Labour leader in his autobiography. Remembering the long drawn-out bargaining between the Conservatives and the Liberals over the formation of Asquith's coalition in 1915, 'I was resolved that I would not, by haggling, be responsible for any failure to act promptly.'[25] In his memoirs, Churchill mentioned another reason – his relationship with Attlee and Greenwood. As he wrote, he had known both men for many years in the House of Commons and in the ten years before the outbreak of war: 'I had in my more or less independent position come far more often into collision with the Conservative and National Governments than with the Labour and Liberal Oppositions.'[26]

Churchill, in fact, owed much to the Labour Party. Despite holding only 167 seats in the Commons to the government's 418, Attlee and his colleagues had used the procedure of the House to set up the debate over the conduct of the war and to engineer the vote which provided the occasion for the devastating revolt against Chamberlain. Equally important, by making their presence in a national coalition so indispensible to the successful prosecution of the war, they had created for themselves a de facto veto against a government led by Chamberlain. In the end, it was Attlee's telephone message from Bournemouth which brought about Chamberlain's downfall.

The Labour Party may not have been directly responsible for making Churchill prime minister. On this second issue, Halifax's refusal was the crucial factor. But by not publicly favouring either man, Labour undermined the main argument used by Chamberlain against a Churchill premiership, which was that he would find it difficult to get Labour Party support. In that sense, Labour's decision (or non-decision) at Bournemouth made Churchill's assumption of power easier.

Over the weekend, Attlee worked hard to deliver the Labour movement for the new coalition. The key Labour appointment, apart from the two members of the War Cabinet, was Ernest Bevin, the most powerful trade union leader in the country. Bevin was supportive of Labour joining the government. He pointed out: 'In view of the fact that you helped bring the other fellow down, if the party did not take its share of responsibility, they would say we were not great citizens but cowards.' Attlee explained to Bevin: 'We want someone from the industrial movement from outside parliament to come in, not merely to run a department but to help the state in this critical hour.'[27] At a meeting with Attlee at the Commons later that day, Bevin agreed to become minister of labour, provided he had support of his union (the Transport and General Workers), the TUC and the party National Executive Committee (NEC) and that he would be able to convert the Ministry of Labour into a powerful new organisation, in control of the manpower so vital to the running of the war. Churchill, who had expressed his admiration for Bevin in his Norway debate wind-up speech and was anxious to bring him into the government, at once accepted Bevin's terms.

On Monday 13 May, Attlee moved an emergency resolution in support of joining a coalition government at the opening session of the

Bournemouth party conference. He reminded the delegates that they were meeting at a time of the gravest crisis: 'Right along the line in Holland, Belgium and in France, there is an onrush of the Nazi hordes, and our men […] are struggling to withstand that onrush […] We have to stand today for the souls in prison in Czechoslovakia in Poland, yes, and in Germany.' He had told Churchill, he said, that Labour ministers came into government not as individuals but as representatives of the Labour movement: 'If we come in without the Movement, we are nothing to you.' He was blunt with the conference that coalition would require concessions and compromise. It would also mean including in the government 'some people we do not like' (he was referring especially to Chamberlain, whom Churchill intended to include in the War Cabinet as Lord President). But participating in government would bring with it political opportunities: 'I am quite certain that the world that must emerge from this war must be a world attune to our ideals. I am quite sure that our war effort needs the application of the socialist principles of service before private property.' He concluded with the call to 'go forward and win that liberty so essential to life and establish that liberty for ever on the sure foundation of social justice' and left the hall immediately after his speech to return by car to Westminster, with the cheers of the delegates ringing in his ears.[28]

By 2.30 p.m. on 13 May when Attlee, in a vivid symbol of the new coalition, took his place beside Churchill on the government front bench in the Commons, the news had come through from Bournemouth that he had won an overwhelming victory, with 2,450,000 votes in favour of the NEC resolution and only 170,000 against. When he entered the Chamber, Attlee was congratulated not only by his own party (who remained on the opposition benches) but also by anti-Chamberlain Tories and the Liberals. When Churchill came in, it was noticeable that he also received Labour cheers but that it took Chamberlain's entrance to draw the majority of Tories to their feet. It was clear that Churchill was going to need all his magnificent eloquence not only to rally the country but also to unite his own party. He made an impressive start with his first short speech to the Commons as prime minister:

21

I have nothing to offer but blood, toil, tears and sweat [...] You ask what is our policy. I will say: It is to wage war, by sea, land and air, with all our might and with all our strength that God can give us: to wage war against a monstrous tyranny, never surpassed in the dark, lamentable catalogues of human crime.[29]

Over the next few weeks, despite Churchill's brave words, the new coalition was almost completely overwhelmed by a devastating series of military disasters on the Continent. The Low Countries were overrun; the British Expeditionary Force was cut off by the German breakthrough in the Ardennes and forced back to the Channel ports and, biggest catastrophe of all, the French will to resist collapsed. From 17 June 1940, when the newly formed Pétain government requested an armistice from the Germans, the British stood alone against Hitler.

The only saving grace in this succession of disasters was the so-called 'miracle of Dunkirk'; between 27 May and 4 June, 335,000 British and French troops were evacuated back to Britain. The numbers rescued were far greater than Churchill had expected, though Attlee, with his direct Gallipoli experience when most of the British troops had been safely evacuated, had been more optimistic. The embarking troops may have left behind their weapons and equipment but they were safely evacuated from France to form the nucleus of a new army, which, when re-equipped, would be capable of defending the British Isles. 'Wars are not won by evacuations,' Churchill reminded the House of Commons on 4 June, but all the same it was 'a miracle of deliverance'.

It was against the background of Belgian capitulation, of the destruction of the French army, and of the drama being played out at Dunkirk, that a momentous struggle also took place within the British War Cabinet. The issue at stake was the supremely important one of whether to fight on, as Churchill so passionately advocated, or whether, as Foreign Secretary Lord Halifax argued, to try and negotiate peace terms with Hitler.

The War Cabinet minutes reveal that on 26, 27 and 28 May there were five meetings almost entirely devoted to that question and that Churchill had to work extremely hard to win the argument. His problem was the weakness of his position inside the five-strong War Cabinet. While he could count on the firm backing of Attlee and Greenwood, he was anything but certain of the two men representing the majority party in the Commons – Halifax and Chamberlain. Halifax had been an appeaser and he still believed that it was possible to do a deal with Hitler which might preserve British independence. Chamberlain was the crucial vote. He was, of course, the architect of the Munich agreement but since then his views about the Nazi dictator had changed. His relations with Churchill had also improved considerably, especially after his appointment by Churchill to the War Cabinet and the courtesy with which the new Prime Minister had shown him, for example by allowing him to continue to use No 10 Downing Street.

At the 9 a.m. War Cabinet meeting on Sunday 26 May, Halifax made his first move. He told his colleagues that 'it was not so much now a question of imposing a complete defeat upon Germany, but of safeguarding the independence of our own empire.'[30] He argued that the conversation which he had had the day before with the Italian Ambassador about keeping Italy out of the war should be broadened into a general conference about peace and security in Europe. Later that day, the War Cabinet agreed to ask Halifax to prepare a draft of his 'suggested approach to Italy', though, in order to bolster his support inside the War Cabinet, Churchill also insisted on bringing in the leader of the Liberal Party, Sir Archibald Sinclair, to discuss the issue.

The clash between Churchill and Halifax continued next day at the 4.30 p.m. meeting of the War Cabinet.[31] This time Churchill came out more firmly against Halifax. 'Let us [...] avoid being dragged down the slippery slope with France. The whole of this manoeuvre was intended to get us so deeply involved in negotiations that we should be unable to turn back.' Attlee, laconically, and Greenwood, at greater length, backed up Churchill, as did Sinclair. Attlee said that the Foreign Secretary's strategy would be 'very damaging to us', as it would inevitably lead to Britain asking Mussolini to obtain terms, while Greenwood argued that, if it got out that Britain had sued for terms at the cost of ceding British territory, 'the consequences would be terrible.'[32]

The dramatic debate came to a conclusion the following day, Tuesday 28 May. At the 4 p.m. War Cabinet meeting, which took place in the Prime Minister's room at the House of Commons (following a short statement by the Prime Minister in the Chamber about the situation at Dunkirk, warning of 'hard and heavy tidings'), Churchill made it clear that he could not support a joint approach with the French to Italy, as requested by the French government. He said that the French were trying to get Britain onto the 'slippery slope': 'If we once got to the table, we should then find that the terms offered us touched our independence and integrity. When at this point, we got up to leave the table, we should find that all the forces of resolution which now at our disposal would have vanished.'[33] He added, in a memorable sentence, 'the nations which went down fighting rose again, but those which surrendered were finished.'

Attlee gave strong support to Churchill, stating, 'if we did what France wanted, we should find it impossible to rally the morale of the people,' while Greenwood warned that the industrial centres of Britain 'would regard anything like weakening on the part of the government as a disaster'.

When the War Cabinet reassembled at 7 p.m., Churchill recounted a meeting he had had earlier with almost 30 senior ministers who had expressed the greatest satisfaction when he told them that 'there was no chance of our giving up the struggle.'[34] He stressed that he did not remember having ever before heard 'a gathering of persons occupying high places in political life express themselves so emphatically'. As Chamberlain had now fallen in behind the new Prime Minister, who already had the firm backing of Attlee and Greenwood, Halifax knew he was beaten. Eight months later, Churchill would be strong enough politically to send him to the United States as British ambassador.

So Churchill, acting with great skill and courage, had won his first decisive victory as prime minister. He had persuaded the War Cabinet that Britain could and should fight on. John Lukacs, in his gripping book, *Five Days in London May 1940*, argued that this was the moment when

Hitler came closest to winning the war. Had Britain stopped fighting in May 1940 (as Halifax advocated), Hitler would have won his war. By keeping Britain in the conflict, Churchill prevented Hitler winning. In so doing, 'he saved Britain, and Europe, and Western civilization.'[35]

This was clearly Churchill's triumph. But the two Labour leaders gave him invaluable support. Greenwood may have been loquacious and Attlee laconic but, if they had wavered, Churchill would have been in an impossible position. The new coalition and the relationship between Churchill and Attlee had been tested at its most dangerous moment and had survived.

There were further daunting tests ahead. After the fall of France came the Battle of Britain. Asked on 27 May by the Prime Minister for their assessment of national survival, the Chiefs of Staff judged that it was possible that, provided that the Royal Air Force (RAF) could hold out against the Luftwaffe, the Navy (outnumbering the German fleet by ten to one) and the Royal Air Force combined 'should be able to prevent Germany carrying out a serious sea-borne invasion of this country'.[36] This analysis proved correct. From July to September, 2,500 British, Commonwealth, Polish and Belgian pilots managed to keep command of the airspace over the Channel and southern England, more than justifying Churchill's words in his speech to the House of Commons on 20 August: 'Never in the field of human conflict was so much owed by so many to so few.'[37] When, on 7 September, Goering switched the Luftwaffe's attacks from the RAF's airfields to the City of London, it was a sign that the RAF had held firm. Though German night bombing (the so-called 'Blitz') on British cities continued throughout the winter months with considerable loss of life and damage to property, the threat of invasion receded.

The Chiefs of Staff's assessment of the chances of survival had also stressed the role of morale. They said that 'the real test is whether the morale of our fighting personnel and civic population will counter-balance the numerical and material advantages which Germany enjoys. We believe it will.' Here Churchill's defiant and stirring speeches and broadcasts (listened to by well over half the nation) played an absolutely crucial part.

It really was his finest hour. Attlee wrote later, 'If somebody asked what exactly Winston did to win the war, I would say, "Talk about it".'[38] When questioned about his part in rousing his compatriots, Churchill said they had the lion's heart and all he provided was the roar. As one of his biographers remarked, that was to do himself an injustice.[39] His superb oratory had galvanised the British nation.

If Churchill's magnificent defiance and the almost miraculous outcome of the Battle of Britain had prevented Hitler from knocking Britain out of the war,[40] it became increasingly obvious not only that Hitler could only be defeated if the Russians and the Americans came into the war on the Allied side, but also that winning the war would take a considerable time. A long drawn-out struggle meant that the survival of the coalition government, created at a time of extreme national crisis, became all the more crucial. Churchill's authority as a national leader had been greatly enhanced by the events of 1940. The resignation for health reasons of Chamberlain in the autumn of 1940 (he died soon after) gave the Prime Minister the opportunity to reshape his administration. He had brought Lord Beaverbrook, who had proved himself as minister of aircraft production, into the War Cabinet in August. Now he also promoted the minister of labour, Ernest Bevin.[41]

To balance Bevin, Churchill appointed the Tory chancellor of the Exchequer, Sir Kingsley Wood, to the War Cabinet. Herbert Morrison became home secretary and minister for home security (later promoted to the War Cabinet in November 1942). One consequence of Chamberlain's death was that Churchill became leader of the Conservative Party. His wife, Clementine, had advised against this step on the grounds that her husband was a national figure above party. However, Churchill, while sympathising with this argument, was determined, by putting himself at the head of the majority bloc of votes in the Commons, to prevent any other potential Conservative leader emerging.

The Tory party, though still predominant in the Commons, was now very much on the defensive. Leading Conservatives of the 1930s, such as Chamberlain and Halifax, were blamed by soldiers returning from

Dunkirk for the inadequate supply of tanks and aircraft. There were fierce criticisms of the appeasers in the press, while a left-wing polemic, *Guilty Men*, written by three journalists (including Michael Foot), sold over 200,000 copies. Churchill was forced to ask Attlee and his colleagues to try and restrain Labour Party attacks on members of the previous government.

The advent of the coalition and the participation of Labour ministers in it also led to radical measures to sustain the war effort such as the raising of the rate of tax on excess war profits from 60 per cent to 100 per cent, and the rationing of food and clothing; welfare improvements were also introduced such as free or subsidised milk for mothers or their children under the age of five, approved by Attlee's Food Policy Committee, free issue of blackcurrant juice and cod liver oil for the under twos and free school meals. Ideas such as 'equality of sacrifice', fair shares for all and state planning – before the war mainly associated with the left – became popular slogans. Despite Churchill's prestige and the agreement of an electoral truce (there was a formal agreement between the three parties to avoid contests in parliamentary by-elections during the war), the tide of opinion worked against the Tories and in favour of Labour.[42]

The contribution of Labour's leading ministers, especially Bevin and Morrison, was very much a plus for the party. The minister of labour, Ernest Bevin, was the embodiment of trade unionism, a giant figure, heavyweight in personality as well as physique. He had no experience of government or Parliament but, by a combination of will power, creative intelligence and sheer persuasion, he succeeded in making his ministry one of the vital departments in winning the war and getting his pre-eminent position in the administration accepted throughout the country. His rival, Herbert Morrison, was also widely regarded as a top-flight minister. After a few months at the Ministry of Supply (in which he never felt comfortable), Churchill promoted him in October to become home secretary and minister of home security. With the coming of the Blitz, Morrison, with his unrivalled London local government experience, was the obvious choice to improve security and offer reassurance. By the summer of 1941, he had given Britain's home defences a sure foundation – a brilliant effort.

Despite being, from the beginning of the coalition, the de facto deputy prime minister and from 1942 the formal deputy prime minister, Attlee was less publicly prominent than Bevin or Morrison. There were differences of view over Attlee's performance as a minster during the war. The Labour left-winger Aneurin Bevan, who had quickly emerged as an eloquent parliamentary rebel, woundingly described Attlee as bringing 'to the fierce struggle of politics the tepid enthusiasm of a lazy summer afternoon at a cricket match'.[43] Harold Laski made no secret of his dissatisfaction with Attlee's leadership and his failure, as he saw it, to demand more socialist measures from Churchill. He approached Bevin to ask him to run against Attlee for the leadership but was turned down flat.[44] The left-wing professor also encouraged Morrison's ambitions. Morrison had never accepted his defeat by Attlee in 1935 and was always on the lookout for an opportunity to wrong-foot Attlee and promote his own prospects.

Attlee's problem was that, in contrast to Churchill, Bevin and Morrison, the many good things that he did were mostly behind the scenes, while his public persona showed him at a disadvantage, especially when he had to deputise for Churchill in the Commons. Harold Nicolson was critical of Attlee's performance – 'like a snipe pretending to be an eagle', he noted in his diary.[45] It was much the same at Labour Party conferences, where more eloquent speakers such as Morrison and Dalton and more outgoing personalities like Bevin tended to outshine Attlee. The editor of *The Times*, Robin Barrington-Ward, summed up the case against him when he wrote in his diary: 'He is worthy but limited – incredible that he should be where he is now.'[46]

But Barrington-Ward's assessment (which he was later to revise) was seriously to underestimate the abilities and effectiveness of Attlee. As a perceptive analysis by the historian Robert Crowcroft has shown,[47] Clement Attlee established a remarkable dominance over the administration and politics of the wartime coalition. An instinctive patriot, he believed passionately in winning the war and was absolutely convinced that the coalition, very much with Churchill at its head, was essential. At the same time, he was deeply committed to ensuring that the Labour Party, its leaders and its ideas played a prominent role in achieving victory.

Although he was a leading member of the War Cabinet's Defence Committee (where he saw his main role as sorting out the good from the bad from Churchill's inexhaustible supply of ideas), Attlee's chief responsibility was helping run the home front. The key to his power was not the public platform but his mastery of 'the committee system, the private meeting, and, most of all, the simple memorandum'.[48] Only Attlee served (as deputy chairman) on the three main Cabinet committees – the War Cabinet itself, the Defence Committee and the powerful Lord President's Committee, which he had himself proposed to run the civil side of the war (it has been described as 'a Home Cabinet')[49] and of which he became chairman in 1943. He was an exceptionally skilful chairman. Here is a description by a member of the coalition of Attlee presiding over the War Cabinet in Churchill's absence: 'When Attlee takes the chair, Cabinet meetings are business-like and efficient, we keep to the agenda, make decisions and get away in reasonable time. When Churchill presides, nothing is decided; we listen enthralled and go home, many hours later, feeling that we have been present at an historic occasion.'[50]

Attlee was the coalition's 'oiler of wheels' in chief. With the exception of Beaverbrook, whom both he and Bevin loathed, he worked extremely well with his War Cabinet colleagues, especially the outstanding civil servant Sir John Anderson, whom Churchill once called the 'automatic pilot', and the progressive Tory Anthony Eden, whom the Prime Minister had appointed to the War Cabinet as foreign secretary in place of Halifax and with whom Attlee formed an informal alliance. The Labour leader also acted as the Labour ministers' shop steward. The relationship between Attlee and Bevin, which had not been particularly warm before the war, now became exceptionally close. Bevin came to respect Attlee's cool judgement and lack of vanity and recognised in him those qualities of integrity and loyalty on which he himself set such store. When, early in 1942, Churchill appointed Beaverbrook minister of production with powers over manpower, Attlee backed Bevin's vehement opposition and, with Bevin, faced down Churchill. Significantly, it was Beaverbrook, not Bevin nor Attlee, who resigned.

The crucial relationship for the coalition was, of course, the one between Attlee and Churchill. As he movingly revealed in a perceptive appreciation after Churchill's death, Attlee had a great admiration for him as a war leader. Partly it was for his eloquence and ability to project his leadership. He also praised Churchill's creation of the intergovernmental war machine, with Winston as its head as prime minister and minister of defence. He was able, wrote Attlee, 'to solve the problem that democratic countries in total wars find crucial and may find fatal: relations between the civil and military leaders'. His overall assessment was that Churchill was one of the greatest men in history: 'brave, gifted, inexhaustible and indomitable'.[51]

Churchill, for his part, had considerable respect for Attlee. There were some Churchillisms in circulation about Attlee – for example, 'a modest man who has much to be modest about' and 'a sheep in sheep's clothing'. However, when Churchill heard about them, he instructed his private secretary, John Colville, to deny them.[52] Attlee was not, like Brendan Bracken, Beaverbrook or Lord Cherwell, a Churchill intimate or crony. Significantly, Churchill never asked Attlee to join 'The Other Club', the dining club of cronies which he had set up with his close friend, later Lord Chancellor, F.E. Smith, but the Prime Minister always talked to Attlee extremely frankly because he knew he could trust him.

Churchill understood that, so long as the coalition lasted, he had Attlee's total political loyalty. He could go on one of his remarkable wartime journeys in the knowledge that, with Attlee left in charge, business would not only be competently run, but his back would also be securely guarded. Attlee's loyalty did not exclude raising with Churchill difficult questions or stringent criticism when he thought Churchill was wrong. Churchill remarked to Eden that Attlee was 'like a terrier, who, when he gets hold of an idea, will never give it up'.[53] Churchill, though not by nature a good listener, almost always took notice of Attlee. As one of Churchill's aides told Dalton, 'if C.R.A. [i.e. Clement Richard Attlee] digs his feet in he will win.'[54] If, as Attlee said, the country was fortunate in having Churchill as war leader, Churchill was also fortunate to have Attlee as his deputy.

With Hitler's invasion of the Soviet Union on 22 June 1941 and his declaration of war on the United States on 11 December 1941 following the Japanese assault on the American fleet at Pearl Harbor, the long-term strategic balance shifted decisively in favour of the Allies. But, even so, 1942 was a low point for the coalition, with Britain suffering a series of disastrous military setbacks.

This spate of bad news provided the background to the political unrest and ministerial reshuffles (including the rise and fall of Stafford Cripps) which were to test Churchill and Attlee so severely during 1942. Conservative supporters of the coalition suffered a series of parliamentary by-election defeats by independents, prompting Attlee to try and prop up the electoral truce by proposing Labour backing for Conservative and Liberal candidates at by-elections. However, at the Labour conference in May, the electoral truce and, by implication, the continuation of the coalition, was only narrowly upheld. Discontent spilled over into Parliament. There were Labour revolts over what was seen as the coalition's failure to nationalise the coal industry, while the Conservatives furiously resisted Dalton's plan for the rationing of coal. There was also growing criticism of Churchill as a war leader, in both Labour and Tory ranks. A Labour junior minister wrote in his diary, 'Parliament is given over to intrigue.'[55]

It was into this heated atmosphere that Sir Stafford Cripps, a former leader of the radical left, arrived back from Moscow, where he had been Churchill's ambassador, to find that, despite being virtually ignored by the Soviet leadership, he was not only being given the credit for having brought Russia into the war but also being seriously considered as a rival to Churchill.

On 19 February, Churchill, who had already offered Cripps the Ministry of Supply (which he turned down), yielded to the pressure and brought him into the War Cabinet. This appointment was part of the most extensive reshuffle of the war. Cripps took over Attlee's position as Lord Privy Seal and Churchill's role as leader of the House of Commons.

Attlee, who had already deputised for Churchill when he was on his trips to the United States, became deputy prime minister in name also and secretary of state for the dominions. Beaverbrook, furious at his failure to win the struggle over manpower with Attlee and Bevin, resigned, while Greenwood, whose performance as a minister had been undermined by his long-standing drink problem, was sacked.

By making Cripps leader of the House, Churchill had cunningly given a potential rival a job to which Cripps, with his didactic approach, was not well suited. Churchill had, however, been forced to let his close ally, the controversial newspaper proprietor, Max Beaverbrook, go. For his part, Attlee had acquiesced in the dropping of his faithful deputy, Arthur Greenwood. Attlee was unhappy about Greenwood's departure but knew he was no longer up to a government job. In compensation, his own and Bevin's positions had been strengthened, though he had to accept the appointment of Cripps who, before the war, had been expelled from the Labour Party for his advocacy of a popular front. Attlee may have hoped that his good personal relations with Cripps would help him manage the new member of the War Cabinet.

The reshuffle was not, however, enough to pacify the government's critics. Following the news in June about the surrender of Tobruk (which, in Churchill's absence in Washington, Attlee had announced to the House), Tories and Labour rebels coalesced against the government in a heated two-day censure debate on 1 and 2 July. The chairman of the Conservative Foreign Affairs Committee, Sir John Wardlaw-Milne, attacked Churchill for combining the offices of prime minister and minister of defence, while Aneurin Bevan, in a wounding speech, accused the Prime Minister of winning debate after debate and losing battle after battle. 'The country is beginning to say that he fights debates like a war and the war like a debate.'[56]

Churchill, who had hurried back from the United States, made an effective reply which quashed the revolt (only 25 MPs voted against), but, as Bevin had told the War Cabinet, a military victory was now needed more than ever. In an epic journey by Liberator bomber in August,

Churchill, before going on to Moscow to meet Stalin in his lair, flew out to Cairo, where he had replaced Generals Auchinleck and Ritchie by Generals Alexander and Montgomery. The latter were to prove a winning combination. The victory of numerically superior British and Dominion forces at El Alamein over Rommel early in November was followed a few days later by the Operation Torch landings of American and British troops on the coasts of Morocco and Algeria. In his Mansion House speech, Churchill described these successes as 'the end of the beginning'.[57] Although the 'Torch' landings and, above all, the surrender of the German 6th Army at Stalingrad two months later were far more important strategically, the British victory at El Alamein gave a much-needed boost to domestic morale and to Churchill's political authority. By strengthening the prime minister it also effectively dished Cripps. Churchill was able to dismiss him from the War Cabinet, though, wisely advised by Attlee, Cripps was made minister of aircraft production, a post in which his outstanding administrative talents were fully used.

The coalition and Churchill's leadership had survived an extremely testing year. There were times when even the Prime Minister's indomitable spirit had faltered. However, throughout, he had had the steadfast support of Attlee, who had not only acted as his loyal and capable deputy inside government but also, despite vocal opposition both within and outside Parliament, had held the Labour Party firm in support of the coalition.

Following El Alamein, the Prime Minister was increasingly confident about eventual victory. The issues were now rather about how long it would take to achieve it and what would be his country's place in it. At home, there was a decisive change of mood. The church bells which Churchill ordered to be rung throughout the British Isles to celebrate victory in North Africa symbolised a new time of hope, when the thoughts of a war-weary people could at last begin to turn to the future. Not surprisingly after El Alamein, political pressure mounted for reconstruction and reform.

By chance, the Beveridge Report (the work of William Beveridge, the former top civil servant and director of the London School of Economics who had been made chairman of the Social Insurance Committee to get him out of Bevin's way at the Ministry of Labour) was published immediately after the British victory in North Africa. It proposed a comprehensive system of social security, paid for mainly by national insurance. It also assumed a national health service, the introduction of family allowances, as well as a high level of employment for which the state would take responsibility. The report was widely welcomed (according to Gallup, 86 per cent believed that it should be adopted) and its author became a popular hero overnight.

For Attlee and his Labour ministerial colleagues, the Beveridge Report offered both a political opportunity and a difficult dilemma. The Deputy Prime Minister, like most Labour MPs and activists, was strongly in favour of the report. The problem was that the majority of Tory backbenchers were fiercely opposed. As Attlee wrote later, Churchill himself was not so much anti-Beveridge as not prepared to take a firm decision until the war was won: 'He kept, so to speak, pushing the report away from him, because he wanted to get on and win the war.'[58]

With a Commons debate looming and under pressure from his own backbenchers, Attlee sent Churchill a tough memorandum:

I doubt whether in your inevitable and proper preoccupation with military problems you are fully cognizant of the extent to which decisions must be taken and implemented in the field of post war reconstruction *before* the end of the war [...] I am certain that unless the government is prepared to be as courageous in planning for peace as it has been in carrying on the war, there is extreme danger of disaster when the war ends. My contention is that if, as I think it is generally agreed, it is not possible at the present time to have a general election, the Government and the present House of Commons must be prepared to take responsibility not only for winning the war but for taking the legislative and administrative action which is thought necessary for the post war situation.[59]

The War Cabinet minutes of 12 and 15 February reveal a fierce debate between Labour and Tory ministers, with Attlee and Morrison arguing for speedy implementation and the Tories, led by Churchill, replying that a commitment now would be irresponsible. However, pressed by Attlee, Churchill gave a pledge to implement 'Beveridge-type' reforms *after* the war. In the end, the War Cabinet agreed to plan for the Beveridge Report but with no commitment to legislate before the end of the war. The historian Robert Crowcroft shrewdly commented that Churchill's compromise was 'reflective once again of Attlee's ability to sway Churchill'.[60]

In fact, the Beveridge Report caused a serious rift between Labour ministers and their backbenchers – so much so that there were rumours that the coalition was about to collapse. In a vote about the coalition's compromise formula, 97 Labour MPs voted against the government, while only two Labour backbenchers supported it. A worried Dalton warned a meeting of Labour ministers that, if it came to a general election, the Labour Party would be 'scrubbed out' worse than in 1931.[61] Even so, the government compromise on Beveridge, though supported by the Labour leaders, was attacked in the party meeting and repudiated by the National Executive Committee. It took the steadiness of the TUC, which passed a resolution unanimously supporting the Labour ministers, to quieten things down.

Whether coordinated or not, both Churchill and Attlee then made calming and constructive interventions. In late March 1943, Churchill gave a radio broadcast in which he spoke of a four-year plan for reconstruction 'to cover five or six large measures of a practical nature', including national insurance 'for all persons from the cradle to the grave'. Flying a kite, Churchill added that this plan would be put to the voters either by a coalition of the three parties or 'by a National Government comprising the best men in all parties'.[62] Two weeks later, Attlee, in a carefully drafted speech said that, while Labour's first objective remained the winning of the war, the improved war situation meant that the government could begin to make postwar plans, in which Labour ministers would play their part. As to the political future, it was sensible for Labour to keep its options open. Meanwhile, Attlee reassured his party that Labour ministers remained faithful to its policies and decisions. Dalton reported that Attlee's intervention went down well and 'the storms that have been brewing for some time are wholly stilled.'[63]

Labour MPs and activists may have felt that they had suffered a defeat over the Beveridge report. But in public opinion terms it was Labour and not the Tory party which benefited politically. Opinion surveys (then very much in their infancy and largely ignored) showed a consistent Labour advantage. Labour leaders, almost certainly including Attlee, may have thought that, in a general election, Churchill was unbeatable. But the voters, though they greatly admired the Prime Minister as a war leader, were not convinced that he was seriously concerned with postwar reconstruction. The Beveridge Report debate in effect confirmed their scepticism. In that sense, Beveridge was a crucial staging post on the road to Labour's victory in 1945.

In the winter of 1943/4, Attlee was at the zenith of his power within the coalition. In 1943 he presided over the War Cabinet, in Churchill's long absences abroad, almost as many times as Churchill. In September the death of the chancellor of the Exchequer, Sir Kingsley Wood, caused a reshuffle, in which Sir John Anderson became chancellor and Attlee took over Anderson's position as Lord President of the Council. He was now officially in charge of the home front and, backed up on the Lord President's Committee by Bevin and Morrison, was able – to a considerable extent – to shape the domestic agenda. In a key War Cabinet meeting in October, Attlee insisted that the coalition should draw up postwar plans and Churchill gave way, asking the Deputy Prime Minister for a list of four or five major projects. Attlee pointed to exports, food, increased unemployment insurance, a demobilisation scheme and the conversion of industry from war to peace. Churchill complained that he had been 'jostled and beaten up by the Deputy Minister'.[64]

The Prime Minister, as part of his response to Attlee, set up a new Reconstruction Committee, though with a non-socialist minister of reconstruction, Lord Woolton, a businessman who had been a successful minister of food, as its chairman. However, Attlee, Bevin and Morrison were all on the committee. When Attlee wrote to Churchill, asking that a Labour peer should attend the committee, Churchill drafted a reply complaining that 'a solid mass of four Socialist politicians of the highest quality and authority, three of whom were in the War Cabinet, all working together as a team, very much dominates this Committee.'[65] To check the 'force and power' of the Labour ministers, Churchill resorted to blocking tactics, using his two cronies, Lord Beaverbrook and Brendan Bracken (Dalton referred to them as M (Max) and B (Brendan) after the latest sulphur drug, the precursor of antibiotics).

In a magisterial rebuke which he typed out himself, Attlee castigated Churchill not only for the self-indulgent and time-wasting way in which he chaired the Cabinet but also for the unwarranted attention which he gave to his two attack dogs:

> The conclusions agreed upon by a committee on which have sat five or six members of the Cabinet and other experienced ministers are then submitted with great deference to the Lord Privy Seal [Beaverbrook] and the Minister of Information [Bracken], two ministers without Cabinet responsibility neither of whom had given any serious attention to the subject. When they state their view it is obvious that they know nothing about it. Nevertheless an hour is consumed in listening to their opinions [...] It is quite wrong that there should be a feeling among ministers and civil servants that it is more important to have the support of the Lord Privy Seal and the Minister of Information than of Cabinet Ministers, but I cannot doubt that that is a growing impression.[66]

Churchill was infuriated by the Lord President's home truths but was persuaded by those close to him to write a courteous reply. As his wife, Clementine, said, 'I admire Mr Attlee for having the courage to say what everyone is thinking.'

The underlying problem was not so much Churchill's eccentric way of running his Cabinet but that, as the prospect of victory grew nearer and especially after the Normandy landings in June 1944, the common interest which had previously contained party differences and kept the coalition together began to dissolve. MPs started to look ahead to the postwar world, and divisions over policy became more obvious.

The relatively non-controversial 1944 Education Act which established universal secondary education was skilfully navigated through Parliament by the Tory education minister, R.A. Butler, with all-party support. But, though there was political consensus on the principle of a national health service expressed in the 1944 White Paper, there was no agreement on the details. The same was true for other White Papers on employment and on social insurance. The 1944 Town and Country Planning Act only got through Parliament by excluding contentious measures, such as the public ownership of development rights, and by increasing levels of compensation to please the Tories; and in May 1945, at the very end of its life, the coalition managed to pass a Family Allowances Act, paying all families with more than one child 5 shillings per week for each child other than the eldest. Churchill complained in a broadcast in March 1944 that the social progress made under the coalition received little recognition. The reality was that, in most areas, there was not enough agreement to go beyond what the newspapers called the 'White Paper Chase', a process which did not convince an anxious and war-weary electorate.

The question which Churchill and Attlee had to answer was when and how the coalition was to end. Both faced pressures from their parties for an early election. Conservative MPs, hoping to ride to victory on Churchill's coat tails, wanted a poll as soon as possible after Germany was defeated. Ideally, Churchill himself would have liked the coalition to continue at least until the end of the war with Japan (expected to last well into 1946). As he told Eden, he was increasingly worried about the expansionist ambitions of the Soviet Union in Eastern and Central Europe, and 'the support of men like Attlee, Bevin, Morrison and George Hall [Labour under secretary at the Foreign Office] is indispensable to the National Presentation of the Case.'[67] The Prime Minister, who was never a great lover of party politics, was also, as he wrote later, 'distressed at the prospect of sinking from a national to a party leader'.[68]

Labour MPs and activists (though uncertain of electoral victory against the great war leader) were, like the Tories, eager to break free from the compromises of coalition. At the December 1944 party conference, feelings were so strong that the Labour left were able to carry a wide-ranging 'nationalisation' resolution against the platform, calling for the transfer to public ownership of land, large-scale buildings, heavy industry and all forms of banking, transport and fuel and power. Under Attlee's guidance, the Labour Party's National Executive Committee had announced in October 1944 that Labour would fight the next election as an independent party and Labour also agreed in that same month that Parliament should not be prolonged for more than a year. Attlee and Bevin were, however, sympathetic to Churchill's argument that, with the international situation so uncertain, it was unwise to break up the coalition immediately. The Labour leader may also have wanted to allow as much time as possible to elapse between the end of the war and the poll itself to try and reduce the electoral impact of Churchill's prestige.

At the beginning of May 1945, the Germans at last surrendered. The Prime Minister had delayed making a decision on the timing of the election while Attlee was away in the United States with Eden, attending the San Francisco conference that set up the United Nations (UN). On Attlee's return, the two men had a long and friendly late-night meeting at No 10, almost certainly their last as prime minister and deputy prime minister of the coalition government. Churchill produced a draft letter which offered the choice of either an immediate election or the extension of the coalition until the end of the war with Japan. Attlee suggested adding a sentence which said that, if the coalition were extended, the government would do its best to implement the proposals for social security and full employment which had already been presented to Parliament. Attlee told Churchill that this addition might give him a better chance of persuading the Labour Party at its coming conference to stay in the coalition.

However, when the NEC met at Blackpool the day before the conference opened, the tide of party opinion was running strongly against a continuance of the coalition. So, in introducing Churchill's letter, Attlee confined himself to setting out the pros and cons, though Bevin argued for continuing the coalition until the end of the Japanese war. Morrison, who had earlier advocated a continuation of the coalition after the war (mainly because he had expected Labour to lose) was now, as the chairman of the Labour Campaign Committee, the foremost advocate of its end and a general election in October, when a new register of voters would be ready. Backed up by the chief whip, he spoke strongly against the continuation of the coalition and carried the meeting by a big majority.

Attlee, with the help of Morrison, then wrote a reply to Churchill (which was overwhelmingly approved by conference), putting the case for an election in October and explaining Labour's unwillingness to prolong the coalition until after the defeat of Japan. On receiving Attlee's letter, Churchill, who felt, perhaps unfairly, that Attlee had let him down, went to Buckingham Palace to tender the resignation of the government. The great wartime coalition was at an end, Parliament was to be dissolved on 15 June and the general election held on 5 July. Meanwhile, a Conservative 'caretaker' administration, with Churchill at its head, was temporarily in charge.

Labour's Blackpool conference marked the beginning of the general election and provided a fine showcase for the party. Dalton wrote, 'We have a finer body of Labour Candidates, including a large number of young services candidates, than ever before.'[69] In the three-day debate on the manifesto, Attlee, Bevin and Morrison all gave a good account of themselves. Morrison's speech, opening the debate, was cheered to the echo and highly praised by the press, especially by Beaverbrook's *Daily Express*, which mischievously said that he was the 'undoubted leader of the party today'.[70]

During the conference there was, in fact, an attempt by the party chairman, Ellen Wilkinson, and her successor, Harold Laski, to persuade a number of leading MPs that Attlee should step aside in favour of Morrison. They had little success. Dalton's reply to Wilkinson that a change of leadership was out of question at that time and that, in any case, many MPs would prefer Bevin to Morrison probably reflected the general view. Immediately following the conference, Laski, who was to prove a nuisance to the Labour Party during the election campaign, wrote a letter to the party leader, asking him to resign for the good of the party. Attlee's celebrated put-down was as follows: 'Dear Laski, Thank you for your letter, contents of which have been noted.'[71] In his letter, Laski had accused Attlee of lacking 'a sense of the dramatic, the power to give a lead, the ability to reach the masses, the definition of great issues in a great way.'[72] Laski's criticisms were, to some extent, justified but the Labour leader had demonstrated during the war that his own special virtues of reasoned argument, the ability to bring people together, coolness under pressure, honesty and integrity were also formidable qualities. He was also to prove that he could be highly effective at electioneering, certainly superior to Churchill at the 1945 election.

As public opinion polls showed, Labour could arguably have won an election anytime after Dunkirk, certainly after 1943. The leadership of Churchill certainly mitigated the Tories' association with prewar unemployment and the appeasement of Hitler and Mussolini. But, to most voters, he was seen as the heroic war leader rather than a credible postwar reformer. It was to his loyal coalition partners, Attlee, Bevin and Morrison, that the people turned, on the grounds that they would be more likely to bring about the social gains debated but not implemented by the coalition government.

Labour had the good sense to put to the voters a moderate and by now largely familiar programme of full employment, social security, more housing and a national health service, which closely reflected their aspirations. Though Labour did not highlight its nationalisation programme, there was little opposition to the pragmatic piecemeal public ownership which they proposed. In the words of Michael Young, who wrote Labour's manifesto, 'There was a real sense in 1945, one which was well understood by the voters, that it was the Labour Party's leaders, not Churchill, who were speaking for the nation and its concerns.'[73]

In contrast to Churchill, Attlee handled the election campaign with coolness and good sense. Churchill's opening broadcast on 4 June was a massive misjudgement. The great statesman, who had only a week before bid a tearful farewell to Labour ministers, including 'my good friend, Clem Attlee', at a reception in the Cabinet Room, now turned in the most polemical fashion on his former colleagues. 'Socialism', he thundered, 'is inseparably woven with totalitarianism.' If a Labour government carried out its programme, it would require some form of Gestapo, 'no doubt very humanely directed in the first instance'. As a description of a party and its leaders with whom he had been in coalition only two weeks before, it was, as his wife pointed out, totally misconceived. Mass Observation reported 'the disappointment and genuine distress aroused by his speech'.[74]

Attlee's response the following night was far more in tune with the mood of the voters. His beginning was 'more in sorrow than in anger'. He continued:

> When I listened to the Prime Minister's speech last night, in which he gave such a travesty of the policy of the Labour party, I realized at once what was his object. He wanted the electors to understand how great was the difference between Winston Churchill the great leader in war and Mr Churchill the party leader of the Conservatives [...] The voice we heard last night was that of Mr Churchill, but the mind was that of Lord Beaverbrook.

Attlee paid generous tribute to Churchill the war leader, quietly but firmly rejected his attack on the Labour Party, outlined Labour's policy at home and abroad and concluded by projecting Labour as a great democratic party, representing the whole nation. It was a devastating reply heard by 40 million people and was the making of Attlee as a campaigner.

Churchill's campaign was a semi-royal procession. Crowds lined the streets to cheer the great man as he passed in an open car. By contrast, Attlee's election tour was a far more modest affair; as Roy Jenkins put it, 'he chugged around in a family saloon with his wife (Vi) at the wheel from one moderate sized meeting to another, with no spectators on his journeys.'[75] Attlee noted that the contrast, which was widely reported in the press, turned out to be an asset.

Attlee also handled with skill Laski's unwelcome intervention in the election (when he issued a statement that Attlee should only attend the Potsdam Conference as an observer) and Churchill's clumsy attempt to exploit it. The judgement of the two academics who wrote the Nuffield College survey of the 1945 election was that Attlee had the better of the exchanges: 'He had the air of a sound and steady batsman, keeping up his wicket with ease against a bowler who was losing both pace and length.'[76]

When the votes were counted three weeks after the election, Labour achieved a great 'landslide' victory, winning 47.8 per cent of the vote to the Conservatives' 39.8 per cent. This translated into a massive Labour overall majority of 146 in terms of seats, with Labour having 393 MPs compared to the Conservatives' 213. As a result, Clement Attlee became prime minister and Winston Churchill went into opposition, a reversal of votes which astonished many people, including both Churchill and Attlee.

* * *

Attlee went on to lead the celebrated Labour governments of 1945–51 which created the welfare state and the National Health Service, nationalised the major utilities, gave independence to the Indian subcontinent and helped set up NATO and implement the Marshall Plan. Churchill remained in Parliament as leader of the Conservative opposition and, after narrowly losing the 1950 general election, scraped home in 1951 with an overall majority of only 17 seats.

On his return to Downing Street, Churchill was already in his seventy-seventh year and there was a general expectation that he would only continue in office for a year or so. But, convinced that he would do a better job than any possible successor and intent on securing a summit meeting with the Soviet Union that would end the Cold War, he stayed on until April 1955, although he had suffered a severe stroke in 1953.

Despite his admiration for Churchill, it was Attlee's view that he should have retired once the war was won. Arguably, Attlee himself should also have stepped down after Labour's 1951 defeat. As leader of the opposition until 1955, he presided ineffectively over divisions between left and right, failed to provide the new direction the party needed and dashed Morrison's chances when he might have provided more decisive leadership. Like most leaders, Churchill and Attlee both suffered from the delusion that they were indispensable.

Churchill and Attlee had different ideas of leadership. In conception and execution Churchill was the democratic 'superman'. He had, as Attlee wrote, the 'heroic' conception of government in which 'everything must be done by, and through, the big national leader.'[77] Attlee's view of the premiership was more prosaic. When he became prime minister, he saw his role, one which suited his temperament and aptitudes, as 'managing' his dynamic Cabinet colleagues and providing the calming yet effective framework within which they could thrive.

In the wartime coalition, Churchill and Attlee, the initiator and facilitator, with their contrasting but complementary abilities, came together, to the great benefit of the country. Churchill, with all his imagination and rhetorical gifts, ran the war machine and inspired the country. Attlee, with his integrity, skills of chairmanship and administrative efficiency, helped direct the home front. It was an exceptional partnership which not only kept the coalition afloat for five long and difficult years but also enabled the United Kingdom and its people to survive the Nazi menace as a free and independent country and emerge from the war, even though worn out and the poorer, as one of the three victor countries.

2

NEW JERUSALEM

Bevin and Morrison

The two biggest 'beasts' in Clement Attlee's highly talented Labour governments which introduced radical change in British society were Ernest Bevin and Herbert Morrison, both of them examples of 'initiating' politicians. There were other formidable Cabinet ministers, including Hugh Dalton, Stafford Cripps, Aneurin 'Nye' Bevan and later Hugh Gaitskell. But none of these could quite match Bevin and Morrison in experience and authority. Born in rural poverty, Bevin became Britain's most powerful trade unionist, a leading member of Churchill's War Cabinet and Attlee's foreign secretary, arguably the most creative holder of that office in the twentieth century. Bevin's colleague and rival, Herbert Morrison, was a brilliant political organiser who rose from being a Lambeth errand boy to become leader of London County Council, Churchill's home secretary in the wartime coalition and Attlee's deputy and, as Lord President of the Council and leader of the House of Commons, responsible for steering Labour's radical legislation through Parliament.

Bevin and Morrison had a notoriously difficult personal relationship which derived partly from their different political backgrounds and partly from their large and sometimes clashing egos. The antipathy between the two was more Bevin's fault than Morrison's. Bevin never forgave anybody whom he believed had crossed him. He called Morrison 'a scheming little bastard'[1] and thought there was a catch to everything he did. On

45

the formation of the Labour government, he instructed Attlee's adviser on public relations: 'Let me know if he [Morrison] gets up to any of his tricks, I wouldn't trust the little bugger any further than I could throw him.'[2] Morrison sometimes made efforts to make it up with Bevin, whom he once described as 'a strange mixture of genius and stupidity'.[3] But these efforts always failed.

This chapter describes how Attlee, with his gift for management, harnessed the two men to work together in his Cabinet, despite their poor relationship. The key was to allocate them different spheres of operation. As Attlee, with typical understatement, said, 'Ernie and Herbert didn't get on together. If you'd put both on the home front, there might have been trouble.'[4] So he appointed Bevin as the heavyweight in charge of foreign affairs, with Morrison as the chief coordinating figure on the home front. This arrangement, characteristic of a good facilitator, proved to be a great success.

In their rise to power, both Bevin and Morrison had to overcome huge disadvantages. Bevin was born on 7 March 1881 at Winsford, a Somerset village on the edge of Exmoor. His mother, a penniless widow, died when he was just eight. Bevin used to say that he had been educated in the 'university of the 'edgerows'. Though he learnt to read and write and do simple arithmetic, his formal schooling ended at the age of 11 when he was sent out to work as a live-in farm boy, at a wage of sixpence a week, paid in arrears in quarterly lump sums. When he was 13, he left the countryside to seek employment in Bristol, the main city of the West Country. There he was, in turn, a baker's boy, a kitchen boy, a grocer's errand boy, a van boy and a tram conductor. He secured what he described as his first 'man's job' when he was 18, as a drayman driving a two-horse van for a mineral water firm.

Over the next decade, Bevin's exceptional abilities gradually revealed themselves. It was at the Bristol Adult School and the Baptist Sunday Bible classes that he learnt to express himself with fluency and authority, so much so that he was chosen as a lay preacher. However, his anger at the poverty and squalor which he witnessed daily in Bristol's slums and at what he saw as the selfish and uncaring attitude of the city's professionals and employer classes drove him to seek political rather than religious redress.

Bevin joined the Bristol Socialist Society, a branch of the Marxist-inspired Social Democratic Federation, and in 1908 became, at a time of rising unemployment, secretary of the Bristol Right to Work Committee. To highlight their plight, Bevin led a procession of 400 unemployed workers into Bristol Cathedral for Sunday morning service. Their ragged appearance and orderly behaviour made such a deep impression that the local council agreed to back various proposals put forward by Bevin and his committee, including digging out a lake in a local park. But he suffered a severe setback when some of the local hotels and restaurants boycotted sales from his van. He was also defeated in the municipal elections. It was a difficult time for Bevin and his young wife, Florence, as they had a baby daughter to keep as well as themselves.

His career, however, now took a new turn. Within a year, Bevin, who was to be the greatest British trade union leader of the twentieth century, had become a trade unionist. His framed certificate of membership, much decorated with Victorian scrolls and dated 27 August 1910, was a prize possession and, at the end of his life, hung above the marble mantelpiece in the study of his official Foreign Office flat in Carlton Gardens.

What happened was that, following a dock strike in the port of Bristol, Bevin managed to recruit the previously unorganised carters to form a branch of the Dockers' Union, with himself as its chairman. He also persuaded the local employers to recognise the union and negotiate a comprehensive agreement, covering wages, hours and conditions. In the spring of 1911, he was taken on to the staff of the Bristol office of his new union as a full-time officer and, after his efforts in building up local branches in South Wales and the West Country, in March 1914 he was offered the post of assistant national organiser. His first biographer described Bevin at this time: 'Powerfully built, with the strong muscular hands of a manual worker and the rolling walk which is almost as common to draymen as to seamen, Bevin had a natural pugnacity and the physical courage to back it up.'[5]

The 1914–18 war transformed the position of the trade union movement, which, for the first time, was taken into partnership by the government. Its leaders, who before the war had been denounced as agitators, were now invited to join important advisory committees. Bevin played a key role on the Port and Transit Committee, set up by the government to organise the ports. He also served on the Ministry of Reconstruction's advisory council and took part in discussions between employers and trade unionists on the future of industrial relations. Bevin so impressed the prime minister, Lloyd George, that in 1917 he was offered a paid post as full-time Labour adviser to the government, an offer which he turned down because he rightly saw his future as a trade union leader and not as a civil servant. By the end of the war, he was recognised as one of the most able of the younger generation of trade union leaders, a spokesman of his union at TUC and Labour Party conferences, and its leading representative on many negotiating bodies and government committees.

The turbulent years after World War I saw Bevin emerge as Britain's leading trade unionist. In 1922, almost single-handedly and through a process of carefully planned amalgamations, he created a new general union, the Transport and General Workers' Union, which was to become the largest union in the country. After the defeat of the 1926 General Strike (in which Bevin and his union were fully involved), he helped the union movement, working through the TUC, to pick up the pieces. He also developed a wider vision of the trade union role, supporting a more cooperative approach between the two sides of industry, starting with the so-called Mond–Turner talks of 1928–9 between prominent trade unionists (including Bevin) and businessmen. After the collapse of the General Strike and its discrediting as a political weapon, he also became actively involved in efforts to create a more effective Labour Party, a process which was to lead eventually to the election of the 1945–51 majority Labour governments.

Throughout this period, Bevin was growing in stature. There was the same energy, force and determination which had made him such an effective trade union organiser and negotiator. But now these qualities were augmented, as his main biographer has written, 'by a maturing of powers, a deepening of character and experience'.[6] In the years ahead, the farm boy from Somerset was to reveal himself as a national leader, policy maker and man of vision, one of the greatest British statesmen of the twentieth century.

In contrast to Bevin, Herbert Morrison was born in relative prosperity on 3 January 1888 in Brixton, South London. As a police constable, his father, Henry Morrison, had a secure job with a rent allowance and a pension. Most of Herbert's brothers and sisters later found clerical jobs. So Herbert Morrison could be said have been brought up as a member of the lower middle classes and thus to be several rungs higher up the social ladder than Bevin.

However, within three days of his birth, Herbert became totally blind in one eye, probably as a result of an infection. Though he claimed in his autobiography that 'my one eye served me well,'[7] the loss of his right eye handicapped and disfigured him for life.

Morrison said of his education: 'I don't have any grievance against the education system that kept me out of the secondary schools which hardly then existed [...] But they taught me the three R's, and they taught me to like reading which is one of the greatest blessings of life.'[8] From his school library, he devoured the stories of G.A. Henty and R.M. Ballantyne. He was also made to learn poems, such as Gray's 'Elegy', by heart and was chosen by his school to deliver a set speech on Trafalgar Day – his first public address.

When he was 14 (in January 1902), he had to leave his elementary school and find a job as an errand boy, first working for his elder brother and then for the local branch of the well-known grocers and wine merchants Walton, Hassell and Port, where his wages were 7 shillings a week and involved carrying baskets, which when fully laden weighed up to 40 pounds. When he was 19, he was promoted to be a junior assistant at the Lupus Street branch, near Victoria. He quickly became the star window-dresser: 'To me it was an expression of proportion, of colour, and of balance.'[9] It showed an appreciation unusual for his age and upbringing.

By night, Morrison read voraciously, mostly in his room above the shop. He had been brought up in a Conservative household where the established order, especially the glaring contrast between rich and poor, was regarded as part of the natural order of things. Now he studied books which condemned existing conditions, such as Karl Marx's *Communist Manifesto* and Robert Blatchford's *Merrie England*, which helped Morrison make sense of his gut feelings about the injustice and unfairness of Edwardian Britain and turned his thoughts towards socialism. He flirted with several different socialist groups, including the revolutionary Social Democrat Party, before deciding in 1906 to join the ILP on a permanent basis, on the grounds that, because it was affiliated to the Labour Party, it was more likely to be able to influence national politics.

It was the start of Morrison's political life. He learnt how to speak fluently without notes. 'I would have my general line of argument mentally prepared but I used to rely on the inspiration of the moment, the atmosphere of the meeting, or on the comments of that invaluable ally of a public speaker, the heckler, to direct my train of thought.'[10] Yet, though Morrison became an eloquent speaker, he quickly grasped that political success depended 'less on street corner rabble rousing [...] than on the slow but steady construction of an organization devoted to running a planned programme of propaganda, social work and organization'.[11] Soon after joining Brixton ILP, he became its chairman, always starting meetings on time, keeping to the agenda and conducting business with dispatch. His reputation as an organiser rapidly spread, and at the end of 1910 he was appointed honorary secretary of the South London Federation of the ILP branches.

In the autumn of 1912, Morrison became circulation traveller and subsequently deputy circulation manager of the *Daily Citizen*, the first official Labour newspaper. He impressed colleagues by his efficiency and flair. Fenner Brockway, the editor of the *Labour Leader*, the ILP newspaper, wrote: 'He had a genius for organization, becoming the leader of his team of workers by natural ability, surmounting difficulties which baffled everyone else [...] and all the time as he went about his duties whistling, joking, laughing in characteristic cockney lightheartedness.'[12] However at the start of the war in 1914, the *Daily Citizen* collapsed.

Fortunately for Morrison, a fresh opportunity opened up at the end of 1914, when, following the sudden death of the first holder of the office, Morrison was chosen as temporary secretary of the newly created London Labour Party. In 1915, he was elected (by one vote) to the secretaryship on a permanent basis, the post from which he not only built up the strongest local party organisation in the country but also launched his long and successful political career.

Both Morrison and the London Labour Party came through the war virtually unscathed. When conscription came into force in 1916, Morrison received his call-up papers. Although his blindness in one eye would have made him unfit for active military service, he was determined to appear before the Military Service Tribunal at Wandsworth in order to voice publicly his objections to the war. His opposition was not on pacifist grounds but because Britain, in his view, was involved in a 'capitalist' war brought about by commercial rivalry and secret diplomacy.

The tribunal ordered him to Letchworth Garden City in Hertfordshire to work for a market gardener who, fortunately for Morrison, turned out to be a socialist. From Letchworth he was able to keep the London Labour Party organisation alive (despite the party split over the war), issuing a regular four-page magazine which contained a mixture of council and party news and arguments for use against Conservatives and Liberal opponents. He also met his first wife, Margaret, to whom he remained unhappily married until her death in 1953.

After World War I, the London Labour Party's growing success in local and parliamentary elections helped establish a national reputation for Morrison. In 1922, he was elected to the London City Council; in 1923 he was appointed chief whip and in 1925 he became Labour leader on the council. In 1920, he was also elected at his first attempt to a constituency seat on Labour's National Executive Committee, losing his seat the following year, but regaining it in 1922 and remained on the NEC for the next 30 years.

At the December 1923 general election, Morrison won the Hackney South seat for Labour in a three-cornered fight. He had hoped to become a minister in the first Labour minority government but in the short parliament of 1924 remained on the back benches. Though he was defeated at the 1924 general election, his local government activities and his campaign for public transport in London kept him in the public eye. He was always adept at public relations, a skill which was to be of value to him throughout his political career. When Labour was returned as the biggest single party in 1929, Morrison, now widely acknowledged as the party's leading transport expert with the added advantage of being chairman of the party in a successful election year, was an obvious choice as minister of transport. He proved to be highly competent: Beatrice Webb noted in her diary on 23 January 1930 that he was 'the only outstanding minister'.[13] At the beginning of 1931, the prime minister, Ramsay MacDonald, brought Morrison into the Cabinet and it seemed as though the errand boy from South London was destined to rise speedily to the very top of British politics.

However, two developments checked Morrison's progress. The first was the loss of his parliamentary seat in 1931, which put him out of the running at a crucial time. The second was a destructive feud which developed between Morrison and Bevin and was to endure throughout their political lives. It proved to be one of the main reasons why Attlee was able to become and remain leader of the Labour Party.

On the face of it, Morrison and Bevin had much in common. They were both exceptionally able, highly practical men who were superb organisers. On some of the major issues of the interwar period, they were on the same side – for example, they both believed in and worked for a Labour Party capable of forming a government and also shared a hostility towards the Communist Party and other left groups. What then were the reasons for their long running dispute?

It was partly that they represented rival centres of power: Bevin stood for the trade union movement and the working man, Morrison for local government and the party membership, especially of the London Labour Party. As Attlee noted,

> Ernest thought mainly in terms of, so to speak, internal organization – the organization of a body bound together by the same single interests – Herbert Morrison had much more experience of government, of genuinely public affairs, of handling things so that enemies as well as supporters could live together with a sense of benefit.[14]

The consequences of these differences of emphasis spilled over into policy, party development and attitudes to parliamentary democracy.

If what was at issue between these two men arose at first out of their different experience, it soon became something more personal. Both had large egos: Bevin, the ego of a trade union leader accustomed to dominating others; Morrison, the ego of a highly ambitious party politician. Bevin came to distrust Morrison as 'a slick wire puller' and 'a bit of a twister'. For his part, Morrison thought Bevin was an unforgiving bully, liable to steamroller over all opposition. Bevin's first biographer commented that 'the two were temperamentally unsuited for intimacy or even confidence and although the breach between them sometimes narrowed and Morrison made many efforts to close it altogether it remained a permanent factor in Labour party affairs from 1931 onwards.'[15]

Throughout much of the 1920s Morrison led the campaign for a local government-controlled London transport. This brought him into direct conflict with Bevin. Bevin preferred a national rather than a local government solution and believed that the unions should be directly represented on the body set up by the 1924 London Traffic Bill to advise the minister. Morrison, who – while a backbench MP in the 1924 parliament – had voted against the second reading of the Bill, maintained that the minister should be advised by local representatives speaking for the public rather than for sectional interests. 'An authority including interests does not attract me,'[16] said Morrison.

The debate between Morrison and Bevin was resumed in 1929 when Morrison became minister of transport. The two men clashed over the composition of the board, set up by Morrison's London Transport Bill to run London's transport services. Bevin wanted trade union representatives on the board, or at least for the trade unions to be consulted before the minister made his appointments. Morrison rejected both these ideas, because he thought that the minister should select solely on the grounds of ability. In addition, Bevin was offended that the self-confident young minister did not treat him with the respect which he felt was his due as Britain's leading trade unionist.

The dispute continued when Labour went into opposition following the 1931 defeat. At the 1932 Labour Party conference Morrison moved a report on behalf of the NEC to set up public corporations to run transport and electricity. He argued that the only criterion in the appointment of the boards running these corporations should be on grounds of ability. The Transport and General Workers' Union (TGWU) representative, Harold Clay, voiced the union opposition: 'I believe in political democracy,' he said, but I don't believe that can become complete until you have industrial democracy.' Morrison withdrew the controversial part of the report for further discussion, but only after Bevin had told the conference that his union had only moved their amendment 'because in our view Mr Morrison was determined to force his point of view through'.[17]

Bevin's hostility was an important factor in Morrison's failure to become party leader after Labour's defeat at the 1935 general election. The leadership had become vacant after Bevin had forced the pacifist George Lansbury to resign following the 1935 party conference. In 1934 Morrison had led the party to an election triumph in London, where Labour had gained control of the London County Council (LCC). He had also played a big part in the 1935 general election, including making the final election broadcast. After the election, Morrison, elected once again to Parliament, made a bid for the leadership, criticising Attlee, who, as a stop gap after the resignation of Lansbury, had fronted Labour's election campaign: 'We ought to have done better,' said Morrison. 'Was our appeal wide enough or constructively concrete enough?'[18]

When the Labour leadership election took place soon after the general election, Attlee led on the first ballot with 58 votes, followed by Morrison with 44 and Greenwood with 33. As had been previously agreed, the bottom candidate dropped out and, on the second ballot, Attlee received 88 votes to Morrison's 48, a decisive victory. What seems to have happened was that, on the first ballot, Attlee received almost all the votes of those MPs (most of them miners) who had sat in the 1931–5 parliament while, on the second ballot, nearly all of the votes of Greenwood switched to Attlee.

Morrison believed that there was a Freemasons' plot behind the switch of Greenwood's votes, but a more likely explanation was that Morrison suffered because he was (wrongly) thought to be 'anti-union'. Bevin, whose union MPs had voted for Greenwood, a TGWU member, on first ballot, was determined to prevent Morrison becoming leader and though, at the time, he was not impressed by Attlee's abilities, he preferred almost anybody to Morrison. He may not have issued instructions to vote for Attlee, but it is significant that, in the second ballot, almost all the votes of trade union MPs went to Attlee.

With the election of Attlee as leader, a new consideration came into play – Bevin's loyalty to Attlee. Although, before the war, Bevin had been critical of Attlee's passive style of leadership (especially over re-armament), the coming of the war, the formation of the coalition government in May 1940 and the appointment of the Labour leader as Lord Privy Seal and de facto deputy to Churchill and then of Bevin as minister of labour and, a few months later, as a member of the War Cabinet, brought the two men much closer together. Bevin began to recognise Attlee's special qualities. Somewhat to his surprise, he found that he could rely on the Labour leader's word and judgement. Despite his middle-class origins, Clement Attlee proved to be a man a trade unionist could trust. It was after experiencing the skill and firmness with which Attlee presided over the War Cabinet in Churchill's many absences abroad that Bevin began to refer to 'little

Clem' as 'our Campbell-Bannerman' (after the modest but effective prime minister who had kept the Liberal Cabinet of the 1900s together).[19]

Meanwhile, Morrison, despite his defeat by Attlee in 1935, still retained leadership ambitions. In his view, Attlee's lack of charisma was totally inappropriate in a modern democratic leader. Characteristically, Morrison, with his speaking ability, flair for publicity and political dynamism, was confident he could do better and, following the publication of the Beveridge Report in November 1942, saw an opportunity to press his claim. After Churchill and Bevin, Morrison was the most publicly prominent member of the coalition government. From the winter of 1942 until the summer of 1943, he launched a controversial campaign of speeches on the themes of postwar reconstruction. One historian has called it 'Morrison's Midlothian moment',[20] while R.A. Butler, education secretary and chairman of the Conservative Party's Postwar Problems Committee, wrote that 'Herbert Morrison is bidding for the treasurership [of the Labour Party] and, some say, the leadership.'[21]

Bevin's suspicions of Morrison were once again roused, on this occasion strengthened by what he saw as his duty to protect Attlee. By then, Bevin's dislike of Morrison had 'hardened into an immovable prejudice',[22] so much so that he often made *sotto voce* sneers and jibes when the Home Secretary spoke in the War Cabinet. At the June 1943 Labour Party conference, Bevin deliberately swung the block vote of the TGWU behind the discredited Greenwood in order to halt Morrison's bid for the treasurership. As Attlee's biographer wrote, 'it was Ernest Bevin who cooked his [Morrison's] goose.'[23]

It should have been a warning to Morrison that Attlee, with Bevin behind him, would be very difficult to dislodge. However, in 1945, as the war came to an end, Morrison attempted to topple Attlee. His tactics were based on the assumption, shared by most politicians, that Labour would be defeated, albeit narrowly, by the Conservatives led by Churchill. He successfully argued for a break-up of the coalition and an early general election in which he, as chairman of Labour's campaign committee, would play a prominent role. At the 1945 party conference, his supporters, who included the party chairman Ellen Wilkinson and her successor Harold Laski, tried to persuade Attlee to stand down. It is possible that, if Labour had lost the 1945 election, Morrison would have been able to supplant Attlee, but Labour's unexpected landslide victory inevitably consolidated Attlee's position.

When on 25 July Attlee had returned home from the Potsdam Conference of the three victorious powers (to which he had been invited by Churchill), he found a letter awaiting him from Morrison. Morrison had written that he had been approached by a number of colleagues asking him to 'accept nomination for the leadership of the parliamentary party'; he went on to argue that, whatever the result of the election, the new parliament was bound to include many new members, who should have 'the opportunity of deciding as to what type of leadership they want'. Morrison had concluded the letter by giving Attlee notice that, if elected to Parliament, he intended to stand for leader.[24]

On the afternoon of 26 July, as it became clear that Labour stood on the brink of power, a crucial meeting took place in Bevin's room at Transport House, the building the Transport and General Workers' Union shared with the Labour Party. With the party's national secretary, Morgan Philips, Attlee, Bevin and Morrison gathered in Bevin's room to discuss the implications of Labour's victory. Attlee began by reading out a message which he had received from Churchill in which the Prime Minister conceded defeat and congratulated Attlee on Labour's victory, adding that he was going to the Palace at 7 p.m. to tender his immediate resignation and would advise the King to ask Attlee to form a government. Instead of accepting Attlee's prior claim, Morrison then interrupted to say that Attlee had no right to accept the King's invitation to form a government until the new parliamentary party had elected its new leader. He also expressed reluctance to serve under Attlee. Morrison based his argument for a fresh leadership election on a dubious reading of the rules drawn up by the Labour Party after the 1931 MacDonald debacle; these stated that there should be a party meeting to decide whether or not to form a government, but they nowhere mentioned the need for a fresh leadership election.

Attlee and Bevin firmly refuted Morrison's case on both constitutional and political grounds. As Attlee pointed out:

If you're invited by the king to form a government you don't say you can't reply for forty-eight hours. You accept the commission and you either bring it off or you don't and if you don't you go back and say you can't and advise the king to send for someone else.[25]

The political point was that the voters had supported the Labour Party in the belief that, if Labour won, Attlee would be prime minister. To change leaders now would give the impression of an indecisive and divided party, incapable of running the country.

During the meeting, Morrison was called away to take a telephone call from Stafford Cripps, whom Morrison claimed agreed with him about the need for a leadership election. While Morrison was out of the room, a crucial conversation took place. Bevin asked Morgan Phillips: 'If I stood against Clem, should I win?' Phillips replied: 'On a split vote, I think you would.' Then Bevin, as if reassured as to the importance of his own position, turned to Attlee and said: 'Clem, you go to the Palace straightaway.'

This was a key moment for Attlee. He already had Churchill's message tendering his immediate resignation and advising the King to send for Attlee in his favour. Now, he had received the vital support of Bevin as well. Bevin had no leadership ambitions for himself. Having spent most of his life as a trade unionist, he found the Parliamentary Labour Party (PLP) and indeed Parliament itself difficult to handle. He was content to serve under a self-effacing leader whom he could trust. He certainly was not prepared to serve under Morrison, whom he disliked and distrusted. Acting with decision, Attlee, after taking tea with his family, went to the Palace (in a prewar Hillman driven by his wife) and immediately accepted the King's commission to form a government.

From the Palace, Attlee and his wife drove to a victory rally at the Central Hall, Westminster. Behind the scenes, Morrison and his friends had been urging Labour MPs to support a fresh vote on the leadership. Morrison said to John Parker, MP for Dagenham, as they entered the gentlemen's lavatory together, 'We cannot have this man as our leader.' But Parker, like most other MPs, felt it was too late to change. Significantly, when the slight figure of Attlee appeared on the platform, it was to ringing cheers which became deafening when Attlee announced that he had been to the Palace and accepted the King's invitation to form a government. Morrison's ill-judged coup had failed.

Still Morrison persisted. On the afternoon of the next day, 27 July, Attlee called a meeting of the administration committee of the PLP, which consisted of the party officers and the elected members of the Parliamentary Executive Committee. After Attlee had made an opening statement in which he stressed the need to establish a skeleton government while he was away in Potsdam, Morrison raised the leadership issue again, repeating the argument he had made at Transport House the previous day. However, while agreeing that the rules required that the party should be consulted before the formation of a government, the meeting concluded that they said nothing about the election of a new leader. The committee also took the view that, in calling the meeting, Attlee was in fact consulting them and authorised him to go ahead and form a government. The meeting was over in 30 minutes, with Morrison completely isolated.

Presumably on the principle that, if you cannot ride two horses, you have no right to be in the circus (as Jimmy Maxton once said), Morrison had, that morning, been to see Attlee and the chief whip, William Whiteley, to discuss his position in the Labour Cabinet. He asked for the Foreign Office. When Bevin heard that Morrison was demanding the Foreign Office, while at the same time pressing for a leadership election, he rang him up and told him: 'If you go on mucking about like this, you won't be in the bloody government at all.'[26]

Although Attlee resisted Morrison's bid for the Foreign Office, he knew that he had to be brought into the government. Like Bevin, he resented Morrison's 'mucking about' but he fully understood that his ability and stature as a former member of Churchill's War Cabinet made him indispensable to the new administration. So, in an inspired move, he offered him the job as 'supremo' on the home front, combining Attlee's former coordinating role in Churchill's coalition government as Lord President of the Council with leadership of the House of Commons. Morrison at first refused, suspecting he was being bought off with a grand-sounding but inferior position. However, the persuasive powers of Whiteley, as well as Attlee's additional offer of the recognition of Morrison as de facto number two in the government, made him change his mind.

The appointment of Morrison as overlord on the home front had an impact on other Cabinet positions. At the Transport House meeting on 26 July, Bevin had taken Attlee aside and told him that he would like to become chancellor of the Exchequer. Attlee asked whom he should make foreign secretary and Bevin replied that it should be the old Etonian Socialist, Hugh Dalton, who was recognised as the party's foreign affairs specialist. Indeed, when Attlee had seen Dalton shortly before lunch on 27 July, he advised him to pack his bag for Potsdam, saying he would confirm the appointment later in the afternoon. However, when Dalton met Attlee at 4 p.m., Attlee had changed his mind and decided that Bevin should go to the Foreign Office and that Dalton (a trained economist) should become chancellor.

Why did Attlee change his mind, if that is indeed what he did? At the Palace meeting on 26 July, the King had pressed the case for Bevin as foreign secretary. However, it is unlikely that the monarch's advice was decisive. Later, Attlee said to Bevin's biographer: 'I thought foreign affairs were going to be pretty difficult and a heavy tank was what was going to be required rather than a sniper.'[27] An equally important consideration may have been the need, given Morrison's home front appointment, to keep Morrison and Bevin apart. Attlee told Dalton: 'If they were both on the home front they would quarrel all the time.'[28] An additional factor could also have been that, having resisted Morrison's claim to the Foreign Office, putting the other major Cabinet heavyweight in the post effectively blocked off any further designs Morrison might have had on the position.

The next day, 28 July, the new configuration was confirmed. Attlee announced his first appointments, including Bevin as foreign secretary,

Morrison as Lord President of the Council and leader of the House of Commons, Dalton as chancellor of the Exchequer and Cripps as president of the Board of Trade. When the first group of ministers arrived at the Palace to kiss hands and receive the seals of office, Bevin did not hide his disappointment. Pointing to Dalton, he said: 'I wanted the job he's got,'[29] and, as they were leaving for a meeting of Labour MPs at Beaver Hall in the City, he told Dalton that he had some ideas about income tax which he would like to discuss with the new chancellor. However, at Beaver Hall, where nearly 400 jubilant Labour MPs had gathered, it was Bevin who, in a highly effective impromptu speech, moved a vote of confidence in the new Prime Minister. As Attlee rose to reply, the meeting gave him a lengthy standing ovation, which finally crushed Morrison's attempted coup. With Bevin, Attlee then left the meeting to catch a plane for Potsdam, leaving Morrison in charge. Attlee's confident gesture may have established Morrison publicly as his deputy but it also underlined that he, and not Morrison, was in overall charge.

Dalton described the 1945 administration as 'a well-balanced government, with a number of strong and combative personalities, and Attlee held it together with much tact and patience'.[30] Attlee saw his role in Cabinet as an impartial chairman, whose job it was to facilitate business and get decisions. He relied on the heavyweights in the Cabinet, especially Bevin, Morrison, Dalton and Cripps, supplemented by the wartime rebel, Aneurin Bevan, whom the Prime Minister had brought into the administration to set up the National Health Service, to supply ideas and impetus. As Bevin's biographer, Alan Bullock, perceptively put it, 'there were half a dozen men in the government with more obvious talents than his own; it was Attlee's strength as a Prime Minister that he turned this to his advantage.'[31]

In Cabinet meetings, Attlee turned first to Herbert Morrison, coordinator on the home front, and concluded with the foreign secretary, Ernest Bevin, before giving a terse summing up. Though abrupt with other ministers, he allowed Bevin latitude to roam, often brilliantly, not only over external affairs but also to intervene in domestic matters as well. At the end of Cabinet meetings, Attlee would ask the Foreign Secretary to stay behind. It has been said that the close personal relationship between the two men – which, as we have seen, had developed during the war – was the linchpin which helped hold the Labour government together. But it was acknowledged, both at the time and by later historians, that Morrison's role on the home front was also crucial.

Not surprisingly, given Morrison's designs on Attlee's job, relations between these two were much less close. Morrison's view of Attlee was that he 'doodled' (Attlee was renowned for his 'doodles') in Cabinet when he should have been giving a lead. Attlee was well aware what Morrison thought of him but he also realised that the Lord President, with his exceptional drive and administrative flair, was the best man to run Labour's domestic programme. The Prime Minister's skill was that, by separating his two most powerful personalities, both symbolically in Cabinet (where Attlee sat between Bevin and Morrison) and, more importantly, in terms of offices (one in charge of foreign affairs, the other the supremo on the home front), he managed to get the two men to work together, to the benefit of his party and government.

After the party's landslide 1945 election victory, Labour was riding high in Parliament but the extreme weakness of Britain's postwar financial and economic situation almost immediately threatened to overwhelm the government. On 21 August, only a week after the Japanese surrender, President Truman signed a document which brought the Lend-Lease Agreement, which had enabled the UK to receive weapons, equipment and materials without charge, to an abrupt and immediate end. Without Lend-Lease or a loan to replace it, the UK was virtually bankrupt. In the stark words of Dalton's chief economic adviser, Lord Keynes, the country was facing 'a financial Dunkirk'.[32]

The Labour Cabinet sent Keynes to Washington to negotiate US assistance. It soon became clear that a free gift (for which Keynes had hoped) was unobtainable and that a loan would only come on strict American terms, including making sterling freely convertible into dollars as soon as possible. The Cabinet minutes show that, after two long sessions of Cabinet, in which both Morrison and Bevin played their part, the government finally accepted the situation. According to the Cabinet secretary's note, Bevin was especially eloquent:

> I believe our bluff is called. We can't ask them [the British people] to face another three years of even tighter living – with industrial unrest. We are in Shylock's hands [...] No alternative now but to accept this unless you are ready to demand these further sacrifices from the British People.[33]

On 6 December, the loan agreement, amounting in total to $4.4 billion, was signed, less than had been originally asked for but still, as Keynes said in his last speech in the House of Lords (he died in April 1946), 'a substantial sum'.[34] Although the US Congress took some months to ratify the agreement, the Labour government proceeded on the basis that it was going to get the American loan. It therefore went ahead with implementing Labour's programme as set out in its manifesto *Let us Face the Future* – 'Socialism on Credit' as one critic called it.[35]

The key figure in getting Labour's programme on the statute book was Herbert Morrison and the key committee was the Future Legislation Committee, with the Lord President in the chair. This was the kind of strategic work at which Morrison was highly skilled: 'Herbert played it like a game of racing demon. He would deal with thirty or forty bills, calling on each minister in turn to explain his bill, how long it was, how much time it needed – Herbert went at great speed.'[36] The *Manchester Guardian* (as it was then called) commented, 'Herbert Morrison is omnivorous for work himself and he is enormously enjoying the job of piling the work on the House of Commons.'[37]

By the end of the 1945/6 session Parliament had passed the following bills: an Act setting up the National Health Service, steered through the Commons by Nye Bevan, which still survives nearly 70 years later; a National Insurance Act establishing a comprehensive system of social benefits on the lines proposed by the Beveridge Report; an Industrial Injuries Act to provide compensation for industrial injuries; the New Towns Act; and Acts nationalising the Bank of England, the coal industry, civil aviation and Cable and Wireless. In total, 83 Acts were put on the statute book in that session. Dalton rightly called 1946 Labour's 'annus mirabilis'.

The Lord President proved to be an outstanding leader of the House of Commons. He not only drove an exceptional amount of legislation through the Commons but also tried to keep his own backbenchers enthusiastic and involved, while at the same time respecting the rights of the opposition. In the afternoon, Morrison was almost always available in Parliament: 'He would settle in his room in the Commons and hold open court for MPs barging in with their troubles,' said a colleague. The Lord President suspended standing orders to give Labour MPs more freedom. He set up a liaison committee between Labour backbenchers and government, as well as establishing party backbench policy groups. And he arranged for all bills, except finance bills and bills of constitutional importance, to be sent to standing committee; this change not only speeded up business but also gave backbenchers a greater role. On all sides, his work as leader of the House and party manager was widely praised. Observing him from the opposition front bench, Anthony Eden called him 'the linchpin of the post-war Labour Government'.[38] With his quip and ready wit, Tories saw him as a cockney 'cheeky chappie'. As so often in politics, his enemies were on his own side, especially on the left.

Through the Socialisation of Industry Committee, which, as the acknowledged party expert on public ownership, Morrison chaired, the Lord President controlled the timing and structures of individual nationalisations. It was an advantage that, with the exception of road transport and iron and steel (about which Morrison himself had always had doubts), which was to cause trouble later, most of Labour's nationalisation Acts were relatively non-controversial. It was, for example, generally agreed that coal was in a mess and that the railways were very run down; gas and electricity were, to a great extent, already in municipal ownership and Labour ministers were usually able to quote in evidence committees of inquiry set up by prewar or wartime governments. The official opposition often did not oppose nationalisation legislation (as in the case of the Bank of England and also of Cable and Wireless and civil aviation), while a Conservative Party pamphlet, *The Industrial Charter*, produced in May 1947 by prominent Tories such as R.A. Butler, Harold Macmillan, Oliver Lyttelton and David Maxwell Fyfe, accepted the public ownership of coal, railways and the Bank of England. In the immediate postwar conditions, Morrison's policy of public ownership of industries vital to the economy seemed to be a sensible and pragmatic response to their problems.

If, throughout much of the 18 months following the 1945 election, Morrison was on the crest of a wave, Bevin, in his role as the foreign secretary having to cope with Britain's precarious economic and strategic position, was tested to the limit. He brought to his new post not only his past experience as the country's leading trade unionist and outstanding member of Churchill's War Cabinet but also his exceptional intelligence, his humane imagination and, above all, his force of character. Like Churchill, Bevin saw himself as playing a national rather than a purely party political role, with responsibility for maintaining the national interests of his country – its security against external attack, its independence as a country and its right to a decent standard of living. He quickly came to recognise that Britain's overseas commitments would have to be scaled down but was firmly opposed to an abrupt withdrawal from Britain's role, which could create a dangerous power vacuum.

When Bevin became foreign secretary in 1945, he tried to negotiate a satisfactory peace treaty with its great wartime ally, the Soviet Union. This was not because he had any illusions about the nature of the Soviet regime. But, as the weaker power, he understood that it was in Britain's interest to settle outstanding disputes and, if possible, to avoid the division of Europe into rival camps. It was his experience of the obstructive behaviour of Russian diplomats at the Council of Foreign Ministers (CFM) and at meetings of the new international organisation, the United Nations, and of Soviet intervention in Greece, Turkey, northern Iran, Eastern Europe and above all in Germany which convinced him that an understanding with Stalin was not possible. Bevin's private secretary, Pierson Dixon, explained the Soviet attitude as: 'The Russians see that the war has left us financially and economically weak and dependent of the US. They also know the American phobia about the British Empire and calculate that we cannot rely fully on American support when defending out imperial interests.'[39]

For the first year and a half after the end of the war, the US did indeed remain aloof from the United Kingdom – so much so that it was Bevin's recurring nightmare that the Americans might do a deal with the Russians over his head. He was increasingly convinced of the importance of the United States to Britain and that British and European security could only be protected by a long-term alliance with the Americans. For Bevin it was an extremely difficult balancing act: if he moved too soon he might be rebuffed. He also had to contend with opposition from the left within his own party. He had to play a waiting game, relying mainly on his own skill and resolution. As his first biographer wrote, 'In a very real sense his chief asset in foreign policy at this period – and that of his country – was his own character.'[40]

The year 1947 was a climacteric for the Labour government. The first three months were dominated by a fuel crisis, exacerbated by the coldest winter of the twentieth century. In August, following the introduction of sterling convertibility on 15 July, there was a major financial crisis which necessitated a humiliating suspension of convertibility after only a month. The near-collapse of the government's financial and economic policies then led to a political crisis, which included an attempt by Stafford Cripps, with support from Dalton, to make Ernest Bevin prime minister. On 13 November Dalton resigned, after an unpremeditated leak, and was replaced by Cripps. The government's reputation for competence was badly damaged by these events and, though it gradually recovered its balance, after 1947 it was 'never glad confident morning again'.

Britain's economic weakness also had a major impact on external policy. In February, Bevin gave notice that Britain would refer the Palestine issue to the United Nations; the Cabinet agreed that British aid to Greece and Turkey would not be renewed after the end of March and that the remaining troops in Greece would have to be withdrawn; and Attlee announced to the Commons that Britain would hand over its responsibilities in India 'by a date not later than June 1948'. A similar announcement was also made about withdrawal from Ceylon (now Sri Lanka) and Burma. As Alan Bullock wrote, 'the British Empire seemed to be in the process of dissolution, and the British lacking either the resources or the will to prevent it.'[41]

The economic and financial crisis weakened Morrison's previously strong political position. As supremo on the home front, he had overall responsibility for economic affairs. In addition, the Lord President had direct control of economic planning and coordination. In practice, although an official steering committee on economic development was set up to report to the Lord President's Committee and an economic survey was produced in 1947, British economic planning (in contrast to the French system) amounted to little more than an extension of wartime controls, above all over essential raw materials. The truth was that Morrison, like Attlee, was out of his depth on economics. As Morrison's biographers pointed out, 'He sat in the Cabinet and in committee from May to July and offered nothing of relevance to the crisis.'[42]

It did not help that from January to April Morrison was seriously ill with thrombosis, so much so that, for at least two months, he was forbidden to work on government papers. When the minister of fuel and power, Emmanuel Shinwell, asked him for advice about the fuel crisis, Morrison had to turn him away. Churchill sent him a bowl of spring flowers, and he was visited not only by the Prime Minister, but by his old sparring partner, Ernest Bevin, who was himself suffering from a strained heart. In Morrison's absence, Cripps emerged as the strong man on the economic front, making a number of impressive speeches, culminating in a brilliant winding-up performance on the second day of a two-day debate on the state of the nation. Combining a grasp of long-term trends with a mastery of detail, he displayed the leadership which Labour backbenchers had been demanding and not getting from either Attlee or Morrison or Dalton. The performance of the Prime Minister was almost entirely passive. He seemed content merely to act as a chairman without giving the lead the Cabinet and the party so desperately needed.

Dalton's account of a meeting between the leading ministers and officials during July illustrates the effect of the crisis on the morale of the Cabinet:

> I put before them my draft of the paper for tomorrow's Cabinet proposing a variety of actions. Bevin, who had obviously had a very good dinner [...] was at his worst. Morrison, after an hour of this, left the room in indignation, declaring [...] that he had had enough of this drunken monologue [...] Attlee showed no power of gripping or guiding the talk. We adjourn at half an hour past midnight, Bevin enquiring as he lurched towards the door [...] Where do we sleep tonight – in 'ere?[43]

The summer crisis over convertibility, following on so closely from the winter fuel crisis, inevitably raised questions about the leadership. Dalton wrote that 'some doubted whether Attlee had the personality, or the strength of popular appeal, to be the leader in these increasingly critical months.'[44]

Two years before, Morrison would have been the obvious successor. But in 1947 Bevin was the name mentioned by Labour MPs during late-night sessions as they discussed a change of leadership. At the end of July, after the Durham Miners' Gala, Bevin and Dalton shared a car back to London. Bevin complained about Attlee's weakness as a leader and failure to make up his mind; he said that Morrison was a sick man and described Cripps as 'more than halfway to Moscow'. But when Dalton passed on his parliamentary private secretary's report that a large number of MPs wanted Bevin to become prime minister, the Foreign Secretary, while admitting that his own PPS had said the same, replied that he did not want to do anyone out of a job. As the car turned into Downing Street, Dalton persisted, urging him 'not to put out of his mind the possibility of becoming PM'. However, the July move to depose Attlee petered out, as summer revolts in Parliament usually do.

The attempted September coup, initiated by Cripps, was a more serious affair. It came from within the Cabinet, with three of the big five – Cripps, Dalton and Morrison – agreeing on the need to topple Attlee, a potentially decisive group if they acted together. Cripps' plan was to make Bevin prime minister and minister of production, with himself as Lord President in charge of economic planning (instead of Morrison) and Dalton as foreign secretary in Bevin's place. Cripps proposed that he, Dalton and Morrison should go to Attlee and force him to resign in favour of Bevin.

Dalton, who doubted whether Morrison would support a scheme from which he would gain nothing, told Cripps that he (Dalton) would go to see Attlee only if Morrison went as well. As Dalton had expected, the Lord President rejected Cripps' plan. Morrison agreed that Attlee ought to be deposed but thought that he and not Bevin should take his place. As he told Dalton the following day, he also feared that, if Bevin became prime minister, he (Morrison) would be 'knifed'. Morrison was also deeply hurt that neither Dalton nor Cripps – both of whom had in the past supported him as a potential leader – any longer saw him as a candidate. Morrison, understandably, blamed Dalton and the Treasury for the convertibility crisis but it had also rubbed off on him. It was his failure as economic coordinator, possibly combined with continuing doubts about his health, which had taken him out of the reckoning.

On 8 September, Cripps told Dalton that, with Morrison out of the picture, he had decided to see Attlee alone. The Cripps–Attlee meeting took place at 10 Downing Street after dinner the next day. If the winter fuel crisis and the summer's financial crisis had shown up Attlee's weakness as a prime minister, his exchanges with Cripps revealed that he remained a master, as an historian of the Labour Party put it, of the 'coup de repos'.[45] When Cripps set out his plan (with Attlee being replaced as prime minister by Bevin, Attlee going to the Treasury, and Dalton to the Foreign Office), Attlee calmly destroyed the Cripps scheme. He pointed out that he had no head for financial matters; Bevin did not want to leave the Foreign Office, and in any case the party did not want him as leader; and that Bevin and

Morrison would never get on in such close proximity.[46] According to Attlee's version of the meeting, the Prime Minister then picked up the scrambler (a device to encode messages) and asked for Bevin. When he came on the line, Attlee said, 'Stafford's here; he says you want to change your job.' Bevin replied that he had no intention of leaving the Foreign Office.[47] So much for Cripps' plan. Attlee followed up with a 'killer' addition. Unmoved by Cripps' scheme to depose him and apparently taking at face value his argument that a coordinated effort should be made to improve the economy, Attlee suggested that Cripps himself should become minister of production and that a small economic committee of senior ministers should be set up – the big five plus Viscount Addison. It was an offer which Cripps, who was in effect being given Morrison's responsibilities as economic coordinator, could hardly refuse. As Dalton noted, 'within the government, the movement, begun by Cripps, with my support, to put Bevin in Attlee's place, had now turned into a movement to put Cripps in Morrison's place, or at least in the most important part of it.'[48]

Attlee had skilfully disposed of the biggest political crisis of his premiership by buying Cripps off with a job which he coveted and by persuading Morrison, who remained Attlee's deputy, to give up, without losing too much face, a job which he did not enjoy. Ironically, it was partly the refusal of Morrison, who did not rate Attlee, to join Cripps and Dalton in replacing the Prime Minister which enabled Attlee to scupper the coup. The Prime Minister's rock was, of course, Bevin. If the Foreign Secretary had wavered during the crisis, it is doubtful that Attlee could have survived. Bevin's comment on Attlee's performance is worth quoting: 'He plucked victory from defeat. I love the little man.'[49] In November, Attlee both strengthened his position and gave the government's economic policy a new beginning when he accepted Dalton's resignation following Dalton's inadvertent leaking of his budget and made Cripps chancellor of the Exchequer in his place.

After the crisis year of 1947, the Labour government staged a strong recovery throughout 1948 and into 1949. Attlee had survived with an enhanced reputation for shrewdness and nerve. Alongside him were not only Bevin and Morrison but now also the new chancellor, Stafford Cripps. Immensely able, exceptionally hardworking and with the moral authority that came both from his approach to his work and from his religious convictions, Cripps was one of the most powerful chancellors of the twentieth century.

With Cripps' new authority over economic affairs, Morrison was no longer quite the predominant figure on the home front that he had been from 1945 to 1947. Maurice Webb, chairman of the Parliamentary Labour Party and a close friend of Morrison's, expressed party feeling: 'I fear the terms of the announcement [that Morrison was giving up his economic role] will be commonly interpreted as notice of your withdrawal from the highest places [...] I suppose this means the end of Morrison is a typical comment made to me.'[50] It was certainly a serious setback but it was by no means the end. As leader of the House of Commons, Lord President of the Council and deputy prime minister, Morrison continued to play a vital role in the government and, with his close links to the party, the nearer the election drew, the more crucial that role became.

For Bevin this was the high point of his time as foreign secretary. The historian of the Attlee governments, Kenneth Morgan, has written: 'The period between [US Secretary of State] Marshall's Harvard speech on 5 June 1947 and the coming into being of NATO in April 1949 is a period of sustained creativity such as few, if any, British Foreign Secretaries have produced since the time of the Elder Pitt.'[51]

Two notes from Bevin written in late February to the US secretary of state, George Marshall, precipitated a dramatic shift in US policy; these informed Marshall that after 31 March 1947 Britain could not continue to be responsible for aid to Greece and Turkey. Added to the prospect of other British withdrawals (from India, Burma and Palestine), these notes confronted the United States with the momentous decision of whether or not to take over from Britain the world role which the British could no longer sustain alone.

The revolution in American foreign policy was initiated first on 12 March 1947 in the Truman doctrine when President Truman announced to an initially sceptical Congress that the United States would stand ready 'to support free peoples who are resisting attempted subjugation by armed minorities or by outside pressures, primarily by providing economic and financial aid, essential to economic stability and orderly political processes'.[52] Three months later, Secretary of State Marshall followed up Truman's historic announcement by his speech at Harvard, in which he put the case for a European recovery programme, with the initiative to come from Europe.

The story goes that Bevin first heard of Marshall's speech on his bedside radio. He reacted immediately. Indeed, his biographer has argued that his prompt action was his most decisive personal contribution as foreign secretary.[53] In a burst of energy, astonishing for a man in his late sixties suffering from heart disease, Bevin spent the next three months masterminding Europe's response to Marshall's life line; this led to the creation of the European Recovery Programme which underwrote the remarkable postwar economic and political renaissance of Western Europe.

The refusal of the Soviet Union and its allies to discuss the Marshall proposals and the subsequent breakdown of the Council of Foreign Ministers' talks in London on the future of Germany marked the beginning of the Cold War. Following the failure of the London conference, Bevin made a big speech to the House of Commons on 22 January 1948, calling for a Western union. Highlighting the ruthless methods which the Soviet Union was using to eliminate opposition in Eastern Europe, he said that 'the free nations of Western Europe must now draw together.'[54] *The Times* commented, 'What Mr Bevin has done is to strike the dominant chord. Just as he was swift to seize the initiative offered by Mr Marshall last June, so he has now been quick to offer an initiative himself.'[55] Showing the United States that Europe meant business, Bevin set in train talks in the Western European capitals which resulted in the Treaty of Brussels, in which the UK, France, Belgium, the Netherlands and Luxembourg agreed to set up the Western European Union, a military alliance for mutual defence which was to last 50 years.

Then, in late February 1948, the Communist coup in Prague had an electrifying effect on the West. Bevin did not think that the Soviet Union was about to go to war, but he believed that the West (including the United States) had to act on the assumption that it was facing a calculated challenge from the Soviets and had, therefore, to show it had the will and unity to resist. In March, Bevin sent Marshall a powerful message in which he urged the need for the British and US governments to consult without delay on the establishment of an Atlantic security system. This was the first mention of what was to become the North Atlantic Treaty Organisation (NATO). After consulting the US President, Marshall replied to the British Ambassador: 'Please inform Mr Bevin that in accordance with your aide memoire of 11 March, we are prepared to proceed at once in the joint discussions on the establishment of an Atlantic Security System.'[56] Talks began at an official level but the plan for a North Atlantic pact could not make decisive progress until after the US presidential election in November.

Meanwhile, the West faced a new danger when the Soviets blockaded Berlin. Once again, Bevin, at a time when France was without a government, acted with firmness and resolution on behalf of Western Europe. He made it clear to the Americans that it would be a disaster for the Western allies to abandon Berlin. With the support of the Cabinet Committee on Germany, he agreed to the stationing of American B-29 bombers in East Anglia, as well as their deployment in Germany. He also gave his backing to the bold idea of supplying the western sectors of Berlin by airlift and persuaded the Americans, with British help, to do it. It was an astonishing success, with up to 7,000 tons of food and fuel being flown in daily by US and British planes. For 323 days, the 2 million inhabitants of Western Berlin were supplied with food and fuel by air.

In November 1948, the re-election of Truman as president gave the green light for serious negotiations on the North Atlantic pact. Bevin's biographer wrote that the signing on 4 April 1949 of the treaty setting up NATO was 'not only the climax of his career as Foreign Minister but with a German settlement at last secured and the prospect of the Berlin blockade being lifted – the greatest ten days of his life.'[57] This was not what Bevin had had in mind in 1945, but his experience of the deliberate snuffing-out of any prospect of democracy in Eastern Europe, above all in Czechoslovakia, and the blockade of Berlin by the Soviet Union convinced him of the need for a powerful consolidation of the West, in the form of a North Atlantic alliance. This was needed, as Bevin realised, to limit Soviet gains in Europe and to allow room for Western Europe to prosper in freedom, a prospect which the implementation of the Marshall Plan had made possible. When in April 1949, Bevin walked forward, with his characteristic rolling gait to sign the North Atlantic Treaty in Washington, he was warmly applauded in 'a fitting tribute to his work'.[58]

After a good 1948, in the spring of 1949, the economic tide began, once again, to turn against Labour. A recession in the United States hit exports, while imports from the US rose, moving the UK balance of payments on current account into deficit. Against this background, speculative pressure against sterling increased, in the expectation that it would soon be devalued.

By 1949 the strain of office was affecting the health of Labour's ministers. Cripps' tendency to overwork and then fall sick, usually from acute colitis, was nothing new. By February 1949 he had made himself ill again. In July he was in such a bad way that he was forced to go for six weeks' rest and treatment to a Swiss sanatorium. Cripps' ill health was an important factor in the slow and uncertain response of the government to the devaluation crisis which dominated the summer and early autumn. Bevin's heart problems also continued to trouble him, particularly when he was attending conferences abroad.

At the end of August, following a Cabinet decision in favour of the principle of devaluation, the Chancellor and the Foreign Secretary were authorised to discuss devaluation with the US authorities and 'to form a view, in the light of those discussions on the amount and timing of this measure'.[59] The same day, the two men boarded the RMS *Mauretania* bound for the United States. Bevin could not travel by air because of his heart and stayed in bed resting, while Cripps used the boat journey to prolong his convalescence. The two ministers did not actually meet for the first three or four days. This was because Cripps rose at 4 a.m., often pacing the deck till dawn, retiring to bed early at around 4 or 5 p.m.; while Bevin did not rise until late afternoon. It was not until well into the voyage when Cripps agreed to stay up a little later that their officials had the opportunity to brief the two statesmen together.[60]

They did not actually decide on the new rate until the British delegation reached Washington. On 12 September, the officials put the alternatives (either $2.80 or $3 to £1) to Cripps and Bevin in Bevin's sitting room at the British Embassy. Cripps, who believed that devaluation was the equivalent of an immoral act, had to be dissuaded from asking the Americans what rate they would suggest. Finally Cripps turned to Bevin, who was still dressed in his pyjamas and dressing gown, and asked his opinion. Bevin's first reaction was to ask Edwin Plowden, a prominent industrialist who was Cripps' chief planning officer, 'what effect will a rate of $2.80 have on the price of the standard load of bread?'[61] Once reassured, the Foreign Secretary settled for a rate of $2.80 to £1. In this almost casual way the new rate, which was to last until the Wilson government devalued in November 1967, was decided.

The coming election dominated the government's thoughts. Morrison, whose stock had risen as the polls drew nearer, had spent an increasing amount of time planning for the campaign. On the face of it, Labour's electoral prospects looked good. It could point to an impressive record of achievement, having successfully implemented the programme on which the government had been elected in 1945. Moreover, despite the economic and financial crises with which the administration had to contend, they had not lost a single by-election. But Morrison was well aware that Labour had owed its great victory in 1945 not just to its working-class vote but to the coalition between the working and middle classes. If there was to be a Labour government, it was essential to retain 'the one, two or more millions of voters, "the floaters" who in the end will in all likelihood determine' the result of the election.[62] As he told the 1949 party conference, 'we do not want to be a narrow party, we want to be the party of all the useful people, the party of the Nation.'[63]

The question was how to construct a programme which could appeal beyond Labour's committed supporters. Morrison was well aware that the presentation of a further nationalisation shopping list was unlikely to win support. He argued for concentrating on making existing nationalised industries more efficient. As he said, 'advance must be followed by detailed consolidation and by exploiting the territory that has been gained; if we go on always stretching our hands for more and not making good the gains we have claimed only disaster can follow.'[64] But 'consolidation' was hardly a ringing battle cry for a centre-left party.

There was also the issue of the timing of the election. Concerned about the charge made by Churchill that he had deceived the public over devaluation, Cripps insisted that there should be a general election before the budget. He took the view that any budget introduced before the election would be 'electioneering' and therefore immoral. At a meeting of ministers on 7 December, he wanted an election early in the New Year. Morrison preferred to wait until spring or early summer because he feared that winter weather would depress the turnout of Labour voters. Bevin, who was recuperating in Eastbourne, sent a note saying that, as he was 'no politician', he would accept their decision. Attlee, who would almost certainly have preferred a later date, came down on the Chancellor's side because he knew that Cripps would have resigned if the election had been delayed. On 17 January 1950, he announced an election for 23 February.

Morrison played a key role in the election campaign in 1950. Not only was he chairman of the special campaign sub-committee, but he spoke at about 80 meetings. His biographers called him 'Labour's election handyman'.[65] At an eve-of-poll press conference he made an appeal to Liberal and middle-class voters, especially the professionals, the technicians and housewives, stressing that they were 'a useful and valuable element in our society'. Bevin's poor health prevented him from playing an active part in the election, though he was persuaded to speak for Morrison in his Lewisham constituency. 'I'll come for you, Mabel,' he told Morrison's agent

Mabel Raison, 'but not that so-and-so candidate of yours.'[66] The meeting went well, though Bevin had to have treatment for his heart before he could go home. On the Labour side, the surprise star of the election was the Prime Minister himself. Driven by his wife, Vi, in a prewar Humber saloon, he made 34 speeches, mostly in marginal constituencies. It was significant that Cripps, so often critical of Attlee as a performer, suggested that the Prime Minister rather than Morrison deliver the final election broadcast.

The turnout on election day was a record 84 per cent. Labour substantially increased its poll compared with 1945 and finished over 0.75 million ahead of the Tories; it won 13,266,176 votes and gained 46.1 per cent of the poll, compared with 12,492,414 and 43.5 per cent for the Conservatives and their allies. In terms of seats, the first returns went well for Labour, with the party polling heavily in its safe urban seats. But the next day, the Tories made substantial gains in rural seats and in the suburbs, especially around London, with the result that Labour's comfortable lead in votes gave the party only a precarious overall majority of five in terms of seats. Morrison commented, 'The British people are wonderful. They didn't mean to chuck us out, only to give us a sharp kick in the pants. But I think they've overdone it a bit.'[67]

The second Attlee government, which was in office from February 1950 to October 1951, had few legislative achievements to its credit. However, it presided over an impressive post-devaluation economic recovery and, until the Korean War started in June 1950, looked as though it might pull through to better times. But the impact of the war and the subsequent heavy re-armament programme overburdened the economy and also led indirectly to a disastrous Cabinet split over health charges and the resignation of Aneurin Bevan – the beginning of the end for the Labour government.

By 1950, the chemistry of the Cabinet was changing. Two old stars, Bevin and Cripps, in very poor health, were operating at half speed. Morrison and Bevan were the dominant voices, soon to be joined, following Cripps' resignation in October, by Gaitskell. Given the risk of conflict between Bevan and the other two leading figures, it was a potentially combustible situation.

The government's inadequate response to the announcement in May of the Schuman Plan (named after the French foreign minister, Robert Schuman) – a revolutionary proposal to pool the coal and steel resources of France and West Germany under a common authority – was in part the consequence of the declining powers of Bevin and Cripps. It is true that the Chancellor's initial reaction was that the UK should join the negotiations. But, when it came to a decision, he would not have opposed the Foreign Secretary, and even a fit Bevin would not have backed British participation in the Schuman Plan.

For Bevin, too close an involvement with plans for greater European unity was likely to be at the expense of Britain's special relationship with the United States (even though the Americans were continually urging the British to play a more active role in Europe) and its world role as leader of the Commonwealth and the colonies and manager of the sterling area. Morrison's off-the-cuff remark, 'the Durham miners won't wear it', summed up his opinion of the issue. The Prime Minister was sympathetic to the French but, as explained to the French Ambassador, 'it was quite impossible for us to sign a blank cheque.'[68] Dean Acheson wrote that the UK's failure to join the Schuman Plan, which was the first step towards the creation of the European Union, was the UK's great mistake of the postwar period: 'It was not the last clear chance for Britain to enter Europe, but it was the first wrong choice.'[69]

In the spring of 1950, Acheson saw Bevin at the US Embassy in London and was shocked by the deterioration in the Foreign Secretary's physical condition: 'I found Ernest Bevin in distressing shape [...] He had recently undergone a painful operation and was taking sedative drugs that made him doze off quite soundly during the discussion.'[70] When, in December, at the height of the Korean War Attlee flew out to Washington to meet President Truman following a press conference at which the US President seem to suggest that the United States was threatening to use the atomic bomb on China, he was not accompanied by Bevin, who was too unwell to face the long air journey.

On 9 March 1951, Bevin resigned from the Foreign Office. He had been ill for months, with most of his routine work being done by his minister of state. Attlee himself often acted as an unofficial foreign secretary. Bevin had been finding it increasingly difficult to speak in public and his continuance in office was coming under attack by the opposition. Attlee decided to move him out of the Foreign Office by making him Lord Privy Seal. Bevin is said to have complained that he was neither a lord, nor a privy, nor a seal, though he accepted the decision. On budget day, Bevin sat next to the new chancellor, Hugh Gaitskell, throughout his hour-long speech, murmuring when Gaistkell sat down, 'That was a great speech.' Four days later he died of a heart attack in his Carlton Gardens flat, with the key to his red box still in his hand. *The Times* wrote in a leading article: 'Like Churchill he seemed a visitor from the 18th Century. He was of the company of Chatham and Samuel Johnson. His place, one felt was among big men, men of strong heart and strong opinions.'[71]

With some misgivings, Morrison stepped into Bevin's shoes. When asked by Plowden whether he wanted the Treasury, Morrison replied, 'I listen to Stafford explaining those figures and I just know I could not do it.'[72] For obvious reasons he was more attracted to the idea of succeeding his old rival at the Foreign Office. He was also concerned to keep Aneurin Bevan out and felt that if he turned down the number-two job in government he might disqualify himself from the succession. But he understood the risk that he would be taking in leaving a post for which he was ideally suited to take on a responsibility outside his experience and interest. In the end Morrison decided to take the plunge. Ernest Bevin had not been impressed by Morrison's appointment. Shortly before his death, he told Francis Williams, 'I'd sooner have had Nye than 'Erbert. He might have turned out quite good.'[73] Attlee's later comment was that it was a bad mistake, 'the worst appointment I made'.[74]

Morrison was unfortunate to face an immediate crisis in his new job. The Iranian prime minister, the nationalist Dr Mohammed Mossadeq, nationalised a major British asset, the Anglo-Iranian Oil Company. Morrison tried to negotiate an agreed solution but talks broke down. The new Foreign Secretary often sounded as though he was determined to use force. The story goes that within 24 hours of taking office he asked to borrow a copy of the life of Palmerston. But in the postwar world of rising nationalism and declining British power, 'sending a gunboat' in the Palmerstonian mode was no longer an option, especially when the United States was against military intervention. At a Cabinet meeting in September, with Attlee strongly in favour of referring the dispute to the United Nations, the military option was finally ruled out. The *Observer* commented that 'our fault was not excessive weakness but empty bullying [...] Mr Morrison is rightly blamed for his disastrous mishandling of the Persian oil crisis.'[75] If he had had more time at the Foreign Office, his reputation there might have improved. As it was, his tenure as foreign secretary was widely judged to have been a failure.

Some of the blame for the resignations of Bevan, Harold Wilson and John Freeman, a junior minister at the Department of Supply, over the introduction of health charges, also rubbed off on Morrison. Attlee, who was in hospital suffering from a duodenal ulcer, later held Morrison responsible, as acting prime minister, for the resignations.[76] Certainly, Bevan believed that Morrison and Gaitskell ganged up against him. There is no evidence that Morrison ever approached Bevan directly to persuade him to compromise, although he did urge Gaitskell to make concessions. But the main responsibility lay with Attlee. Clearly his illness did not help, but an intervention by the Prime Minister before the dispute had come to Cabinet might have made a difference.

At that stage it might have been possible to nip the issue in the bud by persuading Gaitskell to give way on the health changes, perhaps adopting the formula, already used for prescription charges, of accepting the principle without setting a date for implementation. As it was, what the historian of the Attlee governments called the 'destructive and bitter conflict between the two most gifted and eloquent of the younger socialists' was allowed to escalate, ending in Bevan's highly damaging resignation and a long-running feud which split the party throughout much of the 1950s.

While his two chief lieutenants, Morrison and Gaitskell, were abroad, Attlee announced the dissolution of Parliament and the calling of a general election on 25 October. The Prime Minister had long planned holding an election in the autumn, mainly because the King was to make a six-month tour of Australia and New Zealand early in 1952 (in the event, after the election was announced, the King fell ill and cancelled the tour. He died a few months later). Morrison and Gaitskell, who were both abroad, were aware of Attlee's intentions but were surprised not to be consulted. If the government had been able to keep going through the winter, conditions were likely to have been more favourable later. From mid-1952 onwards, the British economy experienced steady growth. But it was the new Tory government, not Labour, which reaped the benefit.

As in 1950, Labour won more votes at the 1951 election than the Conservatives, this time a 0.25 million more. Labour's 14 million total was the largest vote ever won by a political party. But, largely due to a reduced number of Liberal candidates, there was a small shift of opinion which allowed the Conservatives to gain 21 seats from Labour, giving the Tories an overall majority of 17. Labour was out of power for the next 13 years, missing out on the age of affluence.

*   *   *

This is not the place to analyse Labour's depressing decade in opposition. It spent too much time in fratricidal conflict and too little in adapting itself to the economic social changes which its own governments of 1945–51 had done so much to bring about. Attlee stayed on as leader. Two verdicts may be made on his decision. The favourable one is that he prevented the split between left and right becoming worse, blocked off Morrison and Bevan from the leadership and hung on until he was succeeded by the person from the next generation, Hugh Gaitskell, whom the majority of Labour MPs thought most likely to lead the party to victory. The unfavourable one is that he did little to heal the split, failed to provide the new direction the party needed and deliberately dished Morrison's chances of becoming leader in 1951, when he might have provided more decisive leadership.

How successful were the Attlee administrations of 1945–51? Kenneth Morgan, summing up his history of the Attlee governments, wrote; 'It was without doubt the most effective of all Labour governments, perhaps the most effective of any British government since the passage of the 1832 Reform Act.'[77] Attlee and his colleagues had great achievements to their credit, including the creation of the welfare state, the making of the National Health Service, the independence of India, Pakistan and Ceylon, the creation of NATO and the implementation of the Marshall Plan. Moreover, these were realised against a background of extreme difficulty, above all the sharp reduction in British power and resources (mostly to pay for the war), the need to re-equip industry, a succession of financial and balance-of-payments crises, the coming of the Cold War and the outbreak of the Korean War.

Attlee's clever idea of separating the government's two most powerful personalities not only by sitting as a buffer between them in Cabinet meetings but, most importantly, in terms of office (Bevin in charge of external affairs and Morrison the supremo on the home front) was undoubtedly a factor in the government's overall effectiveness. Despite their difficult personal relationship (more Bevin's fault than Morrison's), the two men worked constructively together in Attlee's Cabinet, both making exceptional contributions to Labour's successes, abroad as well as at home.

Domestically, Morrison's skill and advice as Lord President and leader of the House of Commons ensured that Labour's programme was speedily put on the statute book. As Eden said, he was the linchpin of the postwar Labour government. In his role as foreign secretary, Bevin rose to the challenge of the Cold War in a sustained burst of creativity which led to the setting-up of the Western Alliance and the implementation of the Marshall Plan. It was a classic example of how, given the right guidance and political arrangements, even ministers with exceptionally poor relationships can work well together in government.

3

NEVER HAD IT SO GOOD

Macmillan and Butler

Maurice Harold Macmillan and Richard Austen Butler – the first an initiator, the second a facilitator – were the two most intelligent, creative and forward-looking of the postwar Conservative politicians.

Their relationship was partly one of rivalry, a contest which Macmillan almost always won, being by far the more determined and ruthless of the two. In 1957, against media expectation, Macmillan beat Butler to the party leadership and became prime minister. When he resigned six years later, he also played a decisive role in preventing Butler succeeding him.

It would be wrong, however, to see their relationship purely in terms of competition. It was also an exceptionally fruitful working combination. It was Butler and Macmillan who led the Conservative revival after the war and helped the Tories establish a politically invaluable reputation as the party of affluence. They were outstanding members of Churchill's 1951–5 administration, with Butler as chancellor of the Exchequer and Macmillan as minister of housing. The two Macmillan governments, which restored the alliance with the United States after the Suez debacle, helped negotiate the Nuclear Test Ban Treaty, attempted to build a lasting détente with the Soviet Union, carried through the decolonisation of Africa and sought a new role for Britain as a member of the European Economic Community, were crucially dependent on the strong partnership between Macmillan and Butler.

*

Macmillan, who was nine years older than Butler, was born in London on 10 February 1894 in a large house with the fashionable address of 52 Cadogan Place, Chelsea. He was the third and youngest son of Maurice Macmillan and Helen Belles, a strong-willed American Methodist from the Midwest. The Macmillans were upwardly mobile Scots who had made their way by hard work, drive and education. Harold was the great-great-grandson of Malcolm Macmillan, a crofter on the Isle of Arran. Malcolm's son, Duncan, crossed over to the mainland and became a carter of coal at Irvine in Ayrshire. It was his son, Daniel Macmillan, Harold's grandfather, who, with his brother, Alexander, established the publishing firm which, under Harold's father, Maurice, became one of the leading publishers in the country, with celebrated authors such as Charles Kingsley, T.H. Huxley, F.D. Maurice, Lewis Carroll and Alfred Tennyson on its books.[1]

After three years at preparatory school, Harold Macmillan went as a scholar to Eton in 1906. But in 1909, when he was only 15, his mother removed him, in part because he had been diagnosed with a heart murmur but also because, it was said, she sought to protect him from the homosexual advances of older boys.[2] He was tutored at home by Ronald Knox (then an Anglo-Catholic but later to become a celebrated Catholic priest), with whom Harold formed an intense relationship. Alarmed by this development, Mrs Macmillan promptly dismissed Knox. However, despite his disrupted schooling, Harold won a classical exhibition to Balliol College, Oxford and went up to the university in October 1912.

Macmillan loved Balliol and Oxford. He did well academically, getting a first in Mods (the first part of the classical course). He would almost certainly have been elected president of the Oxford Union had it not been for the war. Already adopting a radical line, as a freshman he spoke in favour of the motion 'That this house approves the main principles of Socialism'. In debate, he learnt about epigrams, changes of pace and the use of pauses in speeches. He formed close friendships with some of his Oxford contemporaries, many of whom were killed in World War I. Of his year, only two of the six scholars and exhibitioners (including Macmillan) survived. He also joined the Anglo-Catholic circle around Ronald Knox, now chaplain at Trinity College, the neighbouring college to Balliol, though he decided not to follow Knox into the Catholic Church. For Macmillan, the summer of 1914, the last summer before the outbreak of war, remained a precious memory of carefree happiness.

It was in sharp contrast to what followed. His experience of the Great War was to mark Macmillan for life. He was not able to join up immediately as he was recovering from an operation for appendicitis, but in the autumn of 1914 he was commissioned as a second lieutenant in the King's Royal Rifle Corps. However, following his mother's intervention, in March 1915 he was transferred to the elite Grenadier Guards and in July joined its newly constituted 4th Battalion. He saw action in September 1915 at the bloody Battle of Loos where the British suffered 50,000 causalities. Macmillan established a reputation for bravery and was seriously wounded in the hand, also receiving a potentially more dangerous glancing bullet wound in the head. After a few months recuperating in London, Macmillan returned to the 2nd Battalion, which was stationed in the Ypres Salient. In September 1916, he was severely wounded, this time in the pelvis and left thigh, during the appalling slaughter on the Somme. For ten hours, he lay in a shelter in no man's land, dosing himself with morphine and reading his pocket edition of Aeschylus until he was rescued by a search party. Back in London, he was treated at a hospital in Belgrave Square. He needed a series of complicated operations to remove shrapnel from his wounds and it was not until December 1918 (after celebrating Armistice Day on crutches) that he was finally free of hospital.

The war left Macmillan with 'a limp handshake, a dragging gait, and sporadic pain'.[3] He was altered in other ways. He became more compassionate and more understanding of what he called 'the poorer classes'. He told his mother: 'They have big hearts these soldiers and it is a very pathetic task to have read all their letters home.'[4] Above all, as one of the fortunate survivors, his perspective changed. As he told his Balliol tutor, Sligger Urquhart, in a letter just before the Somme battle, 'God spares my life. Oh Slig, pray that if he spares it till the end, I may make good use of it.'[5]

The question was what to do. He did not wish to go back to Oxford to finish his studies, haunted as the university was for him by memories of his dead friends. Nor did he want yet to devote himself entirely to publishing. Understandably after the horrors of war, he had a desire to see the world. His doctors refused to allow him to go to Bombay, where the governor was looking for aides de camp (ADCs). So, helped once again by his mother, he took up an offer to become an ADC to the governor-general of Canada, Victor Cavendish, the ninth Duke of Devonshire. He later wrote that he was to find in Canada 'health and a wife'.[6] He could also have added that his work with the Duke gave him a taste for politics. On 26 December 1919, the 25-year-old Harold Macmillan became engaged in Canada to Dorothy Cavendish, the Duke's third daughter. Their wedding at St Margaret's Westminster was one of the social events of the 1920 London season; the bride's side was packed with royals, duchesses and peeresses, while the bridegroom's was mainly filled with publishers and authors, though six of these had the Order of Merit. Macmillan wrote to Dorothy on the eve of his wedding, 'I shall always be your lover.'[7] Macmillan, diffident (the Cavendish family found him dull), emotionally stilted and very much the intellectual, was certainly true to his word. But Dorothy, outgoing, warm hearted and a devotee of the outdoor life, found being married to Macmillan difficult to handle, especially when marriage came with an overbearing mother-in-law.

For Macmillan, marriage to a Cavendish led almost inevitably to politics. It was not that he was a dyed-in-the-wool Conservative. Indeed, if the Liberals had not been in an advanced state of disintegration, his admiration for Lloyd George might have attracted him to join the Liberal Party. Privately, he also respected a number of members of the rising Labour Party. Sligger Urquhart remembered him saying that 'the best Conservatives and the best Labour men had so much in common.'[8]

But his father-in-law, the Duke, encouraged him, not by securing for him the traditional Cavendish seat of West Derbyshire (which was reserved for the Duke's eldest son), but by advising him to go for an unwinnable seat. The Conservative Central Office almost casually suggested a Liberal-held constituency in the north-east, Stockton-on-Tees, a mainly industrial town which had been the birthplace of the railways. Meeting the chairman of the local Tories by chance at Central Office, Macmillan went up to Stockton the next day and almost immediately became the Conservative candidate for the borough. At the December 1923 election, called by Baldwin on the controversial issue of protection, Macmillan did far better than expected and was defeated by only 73 votes. At the next election, which took place less than a year later following the defeat of the first minority Labour government in a confidence vote, Macmillan was comfortably elected with a majority of over 3,000. As he wrote, 'for the first time in my life I heard the roar from thousands of throats, acclaiming victory.'[9]

Richard Austen Butler (familiarly known as Rab, from his initials), the eldest of a family of two sons and two daughters, was born on 9 December 1902 in British India at the Attock Serai, the rest house attached to the fort built by the Mughals at Attock, which guarded the confluence of the Indus and the Kabul rivers. His father, Montagu Butler, was then a local revenue official in the Indian Civil Service (ICS). He later had a distinguished career, becoming governor of the Central Provinces and being knighted for his services. The Butlers were a celebrated academic family, whose members had been dons at Cambridge University since 1794; they included a master of Trinity, two headmasters of Harrow and one of Haileybury.

As with most 'Raj' children brought up in India, the subcontinent left its mark on Rab. In his autobiography, he wrote of 'the rich smells of wet marigolds round the neck [...] The burning dung fires [...] the stone bathroom, the tent and rope smells, the horses and ponies, the deluge of the monsoon, the brilliant-coloured shrubs coming out after the rains'. He also remarked that 'we children ever after regarded Indians as friends.'[10] When he was six, he fell off his pony in Simla and broke his right arm in three places. It never fully recovered, so much so that for the rest of his life his arm hung limply at his side.

Again like most British children in India, Rab went back to Britain (in 1911) for his education, accompanied by his much-loved mother and her other children. He was sent to a prep school at Hove. In his memoirs, he described how he failed to get an Eton scholarship:

> I went up and sat the papers. At the end of the second day a man in a gown had the names of those who were requested to stay [...] Mine was not included. I went and spoke to him, asking if there had been a mistake, he said there had not.[11]

Rab refused to go to Harrow, perhaps because there were already other Butlers there, and decided instead for Marlborough College. His cousin, the poet Charles Sorley, had been educated there, and the home of his father's elder brother, who had prospered in the City and had an extensive collection of modern British pictures, was near the college and was to provide a haven for the young Butler.

Rab, whose parents had returned to India, did not much enjoy Marlborough, at least until his last year. Because of his disability, he did not shine at games and found classics, as it was then taught, very uninspiring. However, in his last year, he was able to change to literature, history and modern languages, and it was the French language and France itself which first awoke Rab's enthusiasm and brought out his latent ability. After leaving Marlborough, he spent the first five months of 1921 learning French at the house of a Protestant pastor at Abbeville in northern France. He also went to the local college to master the French classics, such as La Bruyère and Corneille.

His hard work was rewarded when he won an exhibition to his father's old Cambridge college, Pembroke. Rab's Cambridge career, which began three years after the end of the war, was highly successful. He got a first in part one of the Modern and Medieval Languages Tripos, followed in his fourth year by a first in the History Tripos. His papers in the History Tripos, including one on his special subject, Peel and the repeal of the Corn Laws, were so good that he was offered a fellowship at Corpus Christi

College. Like Macmillan at Oxford, Rab combined academic achievement with debating at the Union. He had joined the University Conservative Association (of which his uncle Sir Geoffrey Butler was the president) and was elected secretary of the Union in 1923, becoming president in 1924. Rab later described the Union as a wonderful training ground which 'should not be missed by those at the University aiming at public life'.[12]

In the summer of 1925, Butler was invited to Norway by Sydney Courtauld, a female friend who had been at Newnham College while he was at Pembroke. This Norwegian fortnight was to change his life. By the end of it, Rab and Sydney were unofficially engaged and on 20 April 1926 they were married at a church in the City. The intelligent and strong-willed Sydney was the daughter of Sam Courtauld, one of the country's leading industrialists – Rab described him admiringly as 'the greatest power in business in England'.[13] To the amazement of Rab's father, the wealthy Sam Courtauld gave his new son-in-law £5,000 a year tax free for life. This handsome settlement provided Rab with the financial independence necessary to both embark on a political career and support his wife in the style to which she was accustomed. Rab decided to give up his fellowship at Corpus and set out with Sydney on a year-long world tour.

It was while Rab and Sydney were in Vancouver on the return leg of their voyage that they received the exciting news that the sitting Tory MP for Saffron Walden in Essex (where Courtaulds was the main employer) was not seeking re-election and that the local constituency party would be looking for a new candidate in the autumn. The young Butlers calmly completed their journey across Canada, and six weeks after their return Rab was asked to attend the local Conservative Association selection committee meeting. In his speech, Butler promised to live in the constituency and to devote himself to nursing and representing it. His pledges appeared to satisfy the meeting, as he was chosen as prospective Conservative candidate. It certainly helped that there were no other candidates.

Though Saffron Walden had been won by the Tories with a majority of almost 6,000 at the last election, it had previously been held by the Liberals. Throughout 1928, Rab worked the constituency assiduously, visiting most of its 80 villages and acquainting himself with its problems. At the 1929 election, which the Tories lost and at which Labour became for the first time the biggest single party in the Commons, he comfortably held on to Saffron Walden, though with a reduced majority of just under 5,000. Rab's political future now looked assured.

Butler remarked in his memoirs that there are two paths to the top in politics – one, pursued by Rab himself, was that of the insider, 'serving the establishment with patient if unglamorous tenacity'; the other, followed by Macmillan, was that of the outsider, not averse to 'colourful rebellion' and even 'resignation'.[14] If Butler's view of his own career was broadly accurate, his description of Macmillan's rebellious phase made it sound more glamorous and successful than it really was. In Macmillan's first 16 years in politics, there were far more ebbs than flows.

Considered one of the brightest of the 'coming men' in the 1924–9 parliament, Macmillan became one of a 'ginger' group of progressive, younger Conservative politicians whose number included John Skelton, John Buchan, Duff Cooper and Robert Boothby. They made speeches and produced thoughtful books and pamphlets (some of which were published by the Macmillan publishing firm of which Harold was a director). Macmillan wrote a booklet, *Industry and the State*, a forerunner of his longer work, *The Middle Way*, published in 1938: *Industry and the State* advocated a mixed economy, as well as the setting-up of industrial councils and statutory collective bargaining.

These radical MPs were unpopular with the older 'diehard' Tories, who disparagingly called them the YMCA or Young Men's Christian Association. Macmillan's enthusiastic backing for the Keynesian policies of Oswald Mosley (who had resigned as one of MacDonald's Cabinet ministers to form the New Party and later set up the British Union of Fascists) was widely deemed beyond the Conservative pale. In the fluid political situation leading up to the 1931 crisis, Harold Macmillan even considered joining Mosley but, fortunately for his future career, was persuaded by his friends, above all by Robert Boothby, to stay with the Conservatives.

This wise advice may have helped save Macmillan's political career but Boothby's passionate affair with Dorothy Macmillan effectively destroyed Harold Macmillan's private life. Boothby was a handsome and glamorous bisexual with a taste for high living and fast cars. In August 1929, Dorothy fell madly in love with him and a year later told Macmillan that Boothby was the father of her fourth child, Sarah, and that she wanted a divorce so that she could marry him. Macmillan, still in love with his wife and aware that in the atmosphere of the time a divorce would ruin his political career, refused.

Eventually they agreed on an arrangement whereby Dorothy would be a loyal wife in public, especially at political functions, but in private would lead her own life with Boothby. Following a virtual breakdown in the summer of 1931 and some weeks in a Swiss clinic, Macmillan recovered in time to take part in the October election, at which he was returned once again for Stockton. One of his biographers, D.R. Thorpe, has written that, after the failure of his marriage, Macmillan devoted his energies to his work: 'His confidence could have been destroyed for ever, but in fact the painful experience gave him a sense of detachment and a ruthlessness that channelled his ambition.'[15]

Even though Macmillan was nine years older than Butler and had entered Parliament five years before him, it was the younger man who achieved office first. While the Tory leadership regarded Macmillan as a rebel, they considered Butler a safe and able pair of hands. One of Rab's first political initiatives was to write, in conjunction with three other Conservative colleagues, a sharp reply to a letter to *The Times* from Macmillan in support of Mosley. Macmillan had explained that Mosley was rightly trying to change the rules of the game which, in its present form, was hardly worth playing at all. Butler's riposte was that when a player starts complaining that it is hardly worth bothering to play, 'it is usually the player, and not the game, who is at fault. It is then usually advisable for the player to seek a new field for his recreation and a pastime more suited for his talents.'[16] Butler's waspish intervention may have pleased the Whips' Office but it risked making a long-term enemy of Macmillan.

When Rab was given his first job as under secretary at the India Office in September 1932, he was only 29 and by far the youngest member of the National Government. He owed his preferment partly to luck (his predecessor, the Marquis of Lothian, had resigned over imperial preference), partly to his knowledge of India (he had acted both as PPS to the secretary of state for India, Samuel Hoare, and as a member of the Indian Franchise Committee), and partly to the support not only of Hoare but also of the Tory leader, Stanley Baldwin.

Butler's main task in his new job was helping steer the India Bill (which combined provincial autonomy with the eventual prospect of an all-India federation) through the British Parliament. While Gandhi and the Indian Congress leaders rejected the Bill as not going far enough towards self-government, Tory imperialists claimed that it would lead to disaster for India and the British Empire. Die-hard opposition was led, in one of his most ill-judged initiatives, by Winston Churchill. Writing to Lord Linlithgow, chairman of the Joint Select Committee on India and later viceroy, Churchill tried to explain the rationale behind his extreme position: 'In my view England is now beginning a new period of struggle and fighting for its life, and the crux of it will be not only the retention of India but a much stronger assertion of commercial rights [...] Your schemes are twenty years behind the times.'[17] In fact, as Butler demonstrated, in a series of well-informed and skilful speeches during the passage of the Bill, it was Churchill who was behind the times.

Yet, in getting the Bill onto the statute book in 1935, Butler combined firmness with courtesy towards his chief opponent, so much so that, on the third reading, Churchill was moved to congratulate the young under secretary on establishing 'a parliamentary reputation of a high order'.[18] In July there was further recognition of Rab's achievement, when Baldwin, who had succeeded MacDonald as prime minister, agreed to address a large meeting at Butler's home, Stanstead Hall and, with his wife, stay for the weekend. Waiting for the train on the Sunday morning, the Prime

Minister said to Butler, 'I am so glad to have seen you at home in the country [...] Life in the country makes one see things clearly and will enable you to steer, as I have done, between Harold Macmillan and John Gretton [a right-wing Tory].'[19]

In May 1937, Rab was switched to the Ministry of Labour. Touring the depressed areas of South Wales and the north-east, he was struck by 'the look of hopelessness in the eyes of men standing idly on street corners or queuing drably at the labour exchanges'. He wrote later that, as postwar chancellor of the Exchequer, his message to the apostles of deflation was that 'those who talked about creating pools of unemployment should be thrown into them and made to swim'.[20] However, his stint at the Ministry of Labour only lasted nine months. In February 1938, following the resignation of Antony Eden as foreign secretary, Rab became under secretary at the Foreign Office.

As Baldwin's successor, Neville Chamberlain, made clear to Butler, this was a promotion. Although his ministerial title remained that of under secretary, he was to be the sole spokesman for his department in the Commons, as the new foreign secretary, Edward Halifax, was in the Lords. Rab was thus given the opportunity to shine on the floor of the House. He also worked closely with the prime minister, Neville Chamberlain, who was very much involved with foreign affairs. But Rab's political prominence had a downside: it meant that he was inevitably associated with, and indeed became one of the chief advocates of, Chamberlain's policy of appeasing Hitler, a connection which was to be used against him later in his political career.

In his memoirs, Butler defended appeasement on the grounds that it was necessary to buy time to build up Britain's armaments. Although there is some force to this argument (as the historian John Wheeler-Bennett, in his masterful study of Munich, admitted), it was not one which Rab used at the time. In his speech during the Munich debate in the Commons, Butler concluded by saying: 'It seems to me that we have two choices, either to settle our differences with Germany by consultation, or to face the inevitability of clash between the two systems of democracy and dictatorship.' He went on, 'War settles nothing, and I see no alternative to the policy upon which the Prime Minister has so courageously set himself.'[21] The appeasers, as Butler's peroration showed, mistakenly believed that the Nazi leader's word could be trusted and that it was still possible to construct a European peace system with Hitler as part of it.

In contrast, Harold Macmillan was one of the leading opponents of appeasement. In June 1936, following a foreign affairs debate on sanctions, he resigned the party whip. And, although he returned to the fold a year later, he continued his rebellious ways, abstaining with 21 other Conservative MPs at the end of the debate on Eden's resignation. Again, after the Munich debate, he was one of a bloc of government abstainers. Macmillan increasingly acted as liaison between the Eden group (known by the whips as the 'Glamour Boys') and the Churchill group (called the 'Old Guard'). He also had valuable contacts in the Labour Party, especially with the foreign affairs spokesman, Hugh Dalton, who was a fellow old Etonian and a neighbouring MP in the north-east. As one of his biographers wrote, 'Macmillan was moving from the grey area of cerebral pamphleteering and emerging as one of the most forceful of the discontented.'[22]

On 15 March 1939, Hitler occupied Prague, thus destroying the assumption on which Munich and appeasement had been based. The following day, at a lunch at No 10, Chamberlain admitted as much when he told Halifax and Butler: 'I have decided that I cannot trust the Nazi leaders again.'[23] The British guarantee to Poland, supported by the French, followed two weeks later. The appeasers, including Butler, now had to accept the defeat of their policy and the inevitability of war. On 3 September, Butler was at No 10 when Chamberlain gave his low-key broadcast announcing that 'this country is now at war with Germany.' Later that evening, Rab drank champagne with his wife and sister at his country home at Stanstead and, as they watched the reflections dancing in the moat, they could hardly believe that 'things had gone so badly'.[24]

Macmillan's response to the collapse of appeasement was that Chamberlain should resign. Harold Nicolson noted in his diary that 'Harold Macmillan is enraged that Chamberlain should remain on [...] no man in history has made such persistent and bone-headed mistakes.'[25] On 3 September, Macmillan listened to Chamberlain's radio broadcast with the dissident Eden group at a house in Queen Anne's Gate in London and, after walking back to the House of Commons, heard a practice air-raid siren on the terraces before going into the Chamber to listen to a despondent Prime Minister tell the House that Britain was now at war. Macmillan's reaction was mainly one of guilt: 'We few survivors of the First War seemed to have failed in our duty and to have betrayed our fallen friends.'[26]

It was the Norwegian debate at the beginning of May 1940, followed by the highly damaging vote at the end of the two-day Commons adjournment, which brought the Chamberlain government down and replaced it with the Churchill-led coalition (see Chapter 1). As Macmillan later remarked to Churchill, it took Hitler to make Winston prime minister and Macmillan an under secretary.[27] In the crisis of 1940, the old Tory pecking order was overturned. For a few months, Chamberlain remained in the War Cabinet before resigning in September because of ill health (he was to die of cancer two months later), while, at the turn of the year, Halifax was sent to Washington as British ambassador.

Macmillan, whose out-of-tune singing of 'Rule Britannia' when the division figures were announced at the end of the Norway debate had very much upset the supporters of Chamberlain, was one of the junior beneficiaries of the political upheaval. Churchill invited him to become under secretary to Herbert Morrison at the Ministry of Supply, a post for which Macmillan, with his interest in industrial planning, was well suited. Butler, who had after all been a leading appeaser and had also crossed swords with Churchill over India, quite expected to get the sack. However, when he was called to No 10, the new Prime Minister magnanimously said, 'I wish you to go on with your delicate manner of answering Parliamentary Questions without giving anything away.' Churchill referred to their past disagreements but said that Butler had invited him to his private residence, which had at least showed goodwill. When Rab was halfway to the door, the Prime Minister revealed what was probably the main reason for his survival: 'Halifax asked for you. He seems to get on with you.'[28]

A month later, a curious incident occurred which could have led to Butler's resignation, if he had not received Halifax's unequivocal backing. Returning from lunch on the day that France capitulated, Rab met the Swedish minister Bjorn Prytz in St James' Park. Butler asked him into the Foreign Office for a discussion but unfortunately no official record of the meeting was kept. However, Prytz sent back to Stockholm a telegram summarising the meeting, in which, according to Prytz, Butler appeared to support 'compromise if reasonable conditions could be agreed' and to add that 'no diehards would be allowed to stand in the way.' Understandably, Churchill, who possibly first knew about the telegram through security channels, was incensed at what he took to be Butler's 'defeatism' and asked Halifax for an explanation.[29]

Halifax defended his Under Secretary strongly, replying that he was completely satisfied with Rab's discretion and loyalty to the government. In his memoirs, Butler said that he went 'no further in responding to any neutral soundings than the official line at the time, which was that no peace could be considered prior to the complete withdrawal of German troops from all conquered territories'.[30] But in a letter to Halifax in which he gave a different account of the meeting to Prytz's, Rab – while stressing that he had said nothing which he would wish now to withdraw – admitted that he should probably not have even discussed the subject of 'an ultimate settlement'. A fair assessment may be that, while Butler could certainly be exonerated from the charge of 'defeatism', neither he nor Halifax had yet become attuned to the uncompromising defiance expressed so vividly by Winston Churchill in the summer of 1940.

In different ways, both Macmillan's and Butler's careers prospered during the war. From May 1940 to February 1942, Macmillan served with competence at Supply under successive ministers – Herbert Morrison, Sir Andrew Duncan and Lord Beaverbrook. He then became under secretary at the Colonial Office, which felt, he wrote, 'like leaving a mad house in order to enter a mausoleum'.[31] In December 1942, following the successful North African landings by the Allies, Churchill offered Macmillan the plum job of minister resident in North Africa, working with the US supreme commander, Dwight Eisenhower. He at once accepted because he realised that it was a big opportunity. He was almost immediately involved in the January 1943 Casablanca conference between Roosevelt and Churchill, 'the Emperors of the West and the East', as he called them. This conference agreed a Mediterranean strategy, including plans for an invasion of Sicily. It also tried to deal with the problem of the two French generals, Giraud – brave, handsome but with no political sense – and de Gaulle, difficult, arrogant but a great man. Macmillan at least managed to persuade them to be photographed together shaking hands, which Roosevelt called a 'shotgun marriage'. Later, he helped set up the Comité Français de Libération Nationale (FCNL) under the joint chairmanship of Giraud and de Gaulle; de Gaulle, with Macmillan's support, came out on top.

Macmillan also quickly established warm relations with Eisenhower. To Dick Crossman, director of psychological warfare at Allied headquarters and afterwards a Labour Cabinet minister, Macmillan explained,

> We, my dear Crossman, are the Greeks in this American Empire; you will find the Americans much as the Greeks found the Romans – great big vulgar, bustling people more vigorous than we are and also more idle. We must run allied headquarters (AFHQ) as the Greeks ran the operations of the Emperor Claudius.[32]

Following the Allied invasion of Italy, Macmillan (to the annoyance of the foreign secretary, Anthony Eden) played an important role not only as political adviser but also as acting president of the Allied Commission for Italy. With his American counterpart, Robert Murphy, he brokered an armistice with the Italians, was a key figure in the abdication of King Victor Emmanuel and helped set up a provisional government. Then, as the Germans retreated from Greece, Macmillan's responsibilities also included ensuring that that country was not taken over by the communist guerrillas. As Churchill retorted to criticism in the Commons, 'Democracy is no harlot to be picked up in the street by a man with a tommy gun.'[33] Macmillan's solution was the formation of a provisional government with a colourful and respected figure, Archbishop Damaskinos, as regent. For weeks in December, Macmillan was holed up in the British Embassy in Athens, being sniped at by Communist sharpshooters. However, with the arrival of Churchill and Eden on Christmas Day 1944, a settlement was reached which led to a ceasefire, later described as 'one of Macmillan's deftest diplomatic coups in the entire war'.[34]

In April 1945, as the German army in north-east Italy collapsed, Allied troops met up with Yugoslav forces in Venezia-Guilia and Yugoslav and Russian forces in Corinthia. Two difficult issues arose: the first was how to prevent Tito and the Yugoslav partisans taking over Venezia-Guilia and Corinthia without provoking a major conflict; the second was what to do with the thousands of non-German troops surrendering to the Allies. To solve the first issue (the most important in their eyes), Macmillan and Field Marshal Alexander proposed two zones, an eastern one under Tito and a western one under Allied military government; this plan was eventually accepted and formed the basis of the 1954 settlement. The second issue had tragic consequences as the repatriation of the Cossacks led to suicides, torture, executions and later long-term imprisonment in Soviet labour camps. British troops, as they became aware of the probable fate of their prisoners at the hands of the Russians, were traumatised by their involvement in the enforced repatriations.

Forty years later, (though not at the time) Macmillan's role came under intense scrutiny. In 1986, Count Nicolai Tolstoy accused him of being an accessory to mass murder.[35] However, in 1990, a comprehensive inquiry under the chairmanship of Brigadier Anthony Cowgill concluded that the part played by Macmillan in the return to the Soviets of Cossacks who had fought with the Germans was 'extremely small and only marginal in its consequences' and that he did not participate in any decision 'in handing back against their will of the dissident Yugoslavs'.[36]

The key meeting involving Macmillan lasted only two hours. It was between Macmillan and General Keightley of 5 Corps and took place in a hut by the grass landing strip at Klagenfurt, in Corinthia, on the morning of 13 May 1945. The main item discussed was the threat posed by Tito's

Yugoslav partisans but, at the end of the meeting, Keightley also raised the issue of the 40,000 Cossacks and 'White' Russians who had fought alongside and surrendered with the 400,000 Germans. In his diary, Macmillan wrote:

> To hand them over to the Russians is condemning them to slavery, torture and probably death. To refuse, is deeply to offend the Russians, and incidentally break the Yalta agreement. We have decided to hand them over but I suggested that the Russians should at the same time give us any British prisoners.[37]

It is clear from this extract that Macmillan's advice to General Keightley was full compliance with the Yalta Agreement on the exchange of Soviet citizens and British subjects, in accordance with British government policy. He was aware of the possible consequences but his fear at the time was that failure to repatriate the Cossacks could possibly affect the return of British prisoners. Macmillan returned to Britain on 26 May – before the implementation of the repatriations – to join Churchill's caretaker Cabinet as air minister. It was an appalling episode which reflected little credit on those involved, including Macmillan, but the main blame must, of course, rest with the Stalinist regime of their Russian allies which treated the repatriated so shamefully.

There is no doubt that as 'Viceroy of the Mediterranean', consulted by supreme commanders, prime ministers and presidents, Macmillan's war experience had transformed him. As Charles Williams wrote: 'This was no longer the Balliol educated don. This was somebody who gave the appearance of a serious political figure,'[38] as, indeed, he now was.

As for Butler, his career-changing appointment as president of the Board of Education came in the summer of 1941. After six dutiful, but not always easy, months as under secretary to Halifax's successor at the Foreign Office, Anthony Eden, Rab was delighted by the move. The American ambassador, 'Gil' Winant, had advised him to go to Education: 'This is where you can influence the future of England.'[39] He also had the valuable support of Churchill's confidant Brendan Bracken. On 21 July, the Prime Minister sent for Butler. It was after the great man's afternoon nap and, according to Rab, 'he was purring like a tiger.'[40]

Churchill said: 'It is time you were promoted [...] and I now want you to go to the Board of Education [...] You will move poor children from here [*lifting imaginary children from one side of his blotting pad to another*] to here.' He continued, 'I should not object if you could introduce a note of patriotism into the schools.' When Rab said he had always looked forward to going to the Board of Education, the Prime Minister looked pleased, though slightly surprised that, in wartime, Butler should want such a job. His parting words were friendly: 'Come and see me to discuss things – not details, but the broad lines.'

Rab knew that, despite Churchill's detachment, he had been given a great opportunity. Even before the war, there had been a pent-up demand for educational reform, especially of the grossly inadequate secondary education. In 1926, the Hadow Report had recommended the establishment of separate primary and secondary schools with the break at the age of 11, as well as the raising of the school-leaving age to 15. The 1938 Spens Report further recommended that there should be three types of secondary school – grammar schools for the academically able, technical schools for more practical students and so-called 'moderns' for the rest. Yet most of these proposals had not been implemented; the school-leaving age, which was due to be raised to 15 by 1 Sept 1939, had been indefinitely shelved. However, the war itself provided a spur to reform. The evacuation of urban working-class schoolchildren at its outbreak not only disrupted the school system, it was also a shock to the national conscience. As Butler wrote, 'it was realized with deepening awareness that "the two nations" still existed in England a century after Disraeli had used the phrase.'[41] Rab believed that war was 'a crucial test of national values and way of life' and that the time was, therefore, right for a decisive effort to widen educational opportunities, especially in secondary education. His aim was secondary education for all pupils.

So, after telling the Commons that it was necessary to reform the law relating to education, he sent a letter to the Prime Minister stressing the need to adapt the educational system. Back came a firm 'no'. 'We cannot have any party politics in wartime,' replied Churchill. Basing his strategy on his experience with Churchill over the India Bill, Butler decided to ignore the great war leader. He was confident that if he could circumvent religious controversy and avoid party political struggle, he could win Churchill over. He had the strong support of the Labour Party, especially of his experienced junior minister, Chuter Ede, a former teacher, and – crucially in the War Cabinet – the towering figure of Ernest Bevin. His most difficult task was to win over the churches. The churches, dominated by the Church of England, educated over 1.5 million children, often in small and inadequate buildings. If reform was to go through, Butler had to persuade the churches – Anglican, Catholic and Nonconformist – to accept his ideas.

After much discussion and negotiation, Rab came forward with two options. A church school could choose to be 'controlled' (Butler's preferred option), with the local education authority responsible for all the expenses of the school and appointing most of the teachers, and with religious instruction confined to an agreed syllabus and the majority of governors appointed by public bodies, or it could choose to be 'aided', with the churches responsible for 50 per cent of improvements to and alterations of school buildings but still able to appoint staff and organise religious instruction. The archbishop of Canterbury, William Temple, accepted Butler's scheme, mainly because Rab convinced him both of the poor state of many church schools and also of the cost to the Church if it tried to repair these without state support. The Nonconformists came on board as well, because they rightly believed that most church schools would opt for the 'controlled' alternative. The Catholics, however, stood out, because they said that the 50 per cent state support was not enough.

A letter to *The Times* on 2 November 1942 from the Catholic Cardinal Archbishop of Westminster appeared to threaten the whole enterprise, prompting the Prime Minister to cut out *The Times* letter on a piece of cardboard and send it to Rab with the message, 'There you are, fixed, old cock.'[42] The King's speech a few days later merely said that 'Conversations are taking place between my Ministers and others concerned with the provision and conduct of education in England and Wales with a view to reaching an understanding upon the improvements necessary.' However, public opinion was now moving strongly in favour of national reform, especially following the publication of the Beveridge Report in December 1942. In March 1943, Rab was invited down to Chequers to help Churchill with a speech setting out his 'four-year' plan, which was to include education. Butler took the opportunity to tell the Prime Minister that he was preparing an Education Bill. Churchill replied that Rab should show him the plans when they were ready.

In July 1943, Butler published a White Paper and in January 1944 moved the second reading of the Education Bill. It received the backing of both moderate Tory opinion and the Labour Party. The government, especially the Treasury, had been won over by Rab's insistence that the full implementation of the Act would take at least a generation. He had also defused the public school issue by referring it to a committee chaired by a Scottish judge, Lord Fleming. As Rab somewhat cynically observed in his memoirs, 'the first-class carriage had been shunted onto an immense siding.'[43] On one issue – that of equal pay for female teachers – the coalition government was defeated for the first time in the war. However, the Prime Minister made restoring the status quo a confidence issue, while Ernest Bevin said he would leave the government if Butler's position was in any way prejudiced. The equal pay clause was duly deleted from the Bill.

In August 1944, Rab received the following telegram: 'Pray accept my congratulations. You have added a notable Act to the Statute book and won a lasting place in the history of British Education. Winston S. Churchill.' As the historian D.R. Thorpe remarked, 'The Education Act of 1944 established Butler as an immensely rapid and competent administrator, a fast assimilator of information, a superb chairman [...] It made him the foremost Conservative to be identified with the needs of the post-war world.'[44]

*

By the end of the war, Macmillan and Butler were very much the coming men in the Tory Party. They were both given senior positions in Churchill's short-lived caretaker government, Butler as minister of labour, Macmillan as air minister. However, they shared a pessimistic view of the Conservative Party's prospects in the 1945 general election, especially after Churchill's disastrous 'Gestapo' radio broadcast. The result was even worse than they expected: Labour won a landslide victory, with the Tories losing 190 seats. Rab hung on at Saffron Walden (his 1935 majority of 10,066 was reduced to 1,158) but Macmillan was out at Stockton. Fortunately for him, the death of the Conservative member for Bromley (between the election and the announcement of the results) created an immediate vacancy in a safe seat and, on 16 November, Macmillan was back in Parliament with a majority of 5,557.

If ever there was a right moment for Conservative modernisation, it was after the 1945 election defeat. Prewar Toryism, especially in the form of unemployment and appeasement, had been decisively rejected. The election had also showed that Churchill, though almost universally revered as the man who had won the war, was not considered the right person to introduce the peacetime welfare state. In any case, in opposition, his attention was focused mainly on the Cold War and on European unity. Butler and Macmillan were foremost amongst leading Conservatives who believed that, if it was ever to return to power, the party had to demonstrate to the electorate that, in the words of Rab, 'we had an alternative policy to socialism which was viable, efficient and humane, which would release and reward enterprise and initiative but without abandoning social justice or resorting to mass unemployment.'[45]

In November 1945, Churchill had the good sense to appoint Butler chairman of the then-moribund Conservative Research Department. The Research Department was not only to provide Rab with a firm power base but also to act as a crucial lever in the revival of the party. Another powerful vehicle for regeneration was to be the Industrial Policy Committee, which was given the crucial task of producing a modern statement of Tory policy.

Rab was once more chosen by Churchill as chairman, even though other prominent frontbenchers were appointed to the committee, including Harold Macmillan, Oliver Stanley, Oliver Lyttleton and David Maxwell Fyfe.

This was the first time that Butler and Macmillan had worked closely together. Each admired the other's ability, but both had serious reservations about each other. Rab said about Macmillan:

> He had been reared in a very tough school of politics. Permanently influenced by the unemployment and suffering in his constituency in the North-East, Macmillan had revolted against the Montagu Norman banking school and against the Conservative front bench [...] the fact that he had spent much of his early life as a rebel while I was a member of the despised and declining 'establishment' underlines a difference of temperament between us.

He added, 'It may also lie at the root of our future relationship.'[46]

Macmillan was characteristically waspish about Butler. He told his official biographer, 'I always thought of him wearing a soutane. He would have been marvellous in medieval politics, creeping about the Vatican; a tremendous intriguer, he always had some marvellous plan and he loved the press.'[47] Macmillan had never quite forgiven Rab for being an appeaser or, totally unfairly, for not having fought in either war.

However, whatever their personal and temperamental differences, the two men usually agreed politically. *The Industrial Charter*, of which they were the main authors, marked the beginning of a remarkable partnership. The main purpose of this pamphlet of Tory policy, according to Butler, was to show that full employment and the welfare state were safe in Conservative hands. In addition, the mixed economy, in particular the Labour government's nationalisation of coal, the railways and the Bank of England, was to be accepted as a *fait accompli*. As Macmillan said, 'the Tories had to demonstrate that they could combine the need for the central direction of the economy with the encouragement of individual effort and incentives.'[48] *The Industrial*

Charter, with its mixture of Keynesianism, support for social security, backing for a system of employee rights and a commitment to reductions in taxation and an orderly ending of rationing and physical controls, was a clever piece of positioning which had the effect of bringing the Tories, so crushingly defeated in 1945, back into the political game.

The publication of the charter was preceded by a certain amount of tactical manoeuvring between Macmillan and Butler. Macmillan's attempt to reveal the main points of the statement in a speech at a by-election in the week before the document was published (and thus give himself the main credit for it) was blocked by Rab, who got the Tories' publicity director to point out to Macmillan that 'some of the language of your excellent speech at Jarrow rather coincides with that in the Industrial Charter.'[49] However, this did not prevent Macmillan (despite his strictures about Butler and the press) speaking to the *Sunday Express*, which reminded its readers that he 'once wrote a treatise called *The Middle Way*. This is its second edition.'[50] Quite unabashed, he also dropped a note to Butler, in which he said, 'without you, it would have been quite impossible to have reached any conclusion at all.'[51]

Then, as was to happen often in the future, the two men proceeded to work effectively together, on this occasion to ensure that the Tory party, and above all its leader, accepted the charter. Macmillan, in his role as chairman of the Conservative National Union, presided over the October 1947 conference at Brighton. Choosing a favourable amendment tabled by Reginald Maudling, both a parliamentary candidate and one of the secretaries of the Industrial Policy Committee, Macmillan so guided the debate that, by the time that Butler, with considerable skill, came to wind up, 'the conclusion was already determined.'[52] Despite some mutterings behind the scenes about 'milk and water' socialism, there were only three dissenting voices.

That evening, Churchill summoned Butler and his wife to his hotel suite and said, 'well, old cock, you have definitely won through. I wish now to toast your victory.' As the Pol Roger was produced, Butler said that he realised what the psalmist meant when he sang 'my cup runneth over'.[53] It was less clear that Churchill understood what was in the charter. For, when the Tory leader came to prepare his speech on the last day of the conference, he read the four lines on the charter contained in the draft; he then turned to his speech writer, who, as it happened, was Maudling, and said, 'But I don't believe a word of this.' Maudling replied, 'But, sir, this is what the conference adopted.' Churchill apparently grunted and said, 'Oh well, leave it in.'[54]

So *The Industrial Charter* became the bible of modern Toryism. Subsequent documents – the more comprehensive statement *The Right Road for Britain*, published in 1949, the 1950 election manifesto, *This is the Road*, and the 1951 election campaign document, *Britain Strong and Free* – were all based on the original charter. In this way, R.A. Butler and, to a somewhat lesser extent, Harold Macmillan, can claim to be the architects of postwar Conservatism.

Despite a background of great economic difficulty, the postwar Labour government had many achievements to its credit, including creating the welfare state and the National Health Service, nationalising the main utilities, giving independence to the Indian subcontinent, helping set up NATO and implementing the Marshall Plan. Moreover, during the lifetime of the 1945–50 parliament, Labour had not lost a single by-election to the Tories.

But, by the end of the 1940s, the government was running out of steam. This is how Butler, in a sharp but accurate analysis from the other side of the House, described the scene:

The physical decomposition of the Labour government preceded its political extinction by many months. In the general election of February 1950 its parliamentary majority was reduced to only eight, and by the spring of the following year the Treasury branch had been ravaged by sickness and rent by schism. Bevin, alas, was dead and Cripps dying; Attlee was in hospital, Morrison in *terra incognita*, Bevan in the cave of Adullam and Wilson in there with him.

Rab concluded: 'Though the government clung tenaciously to power, its sorrows came not single spies, but in battalions, and clearly its days were numbered.'[55]

At the 1951 election the Tories won a narrow majority and so were back in power, where they thought they belonged. Butler was summoned to Churchill's London house at Hyde Park Gate, where he was interviewed in the great man's bedroom. He was handed a short list of offices and names: opposite that of 'Chancellor of Exchequer' was the name 'R.A. Butler'. When he expressed surprise, Churchill said, 'I have thought much about this offer and in the end Anthony [Eden] and I agreed you would be best at handling the Commons.' Butler owed his appointment not to his economic expertise but to the death of Oliver Stanley nine months before and to his own high parliamentary reputation; Oliver Lyttleton, who as chairman of the Tory Finance Committee was the obvious alternative, was thought to be less effective at the dispatch box.

Harold Macmillan's name was not on the first published list of appointees and he began to fear that he would be left out altogether. However, over the weekend, Churchill sent for him to come over to Chartwell, his country home. There, the new Prime Minister offered him either Housing and Local Government or the Board of Trade. Macmillan, whose interest in opposition had been mainly focused on European, foreign and defence issues, would have preferred Defence but Churchill told him that he was keeping that portfolio for himself. Advised by his wife Dorothy (who had driven him over from the Macmillan country house, Birch Grove, in Sussex), Macmillan plumped for Housing and Local Government. It was a high-risk choice, as the 1950 party conference had unwisely committed the next Tory government to the building of 300,000 houses a year, 100,000 more than the Labour average. However, as Churchill pointed out, 'It will make or mar your political career. But every humble home will bless your name if you succeed.'[56]

Rab's four years at the Treasury (1951–5) were his 'High Noon'. After a shaky start, when his new advisers warned him of 'blood draining from the system and a collapse greater than had been foretold in 1931',[57] a combination of steady nerves and good luck helped turn the economy round. Butler survived a revolt by the Cabinet against a Treasury attempt to introduce a scheme to 'float' the pound. By the last quarter of 1952 the impact of the import-saving measures which he had immediately introduced, together with a sharp improvement in the terms of trade, had resulted in an impressive recovery in balance of payments and the gold and dollar reserves. The years 1953 and 1954 were 'golden years' of expansion for the British economy, during which Rab was able to cut taxation, get rid of food rationing and dispense with controls.[58] At the 1954 party conference, the Chancellor told delegates that it would be possible to double the standard of living in the next 20 years – a prediction which had the merit both of associating the Tories with affluence and of turning out to be accurate.

Economic success brought Rab a personal political dividend. Sophisticates may have talked about 'Butskellism' on the grounds that there was little difference between Butler's policy and that of his Labour predecessor, Hugh Gaitskell.[59] But the press, the Conservative Party and the voters seemed content that the economy was in safe hands. Indeed, from the end of 1952 through to 1954, Rab was seen very much as a potential leader of the Tory party.

On a number of occasions in 1952 and 1953, Butler presided over the Cabinet. Remarkably, between 29 June and 18 August 1953, he chaired 16 successive Cabinet meetings. This was because, on 23 June, Churchill had suffered a serious stroke, while the heir-apparent, Anthony Eden, was in the United States, recovering from a serious operation. This was the moment, in Butler's later view, when he could have become prime minister. For, during the summer months, Rab was, in effect, combining the roles of chancellor, Foreign Office spokesman in the Commons, and acting prime minister. A more ruthless politician, a Lloyd George, a Macmillan or a Thatcher, would have pointed out that it was bad for the country that two such invalids should remain in office, while he did all the work, but Rab lacked that final 'killer instinct'. Instead, loyal to both Churchill and Eden, he went along with the untrue version put out by John Colville, the

Prime Minister's personal secretary, and Christopher Soames, Churchill's PPS and son-in-law, and endorsed by the great man's doctors that he was merely in need of 'a complete rest'. For Rab, the reluctance to strike was not so much a missed opportunity but rather a reflection of his character.

In a revealing diary entry, Macmillan, who himself had to have a gall bladder operation in the middle of July, wrote, 'Butler is, of course, playing a winning game [...] Churchill cannot really last very long [...] What will Butler do if Eden has to give up? Then he will have to appoint a Chancellor of the Exchequer.'[60] At this stage, Macmillan, older than Butler and Eden, did not see himself as a realistic candidate for the leadership but was clearly interested in the consequence of Butler becoming prime minister, at which time the chancellorship would be up for grabs.

However, Macmillan's stock was also rising, as he proved to be a highly effective housing minister. Working with the brilliant civil servant Evelyn Sharp, whom he described as the ablest woman he had ever known, he brought in as his junior minister Ernest Marples, who had made a fortune in construction, and as his director general Percy Mills, a successful Birmingham businessman. The results came quickly. In 1952, there were 240,000 homes completed; between 1 November 1952 and 31 October 1953, 301,000 and in the calendar year of 1953, 318,000.[61] Macmillan's big day was 10 December 1953, when 300,000 houses were completed. Macmillan delighted in his triumph. 'I've never enjoyed three years more [...] three of the happiest years of my life [...] it was great fun.'[62] Ironically, Butler, although doubtful of the wisdom of allocating resources to one sector at the expense of others, made an important contribution to Macmillan's success, consistently providing the necessary funds, another example of Macmillan and Butler acting effectively together to the benefit of Tory electoral prospects.

The period from the middle of 1953 through to the beginning of 1957 was an unsettled time for the Tory leadership. Astonishingly, Churchill recovered from his stroke but most of his Cabinet colleagues, especially Eden and Macmillan, were anxious that the 80-year-old statesman should announce his retirement. Butler, the youngest of the three, was more ambivalent. On 11 March 1954, he dined with Churchill, who told him, 'I feel like an aeroplane at the end of its flight in the dusk, with the petrol running out, in search of a safe landing.'[63]

Eventually, a year later, after much prevarication and vain attempts to arrange a summit with the Russians, the old man was forced, following a Cabinet which Macmillan described as 'the most dramatic, but harrowing discussion at which I have ever been present', to give a firm date for his resignation. On 6 April 1955, Anthony Eden, for so long the crown prince, became prime minister.

In later life, Macmillan confessed that he was disappointed not to have succeeded Churchill as prime minister.[64] This was never a realistic possibility. But what was becoming increasingly clear was that Macmillan was emerging as a serious contender for the succession, should Eden's health deteriorate. In January 1955, Churchill's doctor, Lord Moran, had presciently told Macmillan that under the strain of the premiership, such a breakdown might well happen.[65]

Macmillan's own career was very much in the ascendant. In October 1954, Churchill had appointed him defence secretary. Under Eden, he now became foreign secretary, a position of considerable influence and prestige, even if he had to put up with persistent interference from the new Prime Minister. At the time, Macmillan claimed that the foreign secretaryship was the zenith of his ambition. But such a determined politician must also have been aware that the occupancy of one of the great offices of state was also an ideal launching pad for the top job, should a vacancy occur.

Meanwhile, the career of his main rival, R.A. Butler, had begun to falter. In December 1954, Butler's wife, Sydney, died of cancer. *The Times'* obituary said that 'her essential quality was that of aim. She flew like an arrow.'[66] Certainly, Rab felt her loss keenly and some of his colleagues, including an unusually sympathetic Macmillan, felt his morale and energy had been undermined by her death.[67]

His grief may help to explain his somewhat uncertain handling of the economy during 1955, which marred his reputation as chancellor.

In February, in response to a rising balance-of-payments deficit and a weakening pound, Rab raised the bank rate and restored hire-purchase restrictions. Then, in his April budget (which preceded the May general election), he reduced income tax by sixpence and raised personal allowances. There is little doubt that his budget was a big political success as the Tories increased their majority to 60, but, after the election, Butler was forced to increase purchase tax across the board by a fifth and extend it to kitchenware and other household goods – hence its name as the 'pots and pans budget'. In a crushing parliamentary attack, which may have helped him win the leadership of the Labour Party, the shadow chancellor, Hugh Gaitskell, said of Butler (whom he, in fact respected): 'He began in folly, he continued in deceit, and he has ended in reaction.'[68]

After the Tories' May election victory, Eden had wanted to move Butler and, as Rab wrote in his memoirs, 'If I had been less scrupulous about the economy I would have retired [from the Treasury] in May.'[69] Instead he hung on, politically weakened, until he was replaced as chancellor of the Exchequer by Macmillan. Macmillan, after only eight months at the Foreign Office, was extremely reluctant to accept the change and drove a hard bargain, insisting, in a highly unusual letter, for a 'position in the government no inferior to that held by the present Chancellor'.[70] In practice that meant a block on Rab becoming deputy prime minister.

Remarkably, negotiations between the Prime Minister and Macmillan continued for some weeks until Eden devised a formula whereby Rab presided over the Cabinet in Eden's absence but without the title of deputy prime minister. Butler became leader of the House and Lord Privy Seal, an appointment without the backing of a government department. Rab was warned by the former Lord Privy Seal, Harry Crookshank, that in accepting such a post, he was committing 'sheer political suicide', a view which was widely shared in the Westminster village.

The year 1956 was a landmark in British politics. It led to a 'humiliating failure'[71] over the Suez imbroglio; to the end of Britain's pretensions to being a world power; and, domestically, to the downfall of Conservative Prime Minister Anthony Eden (who resigned on 9 January 1957). Neither

Macmillan, who profited most from it, nor Butler, who lost out, can be said to have done well over Suez.

Harold Wilson's comment on Macmillan's Suez performance was that he had been 'first in, first out'. From 26 July 1956, when Nasser nationalised the Suez Canal, which the British strongly opposed because it was an international trade route, Macmillan was a hawk, if not *the* hawk. He wrote in his diary entry for 1 August: 'we must have a) international control of the canal and b) humiliation and collapse of Nasser.' He also said, 'we must either get Nasser out by diplomacy or by force.'[72] Macmillan was enthusiastic for Israeli involvement. He backed the so-called Challe Plan (secretly agreed at Sevres with the French and Israelis),[73] whereby Israel would attack Egypt across Sinai, and Britain and France would then intervene to call 'both sides' to withdraw, using the conflict as a pretext for taking over the Canal and toppling Nasser. This was the 'collusion' which Eden, to his discredit, was later to deny in the Commons.

But without American support or at least neutrality, the whole bizarre enterprise had little chance of success. Despite a visit to the United States at the end of September, Macmillan completely misjudged the views of President Eisenhower and members of his administration, wrongly assuring Eden that the Americans would acquiesce. In fact, Eisenhower, facing re-election, was incandescent with rage when he was informed that British planes were bombing Egyptian airfields. On 2 November, the US, for the first time, combined with the Soviet Union in voting against Britain and France at the UN. The initiative of the two superpowers was a major shock for Macmillan. When he also heard that the United States was considering oil sanctions against its allies, he apparently threw his arms in the air and exclaimed, 'Oil sanctions. That finishes it.'[74]

By 6 November, Macmillan had switched from being a super-hawk to a super-dove, going so far as to give his Cabinet colleagues a much-exaggerated account of the pressure on sterling and the losses to British reserves.[75] The defence minister, Anthony Head, said that 'Harold was very strong in his warning of what the US would do [...] he put the fear of God into the Cabinet, as Chancellor.'[76] The Cabinet, which by this time had, in any case, lost the will to continue, decided to pull the plug on the ill-conceived expedition by agreeing to a ceasefire, although British forces were still 60 miles from Suez.[77]

Initially Butler was little involved in the Suez crisis. He was suffering from a virus when Nasser took over the Canal and therefore was not present at the crucial Cabinet meeting of 27 July when it was decided that the British reaction should be backed up by the threat – and, if need be, the use – of force.[78] Unlike Macmillan, he was not made a member of the 'Egypt Committee', set up to manage the British response. In October, he was also kept out of discussions of the Challe Plan.

Throughout, Rab's attitude was one of cool detachment. He agreed with his Cabinet colleagues that Nasser should not be allowed to keep the Canal. But he did not share the view of Eden and Macmillan that a key British objective should be to topple Nasser. He also believed that Britain should act in accordance with international law and in line with UN resolutions. He consistently supported attempts to negotiate a settlement and remained sceptical about unilateral British and French military action.

However, on 18 October, Rab had a meeting with the Prime Minister at No 10. Eden informed him about the scheme for Britain and France 'to separate the combatants [Israel and Egypt] and occupy the Canal'.[79] Unwisely, after questioning the Prime Minister closely and expressing concern about the public reaction, Butler said that 'in all the circumstances [...] I would stand by him.' At the subsequent Cabinet meeting, Butler went along with the rest of the Cabinet in agreeing to British and French intervention. This was a bad mistake. At this late stage, merely voicing doubts was not enough. He should have either, like Walter Monckton, stated his opposition unequivocally or even resigned, as did his close ally, Sir Edward Boyle, the economic secretary to the Treasury.

As his *Dictionary of National Biography* entry concluded, 'Butler ended up pleasing virtually no one.' His lack of enthusiasm for the use of force displeased the Tory pro-Suez wing, while his failure to prevent it disappointed the antis.[80] Loyal to the government in public, in private he was often indiscreet. Reginald Maudling wrote in his memoirs that Rab had given 'the impression that he was lifting his skirt to avoid the dirt'.[81]

Following the collapse of his Suez policy, Eden's health broke down and, on his doctor's recommendation, he and his wife flew to Jamaica for him to recuperate, leaving Butler in charge. Rab considered that this period 'was the most difficult of my career'.[82] Although he had been sceptical about the government's Suez policy, he had now been landed with the responsibility of clearing up the mess – 'withdrawing the troops, re-establishing the pound, salvaging our relations with the US and the UN'.[83] As was the case at the time of Churchill's stroke in 1953, Butler ran the administration with commendable efficiency. But the right of the Conservative Party, who wrongly blamed him for the Suez fiasco, gave him little credit for it.

In Eden's absence, Butler and Macmillan worked in tandem to keep the restive Tories together. On the evening of 22 November, they both addressed the 1922 Committee of background Conservative MPs. They had agreed beforehand that Macmillan should aim his remarks at the centre and the left of the party and Rab at the right. This strategy may have achieved the objective of uniting the party; it also worked very much to Macmillan's advantage. The right were never going to support Rab, while the centre and left were able to see the merits of Macmillan, especially as – unlike Butler, who spoke briefly and flatly – he gave a vigorous performance, pulling out all the emotional stops.

For Macmillan at least, the 1922 meeting had a crucial subtext. It was a chance for the two possible successors to Eden to show their paces. For while Butler hoped that Eden would recover from his illness, Macmillan was certain that he was finished as prime minister and started to campaign for the leadership.

When Eden resigned on 9 January 1957, Macmillan was well prepared. In a procedure which seems totally archaic today, instead of having a ballot of the parliamentary party, Macmillan's friend and ally, the Marquess of Salisbury, aided by Lord Kilmuir, collected the opinions of the Cabinet one by one, which were apparently overwhelmingly for Macmillan. The chief whip, Edward Heath, also reported that a substantial majority of the parliamentary party would prefer Macmillan to Rab, while the chairman of the party, Oliver Poole, told Salisbury that many Tories blamed Butler for the Suez fiasco. It was said that there were even some supporters of Butler who felt that, in the wake of Suez, he was not the man to lead the party. Crucially, Churchill came out for Macmillan, on the grounds that he was the more decisive.

So, at 2 p.m. on 10 January 1957, Macmillan, in a morning coat, was summoned to the Palace to 'kiss hands'. He told the Queen (who had been advised by Salisbury that Macmillan had the most support) that the government might not last six weeks. Meanwhile, Butler was informed by Heath that he had not got the job. The Chief Whip wrote later that Rab was 'utterly dumbfounded'.[84] Heath added in his memoirs that every newspaper that morning, save one, had announced that Butler would be the next prime minister. Anthony Eden's wife, Clarissa, sent a consolatory letter to Rab: 'Just a line to say what a beastly profession politics are – and how greatly I admire your dignity and good humour.'[85]

In truth, Butler had been completely outmanoeuvred by Macmillan. From mid-November onwards, Macmillan had seen his opportunity to become prime minister. In his sixty-fourth year, he was three years older than Eden and nine years older than Butler and was, therefore, unlikely to get another chance. If, viewed objectively, his Suez performance was, as he said himself, 'a very bad episode in my life',[86] it also revealed him as a man of decision, determined on action at the beginning and then, when it was obvious that the operation was a failure, equally determined to 'cut his losses'. In the same way, he was ruthless about seizing his opportunity to become premier, pushing himself forward and Eden and Butler aside.

By contrast, Rab, whose scepticism about Suez had in fact, been proved right, seemed to many an equivocal figure, a doubter but not prepared to make a firm stand. In Eden's absence in the West Indies, he had run the government with complete loyalty and great competence, but had failed to convert his temporary position into a permanent one. In January 1957, he behaved more like a public servant than a politician, holding back when he should have struck. As D.R. Thorpe, Macmillan's biographer, put it, 'Butler found – and was to find again in October 1963 – that few were presented with the key to No 10 on a velvet cushion.'[87] In short, Rab lost out to a more ruthless and determined colleague.

In forming his government, the new Prime Minister's key appointment was obviously that of Butler. Macmillan wrote in his autobiography: 'It was, therefore a great relief to me when Butler chose the post of Home Secretary.'[88] This was an inaccurate description of what happened. In fact, as his own memoirs show, Rab asked for the Foreign Office and was turned down, according to Macmillan, on the grounds that one head on the charger should be enough.

Rab's biographer expressed surprise that 'Macmillan was able to deflect his former rival's aspirations as easily as he did'.[89] It was a further example of Macmillan's determination and Butler's dutiful compliance. Macmillan was intent on keeping Selwyn Lloyd as foreign minister, partly because Lloyd knew where 'the Suez bodies were buried' and partly because he wanted to be his own foreign secretary; he also knew that Butler, if pressed, would put the survival of the government before his own personal ambition. As Rab told a journalist, 'In public life one has to do one's duty. I would certainly not desert the ship at a time like this.'[90]

The Macmillan premiership was crucially dependent on the partnership between Macmillan and Butler. The two men may not have liked each other. But their complementary abilities were essential for the success of the Tory government, so vulnerable at its outset, so dominant two years later. Macmillan was decisive, courageous, the 'Supermac' who became the supreme 'actor manager' of British politics. Butler was more enigmatic, the consummate Whitehall politician, brilliant at chairing committees, also, like Macmillan (who disguised it better) a progressive 'One Nation' Conservative to his fingertips. Rab may have had good reason to feel bitter towards his rival, but throughout he served Macmillan with admirable loyalty and diligence. One of Macmillan's biographers has described Butler as 'the essential glue that bound the team together'.[91]

At the heart of his administration, the new Prime Minister, in contrast to Eden, attempted to create an atmosphere of confidence, symbolised by the quotation from Gilbert and Sullivan's *The Gondoliers* which he printed on the door of the private secretaries' room at No 10: 'Quiet calm deliberation disentangles every knot.' Macmillan was well aware that, if the Tories were to make a recovery, the Suez affair had to be put behind them. He resolutely resisted any idea of an inquiry, as happened after the Iraq War the following century. He was also determined to restore good relations with the United States at the earliest possible moment, enthusiastically accepting the suggestion of his wartime friend, President Eisenhower, for a March summit in Bermuda. The summit was a success, Macmillan describing it as being 'not at all like an experience in the modern world. More like meeting George III at Brighton',[92] though the British left Bermuda with a US commitment to supply them with 60 intermediate nuclear missiles. On his return, the Prime Minister demonstrated his control of the government by calmly accepting Salisbury's resignation in protest at the release of Archbishop Makarios from imprisonment in the Seychelles.

For Butler, this was the period of what (after the character in Gilbert and Sullivan's *Mikado*) he called the years of 'Pooh Bah', during which he acquired a number of grand posts. He was both an active and modernising home secretary and leader of the House of Commons and Lord Privy Seal. With the departure of Salisbury, he moved up to the number-two position on the official list, which meant that he not only chaired the Cabinet in Macmillan's absence but also acted as temporary head of government when the Prime Minister went abroad, notably on his six-week Commonwealth tour in early 1958 and the African trip of similar length in 1960, when Rab was left, as he said, 'holding the baby'.

In January 1958 Macmillan's Commonwealth tour coincided with a major political crisis, caused by the resignation of the chancellor of the Exchequer, Peter Thorneycroft, and his two Treasury colleagues, Nigel Birch and Enoch Powell. Ostensibly, the dispute between the Chancellor and the rest of the Cabinet, including Macmillan and Butler, was about a mere £50 million in public spending, but an underlying issue was also at stake. Thorneycroft wanted to squeeze inflation out of the economy by preventing the following year's current spending rising above that of the current year, while Macmillan, still scarred by his prewar experience as a Stockton MP, worried more about the impact of deflation on employment.

Despite the resignation of his Chancellor, Macmillan and his wife set off on his Commonwealth trip, leaving Butler in charge and telling journalists at the airport, 'I thought the best thing to do was to settle up these little local difficulties and then turn to the wider vision of the Commonwealth.'[93] The Prime Minister could afford to adopt such an apparently detached attitude because he knew that he had the support of Rab (whom he described in his diary as having been 'excellent' throughout the crisis)[94] and could rely on him to run the government in his absence with complete competence and loyalty.

Consummate politician that he was, Macmillan, from his first day in Downing Street, had his eyes fixed firmly on the next election. His strategy (similar to Butler's in 1955) was to ride to victory on a tide of affluence. The famous phrase 'most of our people have never had it so good' in his 20 July 1957 speech at Bedford football ground (which, to be fair, was also meant to be a warning against complacency) both epitomised his approach and, to a considerable extent, described the new realities of postwar Britain.

As the election approached, the economy was expanding, unemployment and inflation were low, the standard of living was rising. In 1958, for the first time, homeowners outnumbered those who rented their homes.[95] To accentuate the 'feel-good' factor, Macmillan's chancellor of the Exchequer, Derek Heathcoat-Amory, introduced a tax-cutting 1959 budget, including taking ninepence off the standard rate of tax, a one-sixth reduction in purchase tax and a reduction in the duty on beer. The tax reductions were calculated to increase consumers' spendable incomes by some £300 million in a full year, on top of which repayments of postwar credit added a once-for-all increase of £70 million. Harold Wilson, then shadow chancellor and later prime minister, sardonically wrote that Macmillan saw the Treasury 'as the means of creating a favourable financial system for winning elections'.[96]

Macmillan buttressed his electoral strategy by exploiting the politics of personality. Using television (1959 was the first televised election), he projected himself as 'Supermac', the soubriquet given to him by Vicky, the *New Statesman* cartoonist. Apparently unflappable, self-confident and with an impeccable sense of timing, the Prime Minister commanded the political stage. Wearing a white fur hat in February, he undertook a much-publicised trip to Moscow and, just before the election was announced, he acted as host to President Eisenhower in Britain. In a blatant example of electioneering, the two wartime colleagues, both wearing dinner jackets, were televised in a so-called informal conversation at No 10 Downing Street, thus highlighting the statesman-like credentials of Macmillan. The *Manchester Guardian* quipped that Macmillan had written his own 'commercials'.[97]

The Tories went into the general election with a comfortable lead in the polls. Although a spirited and professional Labour campaign appeared to narrow the Conservative lead, Macmillan remained confident of victory. When the Labour leader, Hugh Gaitskell, in a speech in Newcastle, pledged that Labour would not, in normal peacetime circumstances, raise income tax, Macmillan pounced, saying that, for their part, the Conservatives would not indulge in an electoral auction. Afterwards, he claimed that Gaitskell's pledge had been a turning point, because it seemed to confirm the Tory charge that Labour could not be trusted with the economy.[98] As the Conservative slogan (designed by the advertising agency Colman, Prentice and Varley) put it, 'Life's better under the Conservatives. Don't let Labour ruin it.' When the votes were counted on election night, they revealed a Tory landslide, with gains in the south and Midlands and an overall majority of 100. Macmillan was fully entitled to say, as he wrote in his diary: 'Altogether, the result is remarkable. I don't think any party has won three times running, increasing its majority each time.'[99]

Following the election, Macmillan offered Butler, in addition to remaining home secretary and leader of the House, the role of party chairman in succession to Lord Hailsham. Roy Jenkins wrote that it was like 'a cricket captain piling sweaters upon a patient umpire'.[100] The Prime Minister remarked that the appointment of Butler to the chairmanship was a sign that the Tories intended 'to remain progressive and not slide back into reaction'.[101] It is less clear why Butler accepted, especially in the aftermath of a general election when the post lost much of its importance. As he said later, 'Going to rallies at the weekend in distant parts of England and having to make speeches about how wonderful the government was I found very hard and difficult – and not at all rewarding.'[102]

Although the Home Office had the reputation of being a difficult department to run, Rab found his work there 'rewarding'. He proved to be an outstanding home secretary – arguably, after Roy Jenkins (the reforming Labour home secretary of the 1960s), the most effective holder of the office of the twentieth century. Butler wrote in his memoirs that he was able to bring to the department 'the same spirit of reform and zeal for progress as had called into being the Education Act of 1944'.[103] He noted that Macmillan allowed him a completely free hand 'in a similar spirit of indulgent scepticism [...] as Churchill had shown fifteen years earlier towards my work for education'.[104] The Prime Minister was also no doubt aware that Rab's reforms, while broadly supported by liberal opinion, were not likely to make him popular with the right of the party.

One of Butler's aims, as he told the Conservative Political Centre in early 1959, was to get rid of the 'Victorian corsetry' in which much of Home Office legislation was 'laced'.[105] Hence the changes in the licensing laws extending the hours that pubs could open, the Betting and Gaming Act, which led eventually to the opening of betting shops in every high street, and the modernisation of the law on charities. Rab also gave indirect support to a backbenchers' initiative, the Obscene Publications Bill, which was designed to reform the censorship laws. The Labour MP Roy Jenkins, who sponsored the Bill, said, in thanking Rab for his help, that the legislation would not have gone through 'had you not been basically sympathetic'.[106]

The abolition of capital punishment had to wait for the advent of a Labour government, as the Homicide Bill, which restricted the death penalty to certain specified types of murder, was already on its way through Parliament when Rab was appointed home secretary. This meant that Butler, who, as a result of his experience of office became a convinced abolitionist, was forced to exercise the agonising life-and-death duty of deciding of whether or not to grant a reprieve on a number of occasions, including the much disputed Hanratty case. Although Butler's Street Offences Act of 1959 had the effect of clearing the streets of prostitution, he decided not to implement the other recommendation of the Wolfenden Report on Homosexual Offences and Prostitution – namely, that homosexual relations between consenting adults in private should no longer be a criminal offence – on the grounds that, according to Butler, it did not yet have public opinion behind it.

As he hinted in his memoirs, the legislation which Butler, with his imperial links, personally found most distasteful was the controversial Commonwealth Immigrants Bill which, through a system of labour permits, imposed restrictions on immigration. But the sharp increase between 1950 and 1961 in the annual number of immigrants from the West Indies and South Asia from 21,000 to 136,000, combined with the 1958 Notting Hill riots, persuaded him that restrictions were required if racial tension was to be avoided.

The part of his work at the Home Office of which he felt most proud was the strategy which he devised for penal reform. His White Paper 'Penal Practice in a Changing Society' emphasised the need for research into 'the causes of crime and the effectiveness of various forms of treatment'.[107] A research unit was set up in the Home Office, while a new Institute of Criminology was established at Cambridge. The White Paper also proposed a substantial building programme, intended to relieve the overcrowding of prisons as well as providing detention centres for young prisoners. However, Rab's constructive and measured approach to crime did not satisfy his right-wing Tory critics, whom Butler called the 'Colonel Blimps of both sexes'. Almost every year, Rab had to fend off calls from conference delegates for the reintroduction of corporal punishment, while in April 1961, 69 Conservative MPs, including the newly elected Margaret Thatcher, unsuccessfully backed an amendment to the Criminal Justice Bill, demanding the return of flogging. Later that year at the party conference, Butler took on and routed his critics in a courageous and masterly speech. Even the Prime Minister acknowledged his victory, writing to Rab to congratulate him on 'a real triumph'.[108]

If 1957 to 1959 were years of recovery for the Tories, culminating in the 1959 election victory, the period from 1959 to 1961 was one of reappraisal, during which Macmillan attempted to set out a new role for Britain. It revealed the Prime Minister at his creative best.[109]

In December 1962 the former US secretary of state, Dean Acheson, famously said: 'Great Britain has lost an empire and not yet found a role.' In fact, Macmillan was only too well aware of the relative decline in British power and was determined to do something about it. Before the 1959 election, he had called an informal meeting of his top civil servants on 7 June 1959 to discuss and produce a report on 'what is likely to happen in the world during the next ten years'.[110] The report underlined the extent to which the United Kingdom's relative power had declined and would continue to decline both in relation to the two superpowers and to Western Europe as well: 'The European Economic Community is of immense potential importance [...] if they continue to grow at their recent pace they will approach and perhaps reach the present United States level by 1970. If, therefore, the "six" achieve a real measure of integration a new world however will have come on the scene.' The Commonwealth and the remaining empire would do little to rectify the balance for the UK.

At the beginning of 1960, Macmillan, leaving Butler in charge, undertook a six-week African tour. His appointment of the Tory radical and protégé of Butler, Iain Macleod, as colonial secretary had already given the green light for a rapid acceleration in decolonisation. Macleod later summed up his approach: 'It has been said that after I became Colonial Secretary there was a deliberate speeding up of the movement towards independence. I agree there was. And in my view any other policy would have led to terrible bloodshed in Africa.'[111]

Macmillan broadly agreed with his Colonial Secretary, but he was also acutely aware of the opposition from the Tory right wing at Westminster and of their ties with white opinion leaders in Southern Rhodesia and South Africa. As he wrote to the cabinet secretary, Sir Norman Brook, just before he set out on his tour, 'Africans are not the problem in Africa, it is the Europeans.'[112]

On his trips Macmillan made successful stops in the newly independent Ghana and in Nigeria, which was to become independent later that year. His experience in Salisbury, the capital of the so-called Central African Federation of Southern Rhodesia, Northern Rhodesia and Nyasaland and whose future was in doubt, was much more fraught. But it was his 'wind of change' speech to South Africa parliamentarians in Cape Town which caught the imagination, not only of Africa but of the whole world. Anthony Sampson, journalist and later Macmillan's biographer, who watched the speech from the balcony, said, 'It was a speech of masterly construction and phrasing, beautifully spoken, combining a sweep of history with unambiguous political points. It was probably the finest of Macmillan's career.'[113] Two sentences stood out: 'The wind of change is blowing through the continent. Whether we like it or not, this growth of national consciousness is a political fact.' Macmillan went on to stress the importance of creating societies which respected the right of individuals, including the opportunity to have 'an increasing share in political power and responsibility'. Although it took many years before the 'wind of change' came to South Africa, by the end of Macmillan's government most of British Africa had become independent within the Commonwealth; between 1960 and 1964 17 British colonies – predominantly in Africa – gained independence.[114]

In May 1960, a few months after returning from Africa, Macmillan concluded that Britain must seek to join the European Economic Community (EEC). That same month, the Paris summit between the Soviet Union, the United States, Britain and France had broken up over the shooting-down of an American U2 reconnaissance plane over Russian air space. According to the Prime Minister's aide, Philip de Zulueta, the collapse of the summit, on which he had set great hopes, was a crucial moment for Macmillan: 'The colonial experience was, if not gone, rapidly going, the Commonwealth obviously not being really strong enough, coherent enough as an economic force. So what does Britain do? How does she play a part in the world.'[115]

On 1 June, Macmillan asked the permanent secretary of the Treasury, Sir Frank Lee, to carry out an investigation into the pros and cons of British membership of the EEC. The report, which was presented to the Cabinet on 13 July, concluded that 'They [the six existing members of the EEC] may become a bloc comparable in influence with the United States and the USSR, and if that happens and if we remain outside, our relative position in the world is bound to decline.'[116] A few days earlier, in his diary entry for 9 July, Macmillan had asked himself a penetrating question:

Shall we be caught between a hostile (or at least less friendly) America and a boastful, powerful 'Empire of Charlemagne' – now under French control? Is this the real reason for 'joining' the Common Market (if we are acceptable) and for abandoning a. EFTA [the European Free Trade Association] b. British Agriculture c. The Commonwealth; It's a grim choice.

The Prime Minister set about the complex process of joining the EEC (which he rightly saw as the biggest decision of his premiership) with circumspection, edging his party into Europe, albeit slowly and with plenty of diversions – in the same kind of way that he edged it out of Africa.[117] He put the pro-Europeans into key positions – Sandys as secretary of state for Commonwealth relations, Soames as minister of agriculture and Heath as Lord Privy Seal, in charge of the negotiation with the Six. In July 1961, he was ready to announce to Parliament the decision to seek to join the EEC, provided that satisfactory arrangements could be made for the Commonwealth, EFTA and British agriculture.

Macmillan was well aware that there was substantial opposition in his party and scepticism about the EEC within the Cabinet. He was especially worried about Butler, whom he knew had concerns both about the Commonwealth and about agriculture. In his diary, he noted that there were rumours circulating at Westminster 'that (a) if we reach an agreement in Brussels, Butler will lead a revolt in the Party on the cry of "selling out" the Commonwealth (b) if we fail, the PM's Common Market policy [...] will be humiliated and he must resign.'[118] Macmillan had given Rab the largely honorific title of being in overall charge of the Common Market negotiations, but it was not until August 1962 that Butler finally came off the fence, telling the Prime Minister, at a private dinner at Bucks Club in London that he had decided to support the Common Market because it was 'too big a chance to miss'. He added, however, that 'we might share the fate of Sir Robert Peel and his supporters' (a split in the Tory party over the repeal of the Corn Laws had led to the downfall of Peel).[119]

Between 1960 and 1962, the Prime Minister did his deputy few favours. In the July 1960 shuffle, he once again kept Butler out of the Foreign Office, preferring Alec Douglas-Home. In October 1961, in order to facilitate Iain Macleod's removal from the Colonial Office, he gave Macleod two of Rab's three offices – the leadership of the Commons and the party chairmanship. Butler was upset but, as he wrote in an (unsent) letter to Home, 'I have accepted all without saying anything, and it is Harold's wish.'[120] In March 1962, Macmillan gave Butler responsibility for Central African affairs with the onerous task of 'liquidating' the Central African Federation – a mission which Rab accomplished with exceptional skill.[121] The Prime Minister may have thought that keeping Butler preoccupied with African matters would be to his advantage. If so, he was badly mistaken. The virtual absence of Butler's wise and loyal advice for months on end was to prove a major handicap for a government which was beginning to lose its way.

The first of a succession of setbacks which almost overwhelmed the Macmillan administration was the so-called 'Night of the Long Knives' of July 1962. The background factors to the Prime Minister's botched reshuffle, in which a third of the Cabinet lost their jobs, were deteriorating economic conditions, an unpopular 'pay pause', an ineffective chancellor and a number of by-election setbacks, including the loss of a 'super-safe' suburban seat, Orpington, to the Liberals. In his memoirs, Macmillan concluded that he was right to have replaced his chancellor, Selwyn Lloyd, but 'was led into a serious error'[122] in adding so many other ministers to the casualty list.

There was, in fact, a good case for bringing in younger ministers such as Boyle, Joseph and Powell and promoting Maudling to the chancellorship. Butler himself lost the Home Office but received the high-sounding but basically empty title of first secretary of state (with continuing responsibility for Central African affairs) and the deputy premiership (which he had held in all but name since 1957). Rab, whom some accused of 'leaking' the impending reshuffle at a lunch with the proprietor of the *Daily Mail*, Lord Rothermere, wrote that 'the spilling of so much blood did serious damage to the Prime Minister's hitherto unbroken image of "unflappability".'[123] Certainly, the extent and rushed nature of the purge seemed to indicate a considerable degree of prime ministerial panic.

At the end of that year, on 11 December, the US secretary of defence, Robert McNamara, informed the British defence secretary, Peter Thorneycroft, that the Skybolt missile was a 'dead duck'. This was a major blow, not only for UK defence policy but also for the whole idea of Britain as an independent nuclear power with a seat at the top table. At the Nassau meeting later that month, Macmillan leant heavily on the close relationship which, exploiting the links between the Kennedys and the Cavendishes, he had managed establish with the young American President. Although privately Kennedy dismissed the British deterrent as 'a piece of military foolishness',[124] he fully understood that it was a political necessity for Macmillan and was prepared to help. So, thanks to the President, the Prime Minister came away from Nassau with the promise of Polaris, the submarine missile system.

But, if Kennedy had saved Macmillan's bacon over the nuclear deterrent, the Nassau agreement had a disastrous effect on the British attempt to join the EEC. For, on 14 January 1963, at a press conference at the Elysée

Palace, General de Gaulle, in the most eloquent of speeches, said 'No'. De Gaulle's argument was that the United Kingdom was not yet sufficiently 'European'. Britain had failed to put 'Europe' first 'without restriction, without reserve, and in preference to anything else'. Throughout the previous year, Macmillan had courted his former wartime colleague most assiduously. At successive meetings (at Chateau de Champs and Rambouillet), de Gaulle had been polite but non-committal. Now that the General had finally revealed his hand, Macmillan could only put on a brave face. In private, he was despairing: 'All our policies at home and abroad are in ruins [...] We have lost everything, except our courage and determination.'[125]

In the first half of 1963, the government was hit by a series of security and sex scandals (above all the Profumo affair[126]) which, though individually not perhaps of major importance, cumulatively seemed to reveal the Tories as accident prone and out of touch. The Prime Minister, now in his seventieth year, was derided in satirical shows like *Beyond the Fringe* and the hugely popular BBC programme *That Was the Week that Was* as a figure from a bygone age. Politically, a damaging contrast was drawn between the ageing Macmillan and (following the death of Hugh Gaistskell) the new leader of the opposition, the 48-year-old Harold Wilson. Butler wrote in his memoirs that when he returned from his success at the Victoria Falls conference in July 1963, 'I found it widely assumed among the back-benchers that in a matter of weeks or months Macmillan would have to make way for a new Leader.'[127]

Macmillan himself spent much of the year in a state of indecision, whether to stand down or whether to stay on to fight the next election. If he decided to resign, he favoured as his successor Hailsham, whose path to the leadership – like that of Home – had been opened up by the Peerage Bill which enabled existing peers to renounce their peerage immediately. In January 1962 the Prime Minister had told Butler that if he decided to go before the election 'it all falls to you.'[128]

But this was mere flattery. Macmillan's real opinion, expressed to Hailsham in the summer of 1963, was that 'Rab simply doesn't have it in him to be Prime Minister.'[129] It was this negative view of his deputy that was the main reason why he was so determined to stop Butler becoming leader. For his part, Butler, who could probably have insisted on Macmillan standing down at the height of the Profumo affair, remained loyal to the Prime Minister, telling Churchill's son Randolph, 'I shall always remain loyal to the Prime Minister so long as he remains our leader and Prime Minister.'[130]

The ending of the Macmillan–Butler partnership, which came suddenly, was pure theatre – part tragedy, part farce. On 7 October, on the eve of the Conservative Party conference at Blackpool, the Prime Minister told his closest party colleagues and advisers that he had decided to stay on as leader to fight the general election. However, during the night he suffered an acute prostate obstruction and though, following medical attention, he had recovered enough to preside over Cabinet the next morning, he was in such pain that he had to withdraw from the meeting. That afternoon his doctors told him that he required immediate surgery and at 9 p.m. he was admitted to hospital. The news that he was to have a prostate operation and that Butler was to take charge of the government in his absence was announced on the BBC that evening.

Macmillan was convinced he would have to stand down. But he was determined that, in contrast to Eden, he would play a central role in choosing his successor. The strange process through which Tory leaders at that time emerged – a combination of official consultation and unofficial arm-twisting – suited his purposes admirably. His objectives were to stop Butler (he wrote in his diary on 4 October, 'Butler would be Fatal')[131] and to ensure that the Conservatives picked a credible alternative. On the morning of 9 October, he called Home to his hospital bedside to prepare a resignation note to be read out to the party conference. As they worked, Macmillan suggested to Home that he should put himself forward as a candidate. The Foreign Secretary had already told the Cabinet that he would not run, but agreed to consider the possibility.

Meanwhile, once Home had read out Macmillan's note, the party conference at Blackpool became almost like an American convention.

Hailsham's supporters gave out 'Q' for Quintin buttons, while, at the end of a fringe meeting, Hailsham excitedly announced his intention to give up his peerage – exhibitionist behaviour which turned off the party's elders. Home, canvassing more discreetly, made a decorous and well-received speech to the conference. Butler's end-of-conference address was thoughtful and forward looking but, as in his 1956 speech to the 1922 Committee, his delivery was 'flat and uninspiring'.[132]

The following week the scene shifted back to London. Macmillan, by now recovering from his operation, decided to hasten the leadership process. Interestingly, his private assessment on Monday 14 October, after seeing the Chief Whip and the Vice Chancellor, was as follows: 'the party in the country wants Hogg [Hailsham], the parliamentary Party wants Maudling or Butler. The Cabinet wants Butler. The last ten days have not altered this fundamental fact.'[133]

However, only three days later, on 17 October, when those who had been deputed by the Prime Minister to carry out the consultations (a process endorsed by the Cabinet) met Macmillan at his bedside, the situation had apparently changed. According to the Lord Chancellor, Home had emerged as the leading candidate of the Cabinet, while the Chief Whip reported that Home and Butler had roughly the same level of first-choice support in the parliamentary party. Macmillan was impressed that Home seemed to have less opposition than any other candidate. As he told the Queen in his memorandum of 18 October, 'he seems to be the second choice of everybody.'[134] It was on the basis that nobody was against him that Macmillan advised the Queen to ask Home to try and form a government.

But when the news about the choice of Home leaked out later on 17 October there was immediate protest. Two prominent younger members of the Cabinet, Iain Macleod and Enoch Powell, met at Powell's house at South Eaton Place, and were later joined by the chancellor of the Exchequer, Reginald Maudling and the president of the Board of Trade, Freddie Erroll. Another dissident group, including Hailsham and Thorneycroft, also met at Hailsham's house in Putney. Other dissenting Cabinet ministers included Brooke, Boyle and Boyd Carpenter. There was general agreement that Home would be electorally disastrous. The next morning Hailsham and Maudling met Butler and agreed to support him. Hearing of this potentially powerful rebellion, Home phoned Macmillan and told him that he was inclined to withdraw. Macmillan replied that it was now too late. As Rab remarked in his memoirs, Macmillan acted throughout 'with utter determination and dispatch'.[135]

One of Macmillan's biographers wrote, 'The problem that the rebels had was that Butler himself was not inclined to rebel.'[136] As he later told Home, after his unhappy experience in 1957, Rab was hesitant about competing again. He thought that there was a case for a younger man, somebody such as Maudling, especially now that Wilson was leader of the Labour Party. It was only the special circumstance of October 1963 – Macmillan's illness and Rab's position as acting prime minister – which persuaded him to try once again for the leadership. But to win the crown, he would now have to fight for it with one of his oldest friends in politics (Home), without the certainty of success and with the danger of setting off a civil war in the party. He may have also remembered the observation of Sir John Morrison, chairman of the 1922 Committee, made to him in June: 'The chaps won't have you.' As Macmillan above all was well aware, the single-minded ruthlessness which would have been required was simply not in Butler's nature.

Within 24 hours the rebellion had fizzled out. Although Rab did not immediately sign up, the following morning he accepted the Foreign Office and one hour later Maudling agreed to stay on at the Treasury. Macleod and Powell, however, refused office – an indication that some of the brightest and best were still unhappy with what had happened.

* * *

In Macmillan's hands, the traditional Tory way of choosing the leader – by consultation rather than election – did not enhance the party's reputation. On the contrary, it resulted in 'turmoil and recrimination'.[137] Its inadequacy was devastatingly exposed by Macleod in a review article in the *Spectator* in January 1964, and in 1965 it was replaced by a democratic system of election by Tory MPs.

Macmillan's choice, Sir Alec Douglas-Home (as he became), led the party to an – albeit narrow – defeat at the 1964 election. Labour's victor, Harold Wilson, said that, if Butler had become leader, the Tories would have won the election. Certainly Home's image as an old-fashioned aristocrat and his poor performance on television told against him. Later, both Home and Macmillan himself admitted it might have been better for the party if Butler had been chosen.[138]

These are the might-have-beens of history. What is certainly true is that the tumultuous events of October 1963 provided a sad ending to a most effective combination. Together Macmillan and Butler had launched the revival of the postwar Conservative Party and helped the Tories establish themselves as the party of affluence. The Macmillan governments, with Butler as a loyal deputy, had led the decolonisation of Africa and forged a new direction in European policy for the United Kingdom. It was a great political partnership, one of the most creative in Tory party history.

4
INTO EUROPE
Heath and Wilson

On 1 January 1973, with the Conservative Edward Heath as its prime minister, Britain entered the European Community. Ironically, two years later, the Labour prime minister, Harold Wilson, who in opposition had led his party against the terms of entry negotiated by Heath, recommended that Britain should remain a member. In a nationwide referendum, the British then voted by a margin of 2 to 1 to stay in. Although there were other notable actors in the decision to belong to the EC, including Harold Macmillan and Christopher Soames for the Tories and Roy Jenkins and George Brown on the Labour side, the argument of this chapter is that is was Heath and Wilson who were the two who made the biggest contribution to this momentous change – probably the most far-reaching development in postwar foreign policy and one which still remains controversial today.

In contrast to the other pairings in this book (with the possible exception of Bevin and Morrison), Heath and Wilson were never partners. On the contrary, throughout the second half of the 1960s and the first half of the 1970s, as leaders of opposing parties, they were locked in an often-bitter struggle for power.

After Labour's wafer-thin victory in the 1964 election, Wilson became prime minister; a year later, Heath succeeded the defeated Sir Alec Douglas-Home as Conservative leader of the opposition. In their first electoral

1a. Churchill, who in 1939 most Tories judged to be an unreliable adventurer, was by the end of 1940 thought to be a great war leader. Attlee described him as 'a beacon for his country's will to win'.

1b. Clement Attlee was at the other end of the charisma scale from Churchill. However, the Labour leader's effective management was also crucial to the success of the wartime coalition.

1c. The new British prime minister, Winston Churchill, accompanied by his coalition partner, the leader of the Labour Party, Clement Attlee, makes a last visit to Paris in May 1940 in a vain attempt to keep France in the war.

1d. Winston Churchill returns to London in June 1942 after a meeting in Washington with his new ally President Roosevelt, and is met by his deputy Clement Attlee, in charge of the Cabinet during Churchill's frequent absences abroad.

25 february, 1950

PICTURE
POST

CONGRATULATIONS!

52
PAGES

25 FEBRUARY, 1950

Vol. 46. No. 8.

ELECTION SPECIAL

HULTON'S NATIONAL WEEKLY · PRICE FOURPENCE

HARD LUCK!

e. Two of the greatest twentieth-century prime ministers, Churchill and Attlee, walk ogether after the 1950 election, which Labour had narrowly won. In wartime they combined to form the exceptional partnership which helped save the country.

2a. An unusual photograph of Bevin and Morrison together at a wartime meeting. The two Labour 'big beasts' had a notoriously difficult personal relationship: Bevin called Morrison a 'scheming little bastard', while Morrison said that Bevin was a 'strange mixture o[f] genius and stupidity'.

2b. Attlee, with Bevin and Morrison, celebrate the party's landslide victory at the July 1945 general election. As in the picture, so in his cabinet: the Labour Prime Minister astutely kept the two men apart, with Bevin in charge of foreign affairs and Morrison running the domestic front.

2c. Ernest Bevin at his desk at the Foreign Office; Bevin was arguably the most imaginative Foreign Secretary of the twentieth century, helping create the Western Alliance and implementing the Marshall Plan.

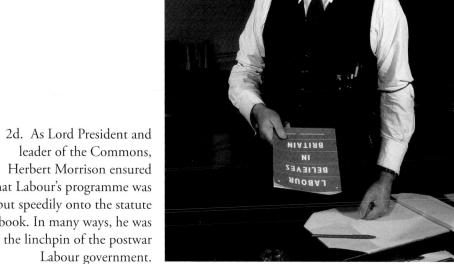

2d. As Lord President and leader of the Commons, Herbert Morrison ensured that Labour's programme was put speedily onto the statute book. In many ways, he was the linchpin of the postwar Labour government.

3a. Harold Macmillan as chancellor of the Exchequer, speaking to the 1956 Tory Party conference, with the Lord Privy Seal, R.A. Butler, beside him. A few months later, after the Suez debacle and the downfall of Anthony Eden, Macmillan ruthlessly outmanoeuvred Butler to become Conservative leader.

3b. However, the two men formed a highly effective partnership with Macmillan as the dynamic prime minister and Butler as his able lieutenant.

3c. Macmillan, with the support of Butler, won the 1959 election with the slogan: 'Life's better under the Conservatives. Don't let Labour ruin it.' He also set in train the decolonisation of Africa and forged a new, European direction for British foreign policy.

"WELL, SO LONG, RAB! I'M OFF TO SEE THE FAMILY, BUT I KNOW THAT YOU'RE THE BEST BABY SITTER WE HAVE!"

3d. This Vicky cartoon illustrates the key role played by Butler during Macmillan's lengthy trips abroad, when Rab was left at home, as he said, 'holding the baby'.

4a. The Labour prime minister, Harold Wilson, and the Tory leader of the opposition, Edward Heath, at the state opening of Parliament. Wilson had just defeated Heath in the 1966 landslide victory.

4b. As this Vicky cartoon implies, the relations between Heath and Wilson were strained. Heath disliked Wilson and Wilson despised Heath, whom he regularly outsmarted in debate.

c. Prime Minister Heath signs the Treaty of Accession in Brussels on 24 January 1972, when the UK joined the European Community.

d. Harold Wilson, with Helmut Schmidt the German chancellor, at the Labour Party Conference in 1974. Wilson was preparing the ground for successful renegotiation and a victory for the 'yes' campaign in the 1975 referendum.

5a. Margaret Thatcher emerges as the outspoken environment spokesman at a Tory Party press conference during the 1974 general election, while the party chairman, William Whitelaw, looks on apprehensively.

5b. Thatcher with Whitelaw during the second ballot for the Tory leadership, following Heath's defeat. Mrs Thatcher comfortably beat Whitelaw but wisely appointed him her deputy.

5c. Mrs Thatcher in characteristically triumphant pose. Arguably the most dominant of the postwar premiers, she once said in a famous but unintentional double entendre, 'Every Prime Minister should have a Willie.'

5d. Whitelaw advises Thatcher. He was her indispensible enabler, conciliator and sheet anchor.

THE
CONSERVATIVE
MANIFESTO
1983

5e. Together Thatcher and Whitelaw launched the 1983 manifesto. When Whitelaw resigned in 1988 following a minor stroke, senior cabinet colleagues saw his departure as a severe blow to the government.

6a. This photograph shows Prime Minister Tony Blair appearing on the BBC's *Breakfast with Frost* programme. By far the best communicator in modern British politics, Blair was stylish and charismatic, with the ability to appeal beyond Labour's heartlands to the aspirational voters of the Midlands and the South.

6b. Brown could make eloquent conference speeches but was less good on television. He was the policy expert of New Labour and also an outstanding chancellor of the Exchequer, at least until the end of the second term.

6c. So long as they were working together, Blair and Brown were an unbeatable partnership. They created New Labour, helped bring it to power, and sustained it by winning three successive elections.

6d. This photograph from the 2001 election shows how frosty the relations between the two men could become. In the end, the government was undermined by Brown's refusal to accept the number two position.

a. The leader of the Tory party, David Cameron, and the leader of the Liberal Democrats, Nick Clegg, announce the first peacetime coalition in the rose garden of No 10 Downing Street.

b. Good personal relations between the two men, as well as self interest, helped the coalition survive such controversial issues as tuition fees, the referendum on the alternative vote, the collapse of House of Lords reform and changes to the health service (which they are announcing here).

7c. Cameron and Clegg launch the so-called midterm review. In practice, the coalition was increasingly dominated by the Conservatives.

7d. Cameron mishandled the European issue by appearing to give more emphasis to appeasing his Eurosceptic critics and winning back votes from UKIP than on keeping Britain in the EU. His unwise commitment to hold an 'in/out' referendum, made in this Bloomberg speech, loomed like a dark cloud of uncertainty over British politics.

contest in 1966 Wilson triumphed over Heath with a large majority, but in 1970 Heath unexpectedly turned the tables, becoming prime minister. In 1974, Wilson won two narrow but, in the end, decisive victories over Heath, which led to Heath's replacement by Margaret Thatcher as Tory leader.

The two men's lengthy political duel was accentuated by personal antipathy. Heath loathed Wilson, whom he dismissed as a blatant opportunist. Wilson had little respect for Heath's political abilities and found him cold and lacking in compassion. Willie Whitelaw, then Tory chief whip, told David Butler: 'There is a real animus between Heath and Wilson. Both are to blame [...] It is embarrassing to be in the same room as them both.'[1]

Although they were similar in age and, to some extent, in attainment and background, Heath and Wilson were different kinds of people. If Wilson was sometimes accused of short-termism and of excessive 'fudging', he was also tenacious and resilient, with, as his *Dictionary of National Biography* biographer, Roy Jenkins, wrote, 'good nerve in a crisis'. He was, above all, a political pragmatist, with a quicksilver mind and a sharp and ready wit, which enabled him to dominate the House of Commons. Heath was more ponderous and often remarkably insensitive to the feelings of others. But he was courageous and had great integrity. Jenkins, who worked closely with Heath during the 1975 referendum campaign, described him: 'as impervious to the waves and as reliable in his beam as a great light house but sometimes blocking the way.'[2]

Their contrasting approach to life and politics spilled over into their attitude towards Europe. The official historian of Britain and Europe, Stephen Wall, has written that 'Heath was a European of head and heart; Wilson of the head.'[3] Heath was a convinced European who made his maiden speech about the Schuman Plan, led the unsuccessful negotiations for British entry at the beginning of the 1960s, and in 1973 took the United Kingdom into the EC. It was appropriate that the City of Aachen should have awarded him the Charlemagne Prize for his services to Europe. In contrast to Heath (and like most of his fellow countrymen),

Wilson was never an enthusiast for Europe. His senior policy adviser, Bernard Donoughue, said of him, 'He would probably have preferred that the European Economic Community did not exist. Now that it did, he adjusted to that reality.'[4] Hence his government's bid to join the EC in the late 1960s and, in 1974–5, the renegotiation and subsequent referendum in which he successfully advocated a 'yes' vote. To secure British EC membership, and then sustain it, needed the contribution of both Heath and Wilson – the visionary and the pragmatist.

James Harold Wilson and Edward Richard George Heath were both born during World War I and in the same year, 1916, Harold on 11 March, a few months before Edward on 9 July. Harold Wilson came from a lower middle-class family, in the West Riding of Yorkshire. His father, Herbert, was a Huddersfield works chemist, while his mother, Ethel, had been a teacher. Ethel's family had relatives in Australia and, in 1926, Harold, the apple of his parents' eye, went with his mother on a six-month trip to see his maternal grandfather and his uncle who was a state legislator in Western Australia. In 1930, as the depression took hold, Harold's father lost his job and it was not until two years later that he found employment as chief chemist at a firm in the Wirral peninsula in Cheshire. This meant a move for the family. In Harold's case, it was a blessing in disguise, because it was at the newly established Wirral Grammar School that his academic ability first revealed itself and, in 1934, before his eighteenth birthday, he won a history exhibition at Jesus College, Oxford.

Ted (as he was called for most of his life) Heath was a southerner, born in Broadstairs in Kent. His father, William, was a carpenter who ended up as a builder. His mother, Edith, had been a ladies' maid at a big house near Broadstairs. Edith, whom Ted revered for 'her beauty and calmness'[5] was the driving force in his early life. It was she who was determined that her sons, especially the eldest, Ted, should make the best of their opportunities.

At the age of ten, Heath won a scholarship to Chatham House Grammar School in Ramsgate. His academic results were satisfactory without being exceptional, but it was at Chatham House that he began to develop an extensive 'hinterland'. He became a promising musician, proficient at both the piano and the organ; he was prominent in the school debating society, and in the school 'mock' general election in 1935, he stood as the National Government candidate, winning in a landslide. After failing to win organ scholarships at St Catherine's College, Cambridge and Keble College, Oxford, Heath tried and failed to win a modern greats scholarship (politics, philosophy and economics) to Balliol College, Oxford, though his economics paper was deemed to be of exhibition standard. He was, however, accepted as a commoner.

The question was how he was to finance his university education. The Kent Education Committee offered him a loan of £120 a year which was made up to £160 by a friend of his father. The rest (a further £60 a year) had to be paid for by his parents; this was a risky decision which was vulnerable to any downturn in his father's business. Fortunately, the organ scholarship at Balliol became available soon after Heath arrived at the college; he entered for it and won. This gave him an extra £80, as well as four years instead of three at university, beginning in 1935 (a year later than Wilson).

Though both Heath and Wilson had 'stellar' university careers, their paths to success were different. Wilson, who worked exceptionally hard, achieved brilliant academic results, obtaining an outstanding first-class degree in politics, philosophy and economics, with 'alphas' in almost every paper. He also won the Gladstone Memorial Prize, as well as the George Webb Medley Senior Scholarship in economics; the latter gave him an extra £300 a year. Although Wilson was briefly treasurer of the Oxford Liberal Club, the future prime minister had little time for involvement in university politics.

By contrast, Heath became one of Oxford's leading student politicians. He was president of the Oxford University Conservative Association in 1937–8 and, in his fourth year, he was elected president of the Oxford Union. The student magazine nominated him as one of its 'Isis Idols'. Heath was a Conservative but very much a left-wing rebel in the Macmillan mode. Like his fellow Balliol undergraduates, Denis Healey and Roy Jenkins, he played an active role in the famous Oxford by-election when the master of their college, A.D. Lindsay, stood in protest against the Munich settlement as an independent against the official Conservative candidate, Quintin Hogg (later Lord Hailsham). In a tumultuous campaign, Lindsay halved the Tory majority. Harold Wilson, immersed in his academic studies, took no part.

On the day after finishing his last exams, Wilson received the news that his father had lost his job. Though the award of the George Webb Medley Scholarship had made it possible for him to stay on at Oxford, he now needed extra money to help out his parents (his father did not find another job until 18 months later). Wilson failed to get an All Souls fellowship but landed a part-time fellowship at New College. It was, however, the acceptance of a research post under the celebrated but domineering social reformer William Beveridge which helped shape Wilson's future. Beveridge was an exacting taskmaster, so much so that Wilson's biographer, Ben Pimlott, wrote that for Wilson the experience was like that of 'a pack animal learning from a muleteer'.[6] The upside was that Wilson not only became a first-rate statistician and, in 1938, research fellow at University College (of which Beveridge was the master), but, more importantly in the long run, Beveridge's patronage was to open up the opportunity of a career outside Oxford.

While Wilson was hard at work for Beveridge, studying unemployment figures and visiting labour exchanges, Heath was getting what the senior tutor at Balliol called 'a very nice second in the schools'.[7] Heath's reaction was one of disappointment but, given all his other commitments and perhaps a lack of academic flair (which Wilson had in abundance), a first was never really on the cards.

In the summer of 1939, as the outbreak of war became imminent, Ted Heath, on the last of his three prewar summer adventures, was with a friend, Madron Seligman, in Danzig, the city which Hitler was threatening to incorporate into Germany. On arrival, they were advised by an official at the British Consulate to leave immediately. Hitchhiking through Poland, they reached Germany, where they found German tanks and trucks moving ominously towards the frontier. Crossing Germany by train as quickly as they could, the two young men got a lift from a French army captain to Paris, where they separated. Heath was met by his parents at Dover just a week before the war broke out. As Ted Heath remarked in his memoirs, 'We had cut things pretty fine.'[8]

On the day that the Germans attacked Poland, Harold Wilson was reading a paper on exports and the trade cycle to the annual conference of the British Association. The coming of war had two immediate consequences for Wilson. First, he had to register at the local Oxford employment exchange under the Military Service Act and was straight-away categorised as a 'specialist'. It is wrong to say that he tried to avoid being called up. As one of his biographers, Philip Zeigler, commented, 'the most that can be said is that he made no effort to escape the current that bore him unprotesting into the maw of the Civil Service.'[9] Secondly, he and his girlfriend, Mary Baldwin, whom he had been courting for five years, decided to get married as quickly as possible. The ceremony took place in Mansfield College Chapel on 1 January 1940, with Mary's father, a Congregationalist minister, officiating; graduate members of the congregation, including the groom, wore academic gowns. Mary Wilson loved the idea of being an Oxford don's wife – 'very old buildings and very young people' – but the future for the Wilsons was, unfortunately for her, to be very different.

When war broke out, Heath immediately volunteered for military service but was told that he would not be required for several months. After consulting the Foreign Office, he decided to take up the opportunity of going on a debating tour in the United States. But he and his fellow debater, a former treasurer of the Oxford Union, were advised not to mention the war. Understandably, this was the subject which most of their American hosts wished to debate. On the advice of the British ambassador, Lord Lothian, they decided to accept the invitation, with one proposing and the other opposing the motion. He was impressed by America and its 'pulsating life', which he contrasted with the lifeless state of the British political elite, which was 'out of touch, uninspired, content to deal with new problems in an old way'.[10] Returning to Britain, Heath had to wait until August 1940 before he was called up in the Royal Artillery.

Early in 1940, Wilson's career as a wartime civil servant began to take off. Apparently he was summoned to the Ministry of Supply, where he was interviewed by the director of statistics on an article in that week's *Economist* on the mobilisation of the economy. As Wilson was able to point out that he had written the article, it was not surprising that he was offered a job. After a brief period as joint secretary of the Anglo-French Coordinating Committee (it was wound up after the fall of France in June), Wilson went on to work with Beveridge at the Ministry of Labour as head of statistics. When, in July 1941, Beveridge was shunted aside by Bevin to chair a new committee on social insurance (the committee which the following year produced the famous Beveridge Report), he asked Wilson to act as its secretary. However, Wilson refused, as he had been offered a job as chief statistician at the Department of Mines.

This decision was not as ill advised as it sounds because the war effort depended, to a considerable extent, on coal. Wilson's performance in improving the department's statistics and thus giving ministers a much clearer picture of coal production was widely praised. Another wartime civil servant, Hugh Gaitskell, whom Wilson was later to challenge for the leadership of the Labour Party, reported to Hugh Dalton, then president of the Board of Trade (which, at that time, was in overall charge of the Department of Mines), that Wilson was 'extraordinarily able' and that 'we must on no account surrender him either to the Army or to any other department.'[11]

As it turned out, Wilson's job at the Department of Mines indirectly led him into Labour politics and to a seat in Parliament. In 1942, his work as joint secretary of a board of inquiry into unofficial disputes in the coal industry brought him into contact with the leaders of the miners' union. In 1943, he was co-opted onto the executive of the Fabian Society, the Labour-linked 'think tank', and was soon drafting papers on the coal industry and on the financing of the railways. In 1944, he allowed his name to be included on the Transport House 'B' list of potential parliamentary candidates. According to his wife, Wilson had always intended to go into politics. Certainly, the special circumstances at the end of the war, with constituency parties looking for suitable candidates, provided him with an exceptional opportunity to establish himself politically. In the autumn of 1944 he was selected as Labour candidate for Ormskirk and, in Labour's 1945 election landslide, Wilson, assisted by a split in the Tory vote, was elected to Parliament with a majority of over 7,000.

While Wilson was winning his spurs in the corridors of Whitehall, Heath and his anti-aircraft battery took part in the defence of Liverpool and other cities in the north and the Midlands against German air attacks. He proved himself a highly competent regimental officer, so much so that in March 1942 he was promoted to be regimental adjutant. Two years later, Heath landed in Normandy with his battery and took part in the bombardment of Caen and the fierce battle to close the Falaise Gap. He saw for the first time 'the full carnage of war',[12] the remains of shattered vehicles, the bodies left behind in ditches and the stinking carcases of animals in the fields. He described the nine months of hard campaigning, during which the Allied armies swept through northern France and Belgium and eventually, after the attempted German breakout in the Ardennes, into Germany, as 'among the most demanding in my life'.[13]

After the German surrender, Heath was put in charge of the reconstruction of Hanover. A few months later he drove across a shattered Germany to the partially destroyed city of Nuremburg to witness at first-hand the Nuremburg trials of the leading Nazi war criminals. It left a lasting impression on him. In contrast to Wilson, he had decided not to try and contest the 1945 election, in part because he felt that he could not abandon his army colleagues at such a time but also possibly because he was unimpressed by the Tories. He was not at all surprised by their disastrous defeat. His wartime experience had, however, given him a political mission. He wrote in his memoirs: 'My generation did not have the option of living in the past: we had to work for the future. We were surrounded by destruction, horrendous hunger and despair [...] Reconciliation and reconstruction must be our tasks.'[14] So began his European commitment.

*

Meanwhile, Harold Wilson's rise was meteoric. In 1945, he was one of only three new Labour MPs to be given immediate office (as junior minister at the Department of Works) and, at the age of 29, by far the youngest. Attlee's explanation was matter of fact: 'I had heard of him as a don at my old college [University College] and knew of the work he had done for the Party.'[15] The latter was possibly a reference to the book which Wilson had recently written, *New Deal for Coal*, which had put forward the case for nationalising the mines on pragmatic, non-doctrinaire grounds. The *News Chronicle*'s description of Wilson as a 'brilliant young civil servant [...] regarded by the Whitehall high-ups as one of the great discoveries of the war',[16] was another, perhaps more compelling reason for his promotion.

Only two years later, in September 1947, Wilson was brought into the Cabinet as president of the Board of Trade, becoming the youngest Cabinet minister since Peel. He owed his spectacular elevation mainly to the patronage of Sir Stafford Cripps, in 1947 very much the rising star of the government. Attlee had made Cripps minister of economic planning in September and in November, following Dalton's resignation, chancellor of the Exchequer; when Cripps moved to Economic Planning, Wilson took his place at the Board of Trade.

Wilson's reputation in the later 1940s was based on his competence as a departmental minister and his technical expertise as an economist rather than on his ability to command the House of Commons. When Cripps resigned in October 1950 because of ill health, he was succeeded by Hugh Gaitskell, who, as minister for economic affairs had already been acting as a kind of deputy chancellor, taking some of the load off a sick Cripps. This was undoubtedly a disappointment for Wilson, who, as the senior economic minister after Cripps, almost certainly had expectations of succeeding the chancellor if, or more likely when, he resigned. However, it was Gaitskell who had come best out of the devaluation crisis of the previous year, impressing ministers and civil servants with his decisiveness. In contrast, Wilson was thought to have prevaricated, so that, when Cripps finally resigned, senior ministers such as Cripps,

Dalton, Morrison and above all Attlee agreed on backing Gaitskell rather than Wilson for the chancellorship.

Despite this setback, over the next decade Wilson emerged as a potential challenger for the leadership. The crucial event both in the party's civil war (which dominated the first part of the 1950s and was a key factor in the lengthy Tory spell in power) and in Wilson's eventual rise to the top was the resignation from the Attlee government of Aneurin Bevan, John Freeman and Wilson himself in April 1951. Bevan, the creator of the National Health Service, was the most prominent figure in the rebellion against the imposition of health changes announced in Gaitskell's budget, with Wilson very much second in command, 'Nye's little dog', as Hugh Dalton used to call him.

Wilson's motives in resigning with Bevan were mixed. These included an understandable concern (set out lucidly in his resignation speech) about the impact on the British economy of the massive increase in defence spending following the outbreak of the Korean War; admiration of and support for the hugely talented Bevan as the coming man in the Labour Party; and possibly also jealousy of Gaitskell, who had got the job which he coveted. Some Labour MPs suspected that Wilson's resignation was a clever exercise in political positioning. Having been overtaken on the right by Gaitskell, he was now making a compensatory move to the left. If so, as Roy Jenkins noted, it needed 'at the very least a very cool nerve'[17] for the youngest member of the Cabinet to resign in such controversial circumstances without any certainty that it would pay off in the future.

Following Labour's narrow defeat in October 1951, the next few years of opposition were dominated by the Bevanite revolt in which Wilson played a prominent part. He acted as chairman of the Bevanite group, was a key member of the Tribune Brains Trust which toured the constituencies putting over an anti-leadership message and, as a reward, succeeded in being elected to the National Executive Committee at the tumultuous Morecambe party conference of 1952 on a left-wing ticket. However, unlike most Bevanites, Wilson was ambitious and, as the Bevanite challenge fizzled out, he gradually began to move towards the centre.

A key moment in Wilson's political evolution came with Bevan's ill-judged resignation from the Shadow Cabinet over Attlee's handling of foreign policy. Wilson, who had been runner-up in the Shadow Cabinet elections, automatically took Bevan's place, provided he was prepared to accept it. It would, of course, mean a break with Bevan (who had not consulted Wilson about his resignation) and the 'hardcore' Bevanites. On the other hand, if he took up the vacancy, it would be welcomed by the Parliamentary Labour Party majority. Urged on by his ally, Dick Crossman, Wilson decided to accept the Shadow Cabinet place, a step which one of his supporters described as his 'first long stride towards No. 10 Downing Street'.[18] When Attlee retired from the leadership in December 1955 (following Labour's defeat in the 1955 election), Wilson's decision to vote for Gaitskell and not for Bevan in the subsequent leaderships contest confirmed his shift away from the left. After Gaitskell's clear victory, Wilson was rewarded with Gaitskell's previous post as shadow chancellor.

It was during the next three years (from 1956 to 1959) that Wilson made his reputation as a parliamentary performer. From being a competent but dull speaker, he became one of the few frontbenchers for whom, when he got up to speak at the dispatch box, the Chamber rapidly filled, especially when there was a clash between Wilson and the then-chancellor, Harold Macmillan. After a brilliant and often witty speech by the Shadow Chancellor, Macmillan would sometimes toss a note of congratulation across the Chamber. He described a Wilson speech thus: 'Epigram followed epigram, and the continual flashes of wit were from time to time relieved by more serious arguments.'[19] Roy Jenkins, himself a powerful House of Commons debater, compared Wilson's daring eloquence to Disraeli's – as he said, 'a very considerable parliamentary comparison'.[20]

Labour's crushing defeat in the 1959 election (which the party had expected to win) raised a tricky problem for Wilson. Up until then, his relations with Gaitskell had been correct, if somewhat wary. But, in Wilson's eyes, the response of the Gaitskellites to electoral defeat – to call for party reform, in particular revision of Clause IV of the constitution – was hasty and divisive. Without directly challenging Gaitskell, Wilson put himself forward as the advocate of unity, producing a formula whereby Clause IV was retained but supplemented by a new statement of aims. In the end, Gaitskell was forced by the weakness of his position to accept Wilson's compromise.

In 1960, a crisis over nuclear defence almost overwhelmed Gaitskell's leadership. However, although Gaitskell was defeated on defence at the Scarborough conference, he made a passionate speech denouncing unilateralism, which won over many constituency delegates and prepared the way for his victory to the following year. When Labour MPs returned to Westminster, the left urged Wilson to stand against Gaitskell for the leadership. Wilson, who was not a unilateralist and was nine years younger than Gaitskell, was hesitant, but the probability that another centre-left candidate (Anthony Greenwood) would stand if he did not forced his hand. Gaitskell defeated the Shadow Chancellor by 166 votes to 81. It was a decisive victory but Wilson had established himself as a credible alternative to Gaitskell.

Early in 1963, Gaitskell, who was riding high in the polls and looking more and more like the next prime minister, suddenly died from a rare immunological disease. In the leadership contest that followed, Wilson, who immediately put his hat in the ring, had two advantages. First, his main opponent from the right, George Brown, was an exceptionally able and eloquent trade union MP but was liable to fly off the handle and was often drunk. Second, partly as a consequence of Brown's widely recognised inadequacies, a third candidate, James Callaghan, was persuaded to run. His candidature split the centre-right vote. In the first ballot, Wilson had 115 votes, Brown 88 and Callaghan 41. Wilson then won the second ballot decisively by 144 to 103. At the age of only 46, he had the political world at his feet.

Heath's political ascent was much slower, certainly less controversial and, arguably, more consistent than that of Wilson. If Wilson's path to the top was characterised by recognition of his exceptional ability, by dramatic resignation and clever positioning, Heath's was more prosaic, marked by loyalty to the leadership as well as hard graft in the Whips' Office.

Heath did not become an MP until 1950, by which time Wilson had not only been in Parliament for five years but had also become a Cabinet minister. Between leaving the army in 1946 and becoming a member, Heath had both to find a seat as well as earn a living; the latter was a difficult task because, despite his ability, most employers were loath to offer him a job once they knew about his political ambitions. He passed the civil service selection board in top place but after he had been adopted as a prospective parliamentary candidate he was immediately forced to resign. Then, following a spell as a subeditor for the *Church Times*, he found a more satisfactory position in the City, working for a small merchant bank, Brown Shipley, which allowed him to devote time and energy to nursing Bexley, a Labour-held suburban marginal seat, and building up Conservative membership in the constituency. At the 1950 election (narrowly won by Labour), Ted Heath gained Bexley for the Tories by 133 votes after a recount. As he admitted, his owed his victory in part to the Communist candidate, who polled 481 votes.

Heath made a promising start to his parliamentary career, delivering a notable maiden speech on the subject of European unity, urging the Labour government to participate in the negotiations over the Schuman Plan in order to develop and coordinate Europe.[21] He became known as a liberally minded Tory, in the mould of Butler and Macmillan. He was a founder member of the 'One Nation' group of young Conservative MPs, alongside such later prominent figures as Iain Macleod, Reginald Maudling, Enoch Powell and Angus Maude. Within a few months, he was offered a junior position as an opposition whip. After some hesitation, he accepted, though he was aware that he would no longer be able to make speeches in the Commons. His virtual silence was to last for eight years.

The compensation was that he was rapidly promoted within the Whips' Office. In March 1952, he became deputy chief whip and, in December 1955, Anthony Eden made him his chief whip. Heath was widely considered to be good at his job. Congratulating him on his appointment, Anthony Wedgwood Benn, then a rising young Labour MP, wrote,

'How you manage to combine such a friendly manner with such an iron discipline is a source of respectful amazement to us.'[22]

The Suez crisis, which divided both his party and country and led to the resignation of Eden, was a test of Heath's qualities. He claimed in his memoirs that he made clear to the Prime Minister his misgivings about the invasion.[23] But, like an officer in wartime, he believed that it was his duty not to resign but to remain in office to steady the government and keep the party from disintegration. Douglas Hurd judged that Heath 'was probably the only substantial figure in the government whose reputation was actually enhanced by the crisis'.[24]

Although, in the leadership contest which followed Eden's resignation, Heath remained publicly neutral, he privately told the Queen's private secretary that the party would prefer Macmillan, a choice which he shared. He admired Butler but considered that, in the critical circumstances that followed Suez, the more decisive Macmillan would be the better choice. On the first evening of his premiership, Macmillan took Heath to an oyster and steak dinner at the Turf Club. This was a mark not only of Heath's importance but also of the new alliance between Macmillan and Heath.

Heath's assessment of Macmillan was that he had 'by far the most constructive mind' of any politician whom he ever encountered.[25] For his part, the new Prime Minister relied heavily on his Chief Whip not only for advice on party matters but also on issues across the political spectrum. In July 1958 Butler noted: 'The Chief Whip's status had been raised to God Almighty by the PM asking him to every meeting on every subject at every hour of the day and night.'[26] After the Conservative victory at the 1959 election, Heath was rewarded by being appointed minister of labour. In his short stay at the department, he proved to be a conciliator, averting a potentially damaging rail strike. Then, in July 1960, following a reshuffle, Macmillan moved Heath to the Foreign Office, with a seat in the Cabinet and with special responsibility for European affairs, an appointment which was to shape the rest of his political career.

Following the Macmillan government's decision to apply for membership of the European Community in July 1961, Heath was put in charge of the negotiations with the Six. He proved to be an outstanding negotiator. He believed passionately that, if possible, Britain's future should be in the EC. He assembled a high-powered Whitehall delegation (known as the 'Flying Knights') led by Sir Pierson Dixon, the British ambassador to France, and with representatives of the key government departments. Eric Roll, a brilliant official from the Ministry of Agriculture, said of Heath: 'He combined in a unique way the qualities of a first rate official having complete mastery of complex technical details with the necessary political touch in his contacts with Ministers and officials of other countries, with the press and with London.'[27] Yet, despite Heath's competence and his impressive team, the negotiations failed.

Jean Monnet, the foremost advocate of European unity, had advised Heath to sign up immediately to the treaties of Paris and Rome and then, once inside the EC, to seek adjustments to Community institutions and policies to meet British requirements. Although this would have saved much time and enabled the UK to take part in negotiations on the Common Agricultural Policy, such a direct approach would have satisfied neither the Commonwealth nor the EFTA countries, nor secured the agreement of the British Parliament. In 1963, there was probably no alternative to lengthy and complicated negotiations over such issues as tariff adjustments, access for Commonwealth foodstuff and arrangements for British agriculture.

Heath had hoped to finalise negotiations by August 1962 but this was not possible. Even so, by January 1963, it seemed as if a successful agreement between Britain and the Six could be reached. At a lunch at the British Embassy in Paris on 13 January, the French foreign minister, Maurice Couve de Murville, told Heath that, providing the economic issues could be solved, 'no power on earth can now prevent the negotiations from being successful.'[28]

However, three days later, the most powerful man in Europe, the French president, Charles de Gaulle, magisterially brushed aside Britain's bid at a press conference in the Elysée Palace, announcing in beautiful French that Britain was not yet ready to join the EC: 'She was insular

[...] maritime [... and] has in all her doings very marked and very original habits and traditions.' If the UK came in, the EC could become an Atlantic community, under American dictation. Patronisingly, he concluded by congratulating Macmillan for having the 'great honour of leading his country on the first steps down the path which one day, perhaps, will lead it to moor alongside the continent'.[29] Two weeks later, the negotiations were brought to a halt by French intransigence and also by the acquiescence of the remaining five members to French intransigence. Heath was deeply depressed by the outcome but made a powerful final statement, concluding with the following sentence: 'We in Britain are not going to turn our backs on the mainland of Europe or the countries of the Community.'[30]

While Heath negotiated, the attitude of the Labour opposition had hardened against British entry. In the summer of 1961, Wilson, transferred from the shadow chancellorship to the foreign affairs portfolio, had made a measured and balanced speech in the debate on the opening of negotiations, making it clear that Labour was not opposed to the principle of negotiations and going so far as to wish the government well in Brussels.[31] But, in his 1962 party conference speech, Gaitskell concluded that the terms of entry, as negotiated by Heath, were inadequate and could mean 'the end of a thousand years of history'. Wilson, who was party chairman that year, immediately proposed that Gaitskell's speech should be printed and distributed to every party member. The reaction of Gaitskell's pro-European supporters was one of dismay and prompted the famous remark of Gaitskell's wife, Dora: 'But all the wrong people are clapping.'

Following Gaitskell's death, Wilson's inheritance from his predecessor was a strong one; however, his own performance as leader of the opposition was a revelation. He brilliantly exploited the growing weakness of the Conservative administration in a series of speeches, arguing for a more dynamic, open and meritocratic Britain. As we have seen, Macmillan's government was undermined by a faltering economy, by the failure of his attempt to join the Common Market and by the scandal that arose when the minister of war, John Profumo, was forced to resign when he admitted lying to the Commons after his affair with a call girl. When Macmillan had to stand down because of ill health, his successor, Sir Alec Douglas-Home, appeared bumbling and amateurish, a figure from another age. By contrast, the new Labour leader was assured in the House, fluent on television (arguably Wilson was the first top-flight politician in Britain who mastered television), always well briefed, a professional to his fingertips. His ratings soared and Labour established a commanding lead in the polls.

However, the 1964 election was a cliff-hanger. Beginning with his conference address at Scarborough in 1963, Wilson – like Blair in the mid-1990s – put forward Labour as the party of modernisation and opportunity, intent on breaking down the barriers of class and privilege. But, as the spring of 1964 turned to summer, Labour's advantage in the polls began to slip. The Conservatives' delaying tactic of postponing the election until the last possible moment, combined with the adoption of a Tory version of modernisation, seemed to be paying off. Heath, promoted by Douglas-Home to be president of the Board of Trade and secretary of state for industry, played a leading role in this rearguard action, giving government incentives to industry to create jobs in areas of high unemployment and abolishing retail price maintenance to encourage competition (RPM was a system of fixing prices across retail outlets). It was Heath's firmness over RPM against fierce opposition which earned him a reputation for determination and, in the eyes of his critics, for obstinacy as well.

As it turned out, the Labour Party, aided by Harold Wilson's campaigning skills, just scraped home. There was a strong feeling on the doorstep that, after 13 years of Conservative rule, it was a time for a change. On the other hand, Labour had been out of office for so long that, for many voters, actually making the change seemed a big gamble. Election night brought many Labour gains, but it was not until 2.48 p.m. on Friday afternoon when Labour held Brecon and Radnor that Wilson was sure of an overall majority. The final figures were Labour 317 seats, Conservatives 304 and the Liberals 9.

Labour's small majority meant that Harold Wilson was forced to devote the period between October 1964 and the March 1966 general election to showing that Labour could provide an effective government and, therefore, deserved to be re-elected. He was triumphantly successful in achieving his objective. Healey, who was often highly critical of Wilson, said that his first two years as prime minister were 'brilliant'. Wilson appeared to be in command of his talented Cabinet, of Parliament, and of the national political scene. Whenever people opened the newspapers or turned on the television, Wilson dominated the headlines.

The symbol of Wilson's first administration was the National Plan. The Labour government was committed to the improvement of the rate of growth to help pay for increased spending on education, health and social benefits; and the instrument of that improvement was to be planning. 'Indicative planning' had been successful in France and there was a consensus among politicians, civil servants, academics and businesspeople that it could work in the UK. By announcing a growth target of 3.8 per cent per year and coordinating resources and investment accordingly, it would be possible, so Wilson and the secretary of the newly established Department of Economic Affairs, George Brown, believed, to improve economic performance in the United Kingdom.

With the Wilson government establishing itself in power, the Tory party, in opposition for the first time for 13 years, had time to settle its own leadership. Although Douglas-Home had done better in the 1964 election than expected, he was no match for the new Prime Minister in Parliament. When in the summer of 1965 Wilson announced that there was to be no election that year, it precipitated a change of Tory leader; and in July, Douglas-Home resigned.

The contest under a reformed procedure whereby the leader was chosen by a secret ballot of Conservative MPs was between Heath and Maudling. The able Maudling was personally popular but it was felt by a significant group of younger MPs that the Tories needed someone more energetic to take on Wilson. Heath had provided vigorous opposition as shadow chancellor while, by contrast, Maudling (who, as the previous chancellor, took some of the blame for the election defeat) had accepted a number of City directorships following the election. In the ballot, Heath polled 150 votes, against 133 for Maudling and 15 for Powell. Dick Crossman, the Labour minister for housing, wrote in his diary that Heath would be the more formidable opponent.[32] There were now two younger men, both grammar school educated and very much professional politicians, at the head of both main parties.

However, Tories who hoped that their new leader would be able to take on and defeat the Prime Minister in debate were disappointed. When Heath moved a motion of censure in the Commons, it proved a flop. Subsequent efforts were little better. Iain Macleod, the shadow chancellor, was surprised that someone so musical should be unable 'to make a speech that anyone can listen to: no feeling for words at all, no feeling for the rhythm of language'.[33] Wilson, confident in his mastery of the Commons, was able to brush aside Heath's attacks. James Griffiths, a Labour elder statesman, wrote, 'I have witnessed many confrontations between rival leaders in Parliament but none which was so uneven as that between Wilson and Heath.'[34]

Wilson, who had handled his minuscule majority with exemplary skill, called a general election for 31 March 1966. The omens looked good for him, as Labour went into the contest with a big lead in the opinion polls. Armed with the confident slogan, 'You know that Labour government works', the Prime Minister fought a campaign which was both cautious and personal, based on his undoubted popularity. On election day Labour swept to an overwhelming victory, with an overall majority of 97. As Callaghan wrote in his memoirs, the party owed its success to Wilson's 'tactical skill, his determination, his orchestration, and the confidence he conveyed to the electorate'.[35]

If it is right to conclude that Wilson's victory in 1966 'was a breathtaking one, and a clear political vindication of his first premiership',[36] his triumph was remarkably short lived. In July 1966, a run on the pound, following a seamen's strike, forced the Labour government to introduce an austerity package, including cuts in public spending and a wages freeze – steps which led to the virtual abandonment of the National Plan, a near-fatal loss of momentum and a devastating blow to the Prime Minister's reputation. A powerful group of Cabinet ministers, including George Brown, Roy Jenkins and Tony Crosland from the centre right of the party and Dick Crossman, Barbara Castle and Tony Benn from the centre left, argued for devaluation on the grounds that it would have to come anyway and that it at least offered the prospect of growth. However, Wilson, perhaps remembering the Labour government's experience when it was forced to devalue in 1949, managed to persuade the majority to resist.

With hindsight, it is clear that the failure to devalue in July 1966 was a big mistake. It meant that the government was forced to squeeze the economy to sacrifice growth, Labour's main priority, in order to maintain the value of sterling, a policy which, by November 1967, proved to be unsustainable. Politically, the events of July 1966 were also a major defeat for Wilson. Until then he was very much 'Super Harold', who seemed to have the answer to almost any problem. Afterwards, Wilson was more often than not on the defensive, intent as much on survival as on implementing the modernising agenda on which he had been elected.

However, Europe offered a possible way forward. Wilson had never been a committed opponent of entry. For him, it all depended on the terms of entry. During the 1966 election, he had declared: 'Negotiations? Yes. Unconditional acceptance of whatever terms are offered? No.'[37] He drew a distinction between Labour's cautious pragmatic approach and that of Heath who, according to Wilson, was 'rolling on his back like a spaniel' at the first hint of encouragement from Paris.

In August 1966, Wilson made George Brown foreign secretary. This was in part to stop the temperamental Deputy Prime Minister from resigning. Appointing Brown as foreign secretary was a risk. Brown's biographer noted that,

George Brown's arrival at the Foreign Office on Friday 12th August 1966 was marked by an element of farce which was to become an inseparable feature of his tenure as Foreign Secretary over the next nineteen months.

The stuffiest, most conservative, and traditionally minded department of State lined up its officials at the imposing quadrangle entrance [...] only to discover that he had slipped in quietly by another door and was already casting a disapproving eye over the furnishings of his new office.[38]

It didn't help that Brown's fondness for drink gave rise to legions of stories about his lack of diplomacy: while drunk at a banquet given by the Belgian government, he told guests, 'While you have all been wining and dining here tonight, who's been defending Europe? [...] the British Army [...] I'll tell you where the soldiers of the Belgian Army are. They are in the brothels of Brussels.'[39]

But Brown's appointment was also an indication that Wilson's attitude towards British membership of the European Community was beginning to change. Brown was one of Labour's most committed pro-Europeans. At the 1962 Labour Party conference at which Gaitskell had made his 'a thousand years of history' speech, Brown had made a brave reply emphasising the positives of entry. More recently, in May 1966, he had given an exceptionally eloquent address to the Socialist International in Stockholm, in which he insisted that Britain was part of Europe and that its central aim was the creation of European unity.

Now, with an energetic pro-European foreign secretary alongside him, Wilson turned to British membership as offering a new goal for a wounded Labour government. After the July crisis, in the words of Roy Jenkins, Wilson 'required constant bounce to get back' and the Common Market option 'looked like a trampoline'.[40]

On 22 October 1966, the Labour Cabinet met at Chequers to discuss the prospects for British entry. The Cabinet agreed that Wilson and Brown should visit the capitals of the Six to explore 'whether the conditions exist – or do not exist – for fruitful negotiations, and the basis on which such negotiations could take place'.[41] On the face of it, Wilson's initial commitment was only to an exploration. But, as Wilson toured Europe with his pro-European deputy, he became visibly more enthusiastic about the possibility of British membership.

The crucial meeting was in Paris with de Gaulle. Wilson had no illusions about what was likely to be the French President's attitude to a second British application. But, as he told US President Johnson, he hoped not to make what he claimed were mistakes made by his Conservative predecessors and so avoid giving de Gaulle grounds for turning Britain down.[42]

On the occasion of their January visit, there is a revealing photograph of de Gaulle towering politely if condescendingly over the two British supplicants. Patronisingly, the French President told Wilson and Brown that, though there had been changes in British thinking, British entry, bringing with it 'all her extra European connections', could alter the EEC's 'fundamental character', making full membership 'difficult, if not impossible'.[43]

Despite de Gaulle's discouraging response, Wilson was paradoxically all the more determined to press ahead with the British application for membership. Following a two-day discussion at Chequers, the Cabinet decided on 2 May to apply for membership and that afternoon the Prime Minister made a statement to the House, announcing the application which was, he said, 'a historic decision which could well determine the future of Britain, of Europe, and, indeed of the world for decades to come'.[44] On 10 May, the House of Commons voted by 487 votes to 26 in favour of Britain applying for EEC membership, the biggest majority in the House for a century; and on 4 July, the foreign secretary, George Brown, made an eloquent opening speech, setting out Britain's application for membership, which was well received by five of the six existing members, with one important exception – France.

The political reality was that de Gaulle, while he remained president of France, was determined to keep Britain out. In his press conference on 16 May, he had made again his now-familiar argument about how different Britain, as an island with its links to the Commonwealth and to the United States, was from the continental Six. In June de Gaulle told Wilson at a meeting in Paris that Britain would always be pulled towards the United States. Wilson's report to Brown was that de Gaulle 'does not want us in and he will use all the delaying tactics he can [...] But if we keep firmly beating at the door and do not falter in our purpose or our resolve I am not sure that he has any longer the strength finally to keep us out.'[45] Wilson was wrong. On 27 November, de Gaulle pulled the plug on Britain's application, saying it was not yet ready to join the European Community, and, on 19 December 1967, France formally vetoed the recommendation of the Commission (supported by the other five member states) that negotiations be opened with Britain. For the second time, de Gaulle had blocked Britain's bid to join the EC.

The question remains whether, with a different approach, the Labour government might have been able to force its way in. Wilson clearly hoped that, with the backing of five of the Six and with a weakening of de Gaulle's position, the French President would no longer have the political strength to use the veto. The Prime Minister certainly underestimated de Gaulle's determination and rocklike immutability.[46] The reality was that there was nothing that Wilson could have done which would have shifted de Gaulle.

So was the Labour government right to have made the application in the first place? Arguably, by insisting throughout that Britain would not take 'no' for an answer, and that, despite the French veto, the British application would remain 'on the table', Wilson was showing the Six that the Labour government was really serious about joining the European Community. The British Prime Minister was often accused, especially by Heath, of 'short termism'. But in the late 1960s, his European strategy was not just an immediate expedient but a longer-term strategy, geared to a future when de Gaulle was no longer in power.

On 28 April 1969 de Gaulle resigned, following his defeat in a referendum on constitutional change. Two months before, there had been a new twist in the increasingly tortuous relationship between Britain and France – 'L'Affaire Soames'. The British ambassador, Christopher Soames, the senior Tory politician whom Wilson had shrewdly appointed to the Paris Embassy, had a lunch meeting with de Gaulle, at which the French President proposed discussions with Britain about his idea of replacing the European Community with a looser free trade arrangement. Rightly judging this to be an important initiative, Soames reported the meeting to London. Wilson's reaction was cautiously favourable, at least to talks with de Gaulle, but his foreign secretary, Michael Stewart, feared a French 'trap' and proposed that Wilson should first tell the German chancellor, Kurt Kiesinger, what de Gaulle had said, even though the French President had made it clear that his proposal should be kept confidential at this stage.

Wilson ended up briefing Kiesinger in Bonn, with the inevitable consequence that the Soames meeting with de Gaulle was leaked to the press, which in turn led to a first-class diplomatic row between Britain and France. Undoubtedly the Labour government, especially the Foreign Office, could have handled the Soames affair 'with', as Wilson admitted, 'greater refinement',[47] but its reaction at least had the merit of demonstrating to the other members that Britain was sticking to its policy of attempting to join the European Community.

After the resignation of de Gaulle and the election of Georges Pompidou as his successor, the prospects for a successful British application greatly improved. However, the new French foreign minister, Maurice Schumann, told Soames that, before opening negotiations with the British, the French wanted the existing members to agree on the Common Agricultural Policy (CAP). At the Labour Party conference that autumn, Wilson made it clear that 'if they, the Six, are ready for negotiations to begin, we are ready.' Optimistically, he also told Soames that negotiations need not be held up by the coming election in Britain. But, with the impact of the CAP on Britain's balance of payments (as revealed by the government's White Paper on the costs of membership), Wilson underlined to the House of Commons the importance of negotiating acceptable conditions for British entry.[48] The Prime Minister began to prepare Whitehall for the British bid, setting up a ministerial subcommittee chaired by George Thomson, the chancellor of the Duchy of Lancaster, who had been put in charge of European matters. Negotiating briefs were made ready and a speech of application was drafted. All that remained was to win the election.

Wilson was confident of victory. The results of the May local elections were good and, after a long period in which the party had been behind the Tories, the polls had turned in Labour's favour. Probably mistakenly, Harold Wilson decided to campaign in a relaxed, folksy, almost non-political manner. He continued to believe in victory right up to election day itself. However, on the final Monday of the campaign, the May trade figures were published, revealing a deficit of £31 million. Although £18 million of this figure was accounted for by the exceptional purchase of two American jets, the news lent some substance to Edward Heath's dire warnings about the real state of the British economy, a message of doom which he repeated in a powerful television broadcast that Monday evening. Against Wilson's expectations, the first few results on election night showed a strong swing to the Tories; the Conservatives ended up with 46.4 per cent of the vote and an overall majority of 30.

Why did Labour lose? Labour politicians tended to point to the trade figures. However, as the standard work on the 1970 election pointed out, if one month's trade figures could create a scare enough to frighten a million votes away from Labour, the electorate must have already been in a fickle and sceptical mood.[49] The underlying problem for Labour was that, after a prolonged period of unpopularity, its recovery in the polls was only very recent and shallowly based, so it did not take all that much to undermine it. Heath's victory in 1970 against the odds owed much to his personal courage and determination. But it also reflected the failure of Wilson to provide potential Labour voters with powerful enough reasons to come out and vote, especially after they had suffered the squeeze on consumption needed to turn around the balance of payments.

It was clear from the start that one of the main objectives of the newly elected Heath government would be to negotiate Britain's entry into the European Community. Although at the time Heath had backed Wilson's attempt to join the EC, in his memoirs he was characteristically highly critical of Britain's application.[50] Yet, when he assumed power, he was able to benefit from the first-class briefs prepared by Whitehall for the Labour government, especially over New Zealand, UK's budget payments and the role of sterling as a reserve currency. Heath's vital contribution was his long-standing commitment to Europe and his determination that this time the bid should be successful.

As in 1963 and 1967, the key to success was to persuade the French that British membership would not disrupt Community arrangements, especially the CAP, and that Britain would play a full part in the European Community. With negotiations dragging on, Heath decided to bring matters to a head by direct talks with the French President. On 20–1 May he met Pompidou in the Elysée Palace, with nobody present except the two interpreters. On the last evening, the two men held a press conference in the Salle des Fêtes, where de Gaulle had announced his veto in 1963. This time, there was a different story. As Pompidou declared:

Many believed that Great Britain was not, and did not wish, to become European, and that Britain wanted to enter the Community only so as to destroy it or to divert it from its objectives. Many people also thought France was ready to use every pretext to place in the end a fresh veto on Britain's entry. Well, ladies and gentlemen, you see before you tonight two men who are convinced of the contrary.

Heath described it as 'a wildly exciting moment' and 'a historic occasion'.[51] It was the moment when it became certain that Britain would join the European Community.

Negotiations on British entry were successfully concluded in June, and on 7 July the Heath government issued a White Paper setting out the terms on which entry had been negotiated. Heath's task now was to obtain parliamentary approval. His problem was that there was a determined group of anti-European Tory rebels whose number (of about 40) was likely to exceed the size of the Conservative majority (30). That meant that he would need the backing of pro-European Labour MPs if he was to get British entry through Parliament.

If Labour had won the 1970 election, there is no doubt that Wilson would have been pleased to have taken Britain into the European Community, and that he would have had the support of most of the

Labour Party. In opposition, it was a different story. The anti-European forces, which had been quiescent while Labour was in government, gathered strength, especially amongst the unions, whose most powerful general secretaries, Jack Jones of the Transport and General Workers' Union and Hugh Scanlon of the Engineers' Union, were both against entry. In the autumn of 1970, the party conference rejected only narrowly a resolution calling for outright opposition to British membership. In late February 1971, Roy Jenkins, the pro-European deputy leader and former chancellor of the Exchequer, who had become increasingly concerned about the growing opposition to Europe, had a meeting with Wilson. Jenkins argued that 'the only way out will be a free vote without recrimination.' Wilson replied: 'I am more optimistic than that. I hope we may be able to get the party to vote in favour, but at the most, the very most, we can fall back on a free vote.'[52] However, although in private Wilson continued to be broadly in favour of entry, as the situation deteriorated he started to shift his public position.

The crucial figure in Wilson's calculations was James Callaghan, who, though an Atlanticist, had supported the Labour government's application for entry. 'Jim was the real villain of the piece on Europe, not Harold,' said David Marquand, a pro-European Labour MP.[53] On 25 May, Callaghan, always a shrewd judge of party opinion, made a powerful anti-European speech at Southampton in which he set out his opposition to British membership in sweeping terms. According to Callaghan, joining the Common Market would mean a complete rupture of identity and a threat to 'the language of Chaucer, Shakespeare and Milton'. He concluded: 'If we are to prove our Europeanism by accepting that French is the dominant language in the Community, then there the answer is quite clear, and I will say it in French in order to prevent any misunderstanding, "Non, merci beaucoup".'[54] Other senior figures, including Healey and Crosland, also ran for cover.

Then at Labour's special conference on 17 July, Wilson himself came out against the terms negotiated by Heath. Contradicting the judgement of his own negotiator, George Thomson, that a Labour government would have accepted the Heath terms, Wilson said, 'I reject the assertions that the terms this Conservative government have obtained are the terms the Labour government asked for, would have asked for, would have been bound to accept.' Jenkins remarked that Wilson's performance was 'like watching someone being sold down the river into slavery, drifting away, depressed but unprotesting'.[55] Wilson himself described this period as 'wading in shit'.[56] It may not have been glorious but Wilson's tactical manoeuvring was probably necessary both to preserve his leadership and keep his party together.

With Labour lining up against entry on so-called 'Tory terms' (a stance which was confirmed in October at the Labour Party conference by a margin of five to one) the question both for Heath and the Labour pro-European group was how many Labour MPs would vote in the 28 October debate for the terms of membership negotiated by the government. The Prime Minister was persuaded by his chief whip, Francis Pym, to give Tory MPs a 'free vote', hoping that it would encourage Labour to follow the Conservative example. However, the Shadow Cabinet and the PLP agreed, in both cases narrowly, to impose a three-line whip. It made little difference. The Labour pro-Europeans, led by Roy Jenkins, stood firm, helping to achieve an impressive majority of 112 for entry. Out of 356 'ayes', 69 were Labour MPs; in addition there were 20 Labour abstentions. Without the pro-European Labour contribution, there could have been a majority of 96 against.

As Heath rightly judged in his memoirs, this parliamentary vote for British membership of the European Community was his greatest success as prime minister and arguably the high point of his political career. After the vote, he retired with his closest friends to his private sitting room at No 10, to play the First Prelude from Book One of Bach's *Well-tempered Clavier* on his clavichord. Then on 22 January 1972, Heath flew in triumph to Brussels to sign the Treaty of Accession. He had invited the leaders of the opposition to accompany him. Jeremy Thorpe, for the Liberals, accepted; Wilson, understandably but to Heath's annoyance, politely refused.

Europe was continuing to divide the Labour Party. After the 28 October 1971 vote, even the boldest of Labour pro-Europeans were reluctant to support the legislation (the European Community Bill) implementing the decision. In Jenkins' words, 'we judged we could make a dash for Europe without endangering out long-term relations with the Labour party.'[57] On the second reading, the government's majority fell to only eight. As the Bill went through its remaining stages with numerous divisions, the pressure on the pro-Europeans was bound to increase, especially as they were relying on the courage of a few older Labour abstentionists to ensure the legislation went through unamended.

It was, however, the referendum issue that pushed Jenkins and most of his closest supporters to resign from the Labour front bench. Using the referendum as a device for settling the European issue was the brainchild of Tony Benn, the born-again Labour left-winger. When Wilson first heard about Benn's proposal, he said, 'I understand you are suggesting a plebiscite on the Common Market. You can't do that.'[58] But now Wilson began to appreciate its merits. Jenkins' view was that the Labour leader, anxious about the possibility of a leadership challenge, was using the issue to provoke his deputy leader's resignation. A more plausible reason was that Wilson saw the referendum as a means of keeping the Labour Party together and, at the same time, keeping Britain in the Common Market. His press aide, Joe Haines, said, 'from the start he believed that he could win a referendum on the Market, for staying in.'[59]

In the short term, Wilson's support for a referendum (which he persuaded the Shadow Cabinet to back) appeased the anti-Europeans, without conceding the case for withdrawal. It proved to be a successful tactical manoeuvre. By the beginning of 1973, Wilson had seen off any threat to his leadership (something which he usually tended to exaggerate), whether from Jenkins, Callaghan or anybody else. He had also kept the party in one piece – at least for the time being. At the same time, despite the strong left-wing pressure to fight the next election as an anti-European party, he had preserved the option of staying in.

As prime minister, Heath sought to govern as a 'One Nation' Tory. But, owing to a combination of circumstance and mismanagement, he ended up going to the country on the ticket of 'Who governs Britain?' He had hoped to lead a competent and fair administration which, through steady economic growth, would provide more opportunities for aspiring workers. He also attempted to reform industrial relations, a move which had popular support. However, the Conservative industrial relations legislation was so complex and clumsy that it acquired the reputation as a union-bashing measure. When the Arab–Israeli Yom Kippur War broke out in October 1973 and oil prices rose dramatically, Heath sought the backing of the unions for a tough pay policy to help control inflation. Unfortunately for the government, the miners, their hand strengthened by the hike in oil prices, were determined to press home their advantage. In January 1974 the TUC proposed that the miners should be treated as a special case but Heath did not trust the union leaders to deliver and rejected their olive branch. When the miners called a ballot on strike action which was backed by 81 per cent of their members, Heath, who had put the country on a 'three-day week', called a general election for 28 February 1974.

It may seem curious for a government to ask the voters 'Who governs Britain?', but most of Labour's leaders were pessimistic about the result. Harold Wilson, expecting to lose, fought a professional but low-key campaign, preaching conciliation and compromise like a latter-day Baldwin and concentrating on prices. At a big Birmingham town hall meeting, Jenkins noted that Wilson 'seemed tired, depressed and expecting defeat, keeping going with some difficulty and gallantry until by the Thursday night he would have completed his final throw in politics'.[60] In fact, though Labour polled fewer votes than the Conservatives, it won five more seats than the Tories, though still 34 seats short of an overall majority. The voters' answer to Heath's question had been inconclusive, but it had left more cards in Harold Wilson's hands than in Edward Heath's. Heath tried but failed to make a coalition with the Liberals. On Monday 4 March, Heath drove to Buckingham Palace and resigned the premiership. Once again the Queen sent for Wilson.

The referendum on whether or not Britain should stay in the European Community was the outstanding issue of Wilson's two governments of the 1970s. It was preceded by a period of renegotiation. Wilson shrewdly put his foreign secretary, James Callaghan, in charge of the renegotiation process. During Labour's period in opposition, Callaghan had established himself as a Eurosceptic. He was also the one person from the British side who could wreck the negotiations. His opening statement on 1 April to the Council of Ministers was described by his deputy, Roy Hattersley, as 'deeply antagonistic to Britain's continued Common Market membership'.[61] Callaghan's reply when Sir Alec Douglas-Home made much the same point was that 'if good diplomacy led to the nature of the bargain that was struck by the previous government, then perhaps a little rougher diplomacy will not come amiss.'[62] In practice, negotiations did not really get started until after the second election in October 1974.

Wilson won the October election with an overall majority of only three, though, because of the 39 minor party MPs elected, the majority over the Tories was substantially larger, a more comfortable lead than Labour had enjoyed in 1964. For Heath it was the end of the road, even though, characteristically, he refused to recognise it. In February 1975, Mrs Thatcher courageously stood against Heath for the leadership and led him on the first ballot by 130 votes to 109. Though under the new rules, which required a margin of 15 per cent, a second ballot was required, even Heath could see that there was no point carrying on.

For Wilson, it was essential to achieve a successful renegotiation of the terms, followed by a referendum which kept Britain in the European Community. The visit of Helmut Schmidt, the German chancellor, to Britain in November proved crucial. Schmidt made a brilliant and moving address to delegates in flawless English, appealing to delegates to remember that Labour's sister parties on the continent wanted the United Kingdom to remain in the Community. He followed up his speech, which received a standing ovation, with talks with Wilson at Chequers, convincing the Prime Minister that there could be a successful outcome to the renegotiations, as well as helping arrange a bilateral meeting between Wilson and the new French president, Valéry Giscard d'Estaing.

162

In March 1975, following the Dublin EC summit meeting, Wilson and Callaghan announced that negotiations had been a success, highlighting the improved deal for New Zealand and the way in which the controversial and costly UK contribution to the Community budget would now be related to the gross national product. Wilson, backed by his foreign secretary, then put the result of the negotiations and a recommendation to stay in to a two-day Cabinet which endorsed the terms by 16 votes to 7. Though the PLP split marginally against staying in, there was a big parliamentary majority in favour.

Wilson handled both the immediate run-up to the referendum and the referendum campaign itself with consummate skill. His aim was to achieve a 'yes' vote, without destroying his party. As a means of keeping his Cabinet together the Prime Minister decided that the minority of dissenting ministers, including Tony Benn, Michael Foot, Peter Shore and Barbara Castle, should be free to campaign against the government's recommendations, though they would not be allowed to speak in Parliament. On 26 April a special party conference voted by nearly two to one against the terms negotiated by the government but, under pressure from Wilson, its impact was blunted by a prior agreement by the NEC that the party as such would not campaign. The backdrop to the conference read: 'Conference advises – the people decide', a message which Wilson underlined in a low-key speech, setting out a pragmatic case for continuing British membership.

As the campaign got under way, the Prime Minister was increasingly confident that the referendum would be won. In the late 1960s and early 1970s opinion polls, influenced first by the de Gaulle veto and then by the unpopularity of the Heath government, had shown a consistent, though shallowly based, majority against entry. However, when the referendum forced voters to answer the question 'Do you think that the United Kingdom should stay in the European Community?', opinion shifted. The uncertain economic and political background was certainly a factor. Christopher Soames, former ambassador in Paris and now a senior British commissioner, was quoted as caustically saying: 'This is not time for Britain to be considering leaving a Christmas Club, let alone the Common Market.'[63] According to Gallup, other issues which were important in persuading people that they were better in than out were Britain's position in the world and the future for Britain's children.[64]

The pro-European campaign was in a much stronger position than the antis, not only financially but more importantly because most of the respected figures in British public life were gathered together on the pro side. Roy Jenkins was president of the umbrella body for the pros' 'Britain in Europe', with Willie Whitelaw, Reginald Maudling and Edward Heath as Tory vice presidents and Jeremy Thorpe and Jo Grimond as the Liberal ones. Wilson and Callaghan were worried that Jenkins, buoyed up by the referendum campaign which he had originally opposed, might be tempted in the future to form a coalition with these moderates. But at this stage, these fears were groundless, though Jenkins found working with his pro-European allies 'a considerable liberation of the spirit'.[65]

Wilson's role was that of the wise, almost detached father figure. During the referendum, he remained aloof from the official 'yes' campaign, intervening in the last fortnight with some well publicised speeches and television interviews. Mixing his metaphors, he argued that Britain would not retain its world influence 'by taking our bat home and sinking into an offshore mentality'.[66] His efforts undoubtedly swayed many Labour voters.

* * *

On referendum day, 6 June, the turnout was 64.5 per cent, with a two to one vote for staying in. Even the *Daily Telegraph* agreed that it was 'Quite frankly a triumph for Wilson'.[67] Peter Jenkins wrote in the *Guardian* that Wilson had skilfully used the referendum 'to keep his party in power and in one piece and Britain in Europe'.[68] Almost a year later, Wilson resigned as prime minister, a resignation which he had planned for two years or more. There was speculation over the reasons for his retirement. The most plausible was the most obvious – he was simply tired of the job of keeping the Labour Party together.

For Heath, the statesman who had taken Britain into Europe, the referendum was his last hurrah. Briefly forgetting his political defeats by both Wilson and Thatcher and casting aside the written texts which had made his speeches as prime minister so leaden, he spoke with a passion and vigour which was especially attractive to younger audiences about why Britain should be a member of the European Community. Heath and Wilson both deserved praise (or criticism if one is an anti) for their contribution to British membership of the European Community. Heath was the believer, Wilson the pragmatist: both attributes were required for securing British entry. Heath took Britain in, Wilson ensured that Britain stayed in.

5

THE THATCHER REVOLUTION

Thatcher and Whitelaw

In a famous but unintentional double entendre, Margaret Thatcher once said, 'every Prime Minister should have a Willie.'[1] Mrs Thatcher, the first woman British prime minister, was arguably the most dominant of the postwar premiers. However, she herself acknowledged that Whitelaw was 'an irreplaceable deputy Prime Minister [...] and the ballast that helped keep the Government on course'.[2]

It was certainly Thatcher's personality, beliefs and policies which shaped her government, but Whitelaw was her indispensable enabler, conciliator and sheet anchor. When, in January 1988, following a minor stroke, Whitelaw resigned after eight years in office, senior colleagues saw his departure as a severe blow to the administration. The chancellor, Nigel Lawson, wrote in his memoirs, 'The Thatcher government [...] was never the same again.'[3] Senior Cabinet colleagues underlined to the author the crucial nature of Whitelaw's role.

Thatcher and Whitelaw were very different – in family and social background, in experience, interest, temperament, style and approach to politics. She was an initiator, the right-wing conviction politician who believed passionately in a number of simple tenets – individualism, private enterprise, the creation and acquisition of wealth, 'sound' money

166

and patriotism. She despised socialists, trade unionists, 'wet' Tories, collectivisation and consensus. He was a facilitator, an old-style, pragmatic Conservative who gave a high priority to loyalty, both to his own party and to his leader. He was, above all, a 'One Nation' Tory who, soon after Thatcher's election as leader, warned that Conservatives would not 'carry conviction if we appear either selfish or narrow-minded in our approach to politics'.[4]

Yet, despite their differences, Thatcher and Whitelaw developed a highly effective partnership. As Mrs Thatcher commented, 'people were often surprised that the two of us worked so well together, given our rivalry for the leadership and our different outlook on economics. But Willie is a big man in character as well as physically [...] Once he had pledged his loyalty he never withdrew it.'[5]

William Whitelaw was born on 28 June 1918 (seven years before Margaret Thatcher) at Nairn in the far north of Scotland. His father came from a line of wealthy industrialists. His great-grandfather, Alexander Whitelaw, was a partner in William Baird and Co., the famous steel-making company, while his grandfather, William, was chairman of the London and North-Eastern Railway Company (GNER) and a director of the Bank of Scotland. The Whitelaw family was almost wiped out by World War I: his two uncles were killed in battle, while his father, William, weakened by his wounds, died from pneumonia in 1919, a year after his son's birth. Willie, as he came to be called, was brought up at Nairn by his mother, Winnie, a strong-willed woman who remained a widow. Winnie Whitelaw served for many years as a councillor in the Nairn area but she had more ambitious ideas for her son; he was not to be, like her, a large fish in a small pond, but 'a large fish in a large pond'.[6] So, financed by his grandfather, he was sent south to school in England, first to a preparatory school, which he loathed, and afterwards to Winchester College, which had a high academic reputation.

Willie had surprised his grandfather by passing the special examination into Winchester. However, his scholastic achievements at the school were relatively modest. One of his teachers, Donald MacLachlan, wrote that he was not spoiled by 'premature intellectualism'.[7] His passion, first fostered by the Nairn club professional when he was only four, was for golf – so much so that at 15 he competed in the British Boys' Championship.

Having gained the necessary credits in the School Certificate, Willie went up to Trinity College, Cambridge, determined to win a golf Blue. His grandfather insisted that he must also get a degree. So the undergraduate Whitelaw played golf in the winter and worked at his books in the summer. He got his golf Blue and, if there had been no war, would have been university captain in 1940. He also managed to scrape a third in law in his first two years and, in his last year, achieved a more respectable second in history. However, in contrast to his contemporaries at Oxford, such as Edward Heath, Denis Healey and Roy Jenkins, he showed almost no interest in politics, though the threat of war persuaded him to join the university Officers' Training Corps and, in the summer of 1939, to carry out an assignment with a Scots Guards battalion at Windsor. The latter move led to a regular commission in the Scots Guards soon after the war broke out in September.

The war proved to be the most formative period of Whitelaw's life. At its beginning, he was an immature and inexperienced student. By its end, he was a major, second-in-command of his battalion, holder of the Military Cross (presented to him by Field Marshal Montgomery) and a married man (to Celia Sprot) with a child. He had survived the bloody Battle of Caumont (eight weeks after the Normandy landings) in which many of his squadron had been killed or wounded. The regimental historian, describing the battle, wrote that it had been 'at once glorious, tragic and exceptional'.[8] The Churchill tanks of Whitelaw's squadron, part of the armoured Scots Guards battalion attached to the 6th Guards Tank Brigade, had advanced successfully through the *bocage* (fields criss-crossed by hedges and trees), penetrating the enemy lines and virtually destroying a German division on the way. But they were then ambushed by more powerful Panther tanks armed with high-velocity guns which proceeded to knock out most of the squadron's Churchills. Whitelaw, however, kept his nerve and rallied the rest, until the infantry arrived with anti-tank guns. The memory of the episode, which had lasted only five minutes, remained with him for the rest of his life. He wrote in his memoirs: 'Then and now I would gladly have given up all the glory in return for the lives of my friends and colleagues [...] I have never forgotten those five minutes – indeed they signalled a great change in my attitude to life and to my fellow human-beings.'[9]

It took a few years for Whitelaw to be drawn into politics. At the end of the war he became a regular soldier and was sent as a staff officer to join the 1st Guards Brigade in Palestine, dealing with Jewish insurrection and terrorism. Then, early in 1946, his grandfather died and left him substantial properties near Glasgow, including the Scottish baronial mansion of Gartshore. It was obvious that it would not be possible to combine soldiering with running a large agricultural estate and so in 1947 Willie resigned his commission, though he remained closely linked to the Scots Guards for the rest of his life.

It is not clear from Whitelaw's memoirs precisely when and indeed why he decided to stand for Parliament. With his war record and social connections, he was undoubtedly a catch for the Conservatives, still smarting from their landslide defeat at the 1945 election. In the Moray and Nairn constituency Whitelaw had voted for James Stuart, Churchill's chief whip and a Whitelaw family friend. But he did not actually join the Conservative Party until 1948. In his memoirs, Whitelaw mentions that his estate manager was a leading official of the Dunbartonshire Unionist Association (as the Conservatives were called in Scotland) and that he, Willie, thought 'it would be fun to gain political experience in the newly formed East Dunbartonshire constituency.'[10] It was as if standing for Parliament was one of the recognised duties of a leading county land-owner. His Winchester tutor, Donald McLachlan, wrote that Whitelaw simply felt that 'anyone who had been as lucky as he had owed something to others to adjust the balance.'[11]

East Dunbartonshire was certainly a suitable constituency for a political novice. Though there were significant pockets of Tory support, the combination of the tightly knit shipbuilding community of Clydebank and some mining villages ensured that it would be a safe Labour seat. The sitting Labour MP, Davy Kirkwood, one of the 'Red Clydesiders' of the 1930s, treated Willie and his wife with a kindness and courtesy which the Whitelaws never forgot.[12] In the days before the coming of television, when political meetings were still packed, Whitelaw learnt how to make speeches and to deal with hecklers. In the 1950 election, he lost by 4,576 votes. Standing again in 1951, this time against a new Labour opponent, Willie was defeated by the smaller margin of 3,426.

The experience of fighting two elections had, however, given Whitelaw the taste for politics and he was now determined to become an MP. No Scottish Conservative members had yet announced their retirement but in 1954 a Scots Guards friend, Charles Graham, approached Willie about the possibility of him becoming the candidate for the 'safe' Cumberland seat of Penrith and the Borders, where the sitting Tory MP was retiring. The constituency chairman, also a former military man, decided to back Whitelaw and proceeded to ensure that the selection committee also supported him. Though there were three other candidates (one of whom dropped out), Willie gave the best performance and, without a formal vote, the chairman declared him to be the winner.[13] After a short period nursing the widespread constituency (which covered scores of villages and 160 polling stations), Willie fought an energetic election campaign, often involving five meetings a night, and was returned to Parliament in June 1955 (by his friend, Charles Graham, who was also a returning officer) with a record majority of 13,672.

Margaret Thatcher's journey to Westminster and indeed to the top of politics was much harder than that of William Whitelaw. In three crucial respects, Whitelaw was better placed than Thatcher – in terms of class, sex and the backing of powerful friends and networks. Only her exceptional ability and determination, combined with good fortune, enabled her to overcome these initial handicaps.

Margaret Thatcher was born Margaret Roberts on 13 October 1925 at 1 North Parade, Grantham, the small south Lincolnshire market town. Her father, Alfred, the most important early influence in her life, was a successful grocer who was also a local politician, a powerful figure on the town council, chairman of the finance and library committees, an alderman and later mayor – very much a big fish in a small pond. In politics, he ran as an independent, though he was firmly anti-Labour. If anything, he was a Liberal but, at the 1935 general election, he backed both the National Government and the Conservative candidate for Grantham.

Alfred Roberts had ambitious plans for his younger daughter, Margaret, who, from the first, proved to be bright and hardworking. She did well at her primary school and won a scholarship to the girls' grammar school, where she was generally at the top of the class. Her reports commended her 'power of sustained interest'.[14] Her father was determined that she should go to Oxford, a goal which Margaret shared. In the autumn of 1943 she was accepted by Somerville College.

Wartime Oxford was a crucial experience for her, not in the conventional sense of becoming a university star or experiencing a great intellectual awakening. Indeed, one of her contemporaries remembered her as quiet, rather mousey, 'someone who hadn't got the style' to make up for her background.[15] Janet Vaughan, the left-wing principal of Somerville, patronisingly described Margaret as 'an oddity [...] She was a conservative [...] we used to entertain a good deal at weekends, but she didn't get invited. She had nothing to contribute, you see.'[16] In fact, she was reinforcing her powers of concentration by studying chemistry, working under the Nobel Prize winner Dorothy Hodgkin and spending long hours in the laboratory. She stayed at Oxford for a fourth year and, without becoming a brilliant student, achieved a good second.

Perhaps more important for Margaret was joining the Oxford University Conservative Association (OUCA). At OUCA, she learnt the mechanics of politics – leafleting, canvassing, speaking. She also met well-known Oxford Conservatives such as Edward Boyle and the Earl of Dalkeith and heavyweight visiting speakers like L.S. Amery and Lord

Woolton. In the 1946 Michaelmas term, she was elected president of OUCA, a post which gave her standing at Conservative Central Office. In October she attended her first party conference at Blackpool, at which she felt very much at home: for the first time, 'she felt surrounded by people who thought as she did.'[17]

After coming down from Oxford, Margaret got a job as a laboratory researcher at a plastics firm in Essex. In her spare time, she was busy with her political interests, going to Young Conservative meetings and attending weekend conferences. It was at the 1948 Tory party conference that she got her lucky break when she was introduced to the chairman of the Dartford Conservative Association. Though he was initially doubtful about the idea of a woman candidate fighting an industrial seat which was also rock-solid Labour, he was very impressed by Margaret Roberts, as were other members of his committee. The deputy area agent wrote that 'her political knowledge and her speaking ability are far above those of the other candidates.'[18] At a packed adoption meeting, she defeated the four other candidates. Her speech was notable for a vigorous attack on the Labour government.

Thatcher's authorised biographer, Charles Moore, commented that her selection for Dartford was even more important for her than Oxford: 'It revealed to her the extent of her political talents, threw her into the combat she always enjoyed and set her on the course of her life.'[19] Contesting both the 1950 and 1951 elections, she proved to be a well turned-out, well-briefed, eloquent and, above all, energetic candidate who provided leadership for the upwardly mobile party activists. They admired her boldness and sincerity and the way she took the fight to Labour by advocating a return to sound finance and support of private enterprise. In 1950, she reduced the Labour majority by 6,000 and, in 1951, by a further 1,300. Her growing reputation was demonstrated when she was chosen to be the youth speaker offering a vote of thanks to Winston Churchill at a party rally at the Albert Hall.

At Dartford, Margaret Roberts met the man whom she was to marry. Managing director of his family paint firm, Denis Thatcher was comfortably off and had his own flat in Chelsea. Ten years older than Margaret, he had, as she wrote in her memoirs, 'a certain style and dash'[20] and, remarkably for a man with pronounced conservative views, was prepared to accept the importance of her political career. Marriage to Denis gave Margaret both social status and financial security and provided her with the long-term stability and support she needed.

Her early married life was marked by the birth of her twins in August 1953 and then, after taking the law exams, by being called to the Bar in February 1954. It was not until the end of 1954 that she resumed her attempt to get into Parliament; over the next four years, she tried for a number of seats, mostly around London. She was almost always shortlisted but, in the male-dominated world of the 1950s, her sex was invariably the barrier to success. Then, in March 1958, the member for the safe seat of Finchley announced his retirement and Margaret Thatcher applied to be considered for the nomination. Once again she was shortlisted but, as she wrote to her sister, she expected that 'the usual prejudice against women will prevail.' This time, however, she won by three votes in the final round, though there is a story that the chairman allocated two of the other candidate's votes to Margaret. Her biographer commented: 'So Mrs Thatcher probably (unknowingly) won her way to Parliament through fraud.'[21] At the 1959 general election, which the Tories won in a landslide, Margaret Thatcher increased the Conservative majority at Finchley from 12,825 to 16,260. She was now safely in Parliament and was to hold the seat for the next 32 years.

In the 1950s and early 1960s, the Tory side of the House of Commons, like that of Labour, was still populated almost entirely by men (when Mrs Thatcher entered the House there were only 12 Conservative women MPs and 13 Labour ones) and, to a considerable extent, by the 'knights of the shires', by the upper ranks of the professional classes and by the public schools. With his ability to get on with people, Willie Whitelaw (who got into Parliament four years before Thatcher) was very quickly at home. James Stuart, the secretary of state for Scotland, was a long-standing family friend, the deputy speaker, Charles MacAndrew, was a golfing partner and, in February 1956, Whitelaw owed his promotion as the unpaid position of parliamentary private secretary to the president of the Board of Trade Peter Thorneycroft to the fact that the Cabinet minister was his cousin. In addition, Thorneycroft's junior minister was Toby Low, who had been at Winchester with Willie.

When Macmillan became prime minister following the resignation of Eden, Whitelaw followed Thorneycroft to the Treasury. Then came what Macmillan called 'a little local difficulty'. In January 1958, Thorneycroft resigned from the government over the level of public spending, taking not only his junior ministers but also his PPS with him. Within the team, Willie argued strongly against resignation on the grounds that it would be damaging to the government so soon after the Suez debacle. Afterwards, he made a public declaration of support for the Prime Minister and added, 'It is often said that silence is golden and I have decided to follow that wise saying.'[22] Whitelaw's intelligently loyal conduct had not gone unnoticed and, at the beginning of 1959, the chief whip, Edward Heath, invited him to join the Whips' Office as a junior whip. This was the start of Willie's frontbench career, which, either in government or in opposition, continued until he resigned almost 30 years later.

If Whitelaw's rise was relatively effortless, Thatcher's advance was far more difficult. It was not so much a question of class by the 1960s. Her marriage to Denis, combined with her Oxford education, ensured her a secure place in the suburban middle class, increasingly well represented in the Tory party. Her sex was more of an issue. The trouble was that on both sides of a male-dominated House, there was a lamentable tendency to patronise female politicians by confining them to so-called 'women's issues', such as pensions, welfare, and education.

Margaret Thatcher was determined to aim for what she considered the top jobs, such as the Treasury. Her confident maiden speech on February 1960 moving the second reading of her private member's bill (legislating for the admission of the press to local government meetings) showed her potential, though a Sunday newspaper tempted her into a minor indiscretion when she said, 'I couldn't even consider a Cabinet post until my twins are older.'[23] Twenty months later, she was given her first government appointment by the Prime Minister, one of the first two of the new intake to be promoted. It was, however, as parliamentary under secretary at the Ministry of Pensions and National Insurance, a post which was normally reserved for women MPs, as much of the work related to pensions for widows. Thatcher spent the next three years in the job, mastering the nuts and bolts of the postwar welfare system. Her performance impressed not only the ministers under whom she served but also the opposition. The Labour MP Dick Crossman, who crossed swords with her in a number of debates, wrote in his diary: 'She is tough, able and competent.'[24]

Whitelaw and Thatcher followed different routes to the top of Tory politics. Willie came up through the Whips' Office. His gregarious nature was well suited to its officers' mess camaraderie and, with his bluff charm and good humour, he quickly learnt how to gather information and gossip not only about his own colleagues but also about opposition MPs and journalists. He became a popular whip who could be relied upon to treat his fellow MPs fairly and, above all, to keep his word. After a spell as junior minister at the Ministry of Labour at the end of the Conservative government, Whitelaw became Conservative chief whip when the Tories went into opposition. In this capacity, he helped manage the resignation of Alec Douglas-Home in July 1965 and the subsequent leadership election, which Edward Heath won. Over the years of opposition, Willie had to deal with several crises, including the vote over Rhodesian sanctions (when the Tory party split three ways) and the sacking of Enoch Powell over his unauthorised speech on race relations. Despite these difficulties, there was cross-party agreement on the merits of Whitelaw as opposition chief whip. Heath described him as a 'tower of strength', while in 1967 Wilson made him a privy councillor. When the Tories unexpectedly won the 1970 election, Whitelaw became Lord President of the Council and leader of the House of Commons. In all but name, he was now Heath's second in command.

Thatcher owed her rise not to the support of the establishment but to her own abilities. From 1964 to 1970, she held six shadow posts; she was junior spokesman for pensions, housing and land, and for Treasury affairs under Ian Macleod, before taking up three further posts in the Shadow Cabinet. She was always well briefed, lucid and combative. Moore described her as 'a worker and a fighter in a party which was slightly short of both'.[25]

Following the Tory defeat at the 1966 general election, Heath had considered promoting her to his Shadow Cabinet. At a meeting with Heath and Whitelaw, Jim Prior, who was then Heath's PPS, recommended her as the 'statutory' woman. After a long silence, Heath replied, 'Yes, Willie agrees she is much the most able, but he says that once she's there we'll never be able to get rid of her.'[26] So, for the time being, she was kept out. However, in October 1967, the Tory leader decided that, in view of her effectiveness in Parliament, her sharpness on radio and her popularity with the party rank and file, she had earned the right to a place in the Shadow Cabinet, to begin with as shadow minister for fuel and power. This was followed by a short spell as transport spokesman and then, in October 1969, Heath appointed her shadow secretary of state for education, and, after the 1970 Conservative election victory, gave her the substantive post.

For Whitelaw, the period from 1970 to 1975 was arguably when he was at his political zenith. However, it was also the time when his hopes of leading the party were extinguished and when Margaret Thatcher emerged from relative obscurity to snatch the crown. With his good humour and inimitable speaking style, Willie was well respected as leader of the Commons. Assisted by Tory Chief Whip Francis Pym, he had the arduous task of steering through the Commons the legislation to ratify British membership of the European Economic Community. Both men argued in Cabinet for a free vote for Conservative members at the end of the six-day debate on the principle of membership in October 1971, on the grounds that it would make it easier for Labour's rebels under Roy Jenkins either to vote in favour or to abstain. The tactic paid off as the motion in favour of entry was carried by 112. However, the passage of the 12-clause Bill was long and tortuous, with the majority often down to single figures. A combination of skilful management by the Tories and courageous voting by Labour's dissidents ensured that the Bill became law.

On 24 March 1972, Heath asked Whitelaw to become secretary of state with special responsibility for Northern Ireland. The background to this new appointment and to the imposition of Direct Rule from Westminster (including the transfer of all security powers and responsibility for criminal matters) was the deteriorating security situation in the province, with a growing number of terrorist atrocities, and the disaster of 'Bloody Sunday' when British troops fired on and killed demonstrators in Londonderry. Whitelaw had only been to Northern Ireland twice in his life: once to attend a twenty-first birthday party and the second time on a golf tour in the 1950s. However, characteristically he accepted the post at once because he saw it as his duty. He told Harrow Conservatives: 'We have a duty to the people of the United Kingdom to preserve law and order.' He added that 'the solution will not be found by military means alone. It will only be found in the hearts and minds of men and women.'[27] Whitelaw well understood that he had not only to restore law and order but also to calm 'a bitterly resentful Protestant majority' and give 'a suspicious Catholic minority' hope of 'a new standing in the community'.[28] Over the next 20 months, Whitelaw applied his considerable powers of conciliation to trying to end the conflict in Northern Ireland.

Almost immediately, he released some of the suspected terrorists who had been interned without trial and lifted the ban on marches and demonstrations. Using the army, he opened up the Catholic 'no-go' areas in Londonderry and prevented similar Protestant areas being created in Belfast. In July 1972, following a ceasefire, he met leaders of the Provisional IRA secretly in London. These talks, however, ended in failure and the truce broke down. When the Provisionals then revealed that talks had taken place, Willie's first reaction was he should resign. But, following a sympathetic reception in the Commons, he changed his mind and declared that he was prepared to 'soldier on' as long as his services were required. He realised, however, that a new political initiative was now essential if further progress was to be made. He therefore invited the leaders of all the Northern Ireland constitutional parties to attend a conference at Darlington on their future. Although only three (the Unionists and the Alliance Party and the Northern Ireland Labour Party) came, the meeting provided the ideas for a White Paper, published on 20 March 1973, which set out the government's proposals, including a legislative assembly elected by proportional representation and an executive in which power was shared between Nationalists and Unionists.

Following assembly elections in June, Whitelaw called the main parties together for talks, above all about the setting up of a stable power-sharing executive. After negotiations, which lasted nearly two months, Willie finally broke the deadlock by skilful use of deadlines, arranging for his helicopter to land on the lawn outside Stormont Castle in a successful ploy to produce an agreement. It was decided that there would be 11 voting members of the executive, of whom six would be Unionists, four from the Social Democratic and Labour Party (SDLP – the Nationalist grouping) and one Alliance Party, with four more non-voting members in the proportion 1:2:1.

The next day, 22 November 1973, Whitelaw was received in the Commons 'like a Roman General who had earned a great Triumph'.[29] Willie wrote in his memoirs that 'The press comments were so favourable that when I look at them now I wonder if they can be describing the same person that I have sometimes read about in their columns since.'[30] Willie was rightly praised for his diplomatic achievement but sadly it proved to be short lived, as the power-sharing executive which he helped negotiate was brought down the following year by the Ulster Workers' Council strike. In the longer term, however, the Whitelaw power-sharing model was to be one of the key elements in the 1998 Good Friday Agreement and is now the basis on which Northern Ireland administrations are formed.

On 2 December, Heath brought Whitelaw, bolstered by his success in Northern Ireland, back to Westminster to try and sort out the crisis arising from the 1973 miners' dispute. In his memoirs, Willie wrote that he was 'somewhat unsuitable for the centre of the stage which I had to occupy in the middle of a major industrial and political upheaval'.[31] As he explained, he was physically and mentally exhausted by the strain of his time in Northern Ireland, while his reputation as a skilled negotiator would only be useful if the government decided it wanted to settle with the miners (who were asking for a 35 per cent pay increase – way outside the 7 per cent norm allowed by the third stage of the prices and incomes policy).

However, the Cabinet was divided, with a powerful group arguing for resisting the miners and going for an early general election. The Prime Minister would not make up his mind. Whitelaw, who was strongly against a dash for the polls, asked Heath in exasperation, 'Tell me what you want me the do with this department. Do you want me to settle, or do you want war?' He did not receive a clear answer. In the end, following a strike ballot which was backed by an overwhelming majority, Heath decided to call an election. Whitelaw, who believed that the government should have accepted the TUC's last-minute proposal that the miners should be treated as a special case, found himself 'swept into an election campaign which I dreaded'.[32]

The February 1974 election was a strange one. Though there was a general expectation that the Tories were likely to win, a leaked pay board finding (which turned out to be erroneous) that the miners were earning less than the average worker in the manufacturing sector appeared to undermine the government's case. Above all, the single issue on which the election was being fought – 'Who governs Britain?' – received an answer unfavourable to the government, as the Conservative Research Department had warned was likely.[33] Despite his misgivings, Whitelaw undertook an extensive speaking campaign up and down the country. On the morning of his constituency count he was so exhausted that he collapsed with a high temperature. However, having been elected with more than 60 per cent of the vote, he managed to make a coherent speech and to take part in a television interview with Robin Day, in which Willie said that, as Labour appeared to have won most seats, it should be declared the winner. Confined to his bed by his doctor, Whitelaw did not take part in the unsuccessful attempt by Heath to cobble together a coalition with the

Liberals. On 4 March, Heath resigned and Wilson, despite having polled nearly a quarter of a million votes less that the Conservatives, formed a minority government. Both Whitelaw and Thatcher found themselves out of office.

Thatcher had proved to be a competent, if surprisingly orthodox secretary of state for education and science. She was not opposed to comprehensive schools in principle, arguing that each local authority should be able to make decisions for itself rather than be compelled to change. When she took office, there were 1,137 comprehensives; when she left in March 1974 she had approved 3,286 comprehensive schemes and rejected only 326. She had, in effect, gone with the prevailing trend, one which most Tory authorities supported.[34] She backed increased spending on primary-school building, successfully opposed the scrapping of the Open University (one of Harold Wilson's pet projects), and raised the school-leaving age from 15 to 16.

Her most controversial decision was removing the provision of free milk for primary-school children above the age of seven, directing the savings to primary-school buildings. At the 1971 Labour Party conference, she was called 'Mrs Thatcher, milk snatcher', a jibe which she bitterly resented, especially as she had managed to save free school milk for infants. However, despite the furore, Heath supported her and, in December 1972, she issued her own education White Paper, 'A Framework for Expansion', which, in addition to teacher training and higher education, focused on nursery education. The *Guardian* praised her for being 'more than half-way towards a respectable socialist education policy'.[35]

Thatcher took little part in broader Cabinet discussions. She was recognised as being slightly to the right of centre but at that time her views did not carry much weight. There is no evidence that she objected to Heath's 1972 U-turn, when the Conservative government decided on a price and incomes policy and adopted an industrial strategy. In the crisis of 1973 and 1974 she was in favour of an early general election, but hers was not a decisive voice. In her only general election broadcast in February 1974 (in which she shared a platform with Willie Whitelaw) she spoke up strongly against the idea of a national coalition. But her main worry was holding onto her Finchley seat against a possible Liberal surge; her majority was almost halved but she survived comfortably.

Yet, less than a year after losing her job as secretary of state for education following the March general election, Margaret Thatcher was elected leader of the Conservative Party. As one of her biographers wrote, this was 'a stunning transformation which no one would have predicted twelve months earlier'.[36] Enoch Powell's comment about Thatcher was that she 'didn't rise to power. She was opposite the spot on the roulette wheel at the right time, and she didn't funk it.'[37] There were three main reasons for Margaret Thatcher becoming leader in early 1970. First, there was Heath's unpopularity with his parliamentary party and his obstinacy in staying on. Secondly, there was Whitelaw's loyalty to Heath. Thirdly and by no means least, there was Thatcher's courage and opportunism in reaching for the crown.

In March 1974, Heath's narrow election defeat had the paradoxical effect of sustaining him as leader. Although many Tory MPs told whips that there should be a change, the likelihood of an early general election persuaded the dissidents to stay their hand. Even so, although Heath remained as leader, he was now there only on sufferance.

He tried to shore up his position by appointing Whitelaw, who was popular in the constituencies, as party chairman. Willie regarded the job as a 'poisoned chalice' but characteristically felt that it was his duty to accept Heath's offer.[38] Whitelaw knew that he would share the blame if the party was beaten again. On the other hand, he thought that it was essential for the Conservatives at least to limit the extent of defeat. So during the summer he toured the country, keeping up party morale, relying, according to his family, on his well-tried phrases such as 'Splendid! Splendid! Carry on the good work.'

Heath also moved Mrs Thatcher to the shadow environment portfolio, with a brief covering housing and rates. This was a key time for her, as it was during this period that, under the influence of her close colleague, Keith Joseph, she was increasingly attracted to free market ideas. Heath had refused to appoint Joseph as shadow chancellor but allowed him to act as a roving right-wing intellectual, with permission to set up his own think tank, the Centre for Policy Studies (CPS). Thatcher became vice chairman of the CPS and, within the Shadow Cabinet, gave cautious support to Joseph when, in a speech at Preston, he advocated abandoning incomes policy in favour of relying on the supply of money as a means of controlling inflation.

Thatcher played a significant part in the October election campaign. Encouraged by Heath, who was searching for populist policies which would attract the support of the middle classes, she had announced (at a press conference in August) that a Conservative government would reduce the mortgage rate from 11 to 9.5 per cent and also abolish domestic rates in the next parliament. In addition, council tenants were to be helped to buy their houses at a 33 per cent discount. She put across these electoral attractions with such panache that she was considered by many observers to be the Tories' star performer in the campaign. Whitelaw was the anchorman; presiding with style and skill over 12 of the 15 press conferences. At one conference, he denied that morale within the party was low. Asked for evidence, he replied, 'Well, I have the thermometer in my mouth and I am listening to it all the time.'[39]

However, the Conservatives went down to a second defeat, though it was not as bad as most pundits had expected. Labour's overall majority was only four, but its majority over the Conservatives was 43. Willie regarded the defeat as a relatively successfully rearguard action. However, he knew that it would increase the pressure against Heath's leadership. Margaret Thatcher, whose majority at Finchley was reduced below 4,000, was in no doubt 'that Ted should go'.[40] Her opinion was shared by a substantial number of Tory MPs, including most of the members of the 1922 Committee, above all by its chairman Edward Du Cann. One of Margaret Thatcher's biographers, John Campbell, summed up the extent of the disillusion: 'By his rudeness, insensitivity, and sheer bad manners, Heath had exhausted the loyalty of a large number of backbenchers.'[41]

But Heath, who had now lost three of the last four elections, refused to budge. His closest colleagues and advisers were divided. Sara Morrison,

Jim Prior and Lord Carrington thought he should resign, although Lord Thorneycroft and Lord Hailsham wanted him to remain as leader. In his memoirs, Jim Prior concluded that the Tory leader only heard 'the advice he wished to hear'.[42] Heath genuinely believed that only he was fit to lead the Tory party and to provide the national direction which the deteriorating economic situation required. In the end, by staying on, Heath effectively scuppered the chances of a candidate from his own wing of the Tory party – above all, Willie Whitelaw – and helped pave the way for Margaret Thatcher.

Whitelaw wrote that the period following the second 1974 election was 'the worst time in my political life'.[43] In public, he remained loyal to Heath. On election night, he stressed the importance of loyalty and a week later he issued a statement affirming his support for Heath. In private, however, he told friends that he thought the Tory leader should have resigned. But, when approached by supportive MPs, he told them to hold their hand. In November he turned down a persistent critic of Heath, Airey Neave, who, before turning to Thatcher, offered to run Whitelaw's campaign for him. 'Cross bencher' in the *Sunday Express* cruelly wrote that Willie had 'manoeuvred himself into immobility'.[44] The problem for Whitelaw was that he would only run if Heath stood down. But by the time that happened, it was already too late.

Following the October election defeat, Margaret Thatcher may have wanted Heath to resign but her public position was that she herself was not yet ready to challenge for the leadership and that she would therefore give her support to Keith Joseph. However, on 19 October, Joseph made a controversial speech at Edgbaston in which he appeared to suggest that working-class single mothers should be discouraged from having children. This raised doubts about his suitability as a candidate and on 20 November Joseph informed Thatcher that he had decided not to run. Thatcher said in that case she would stand. A few days later, she met Heath in his room and told him of her challenge. Apparently, he replied, 'You'll lose.'[45] Denis Thatcher's reaction when his wife told him of her decision was similar: 'Heath will murder you,' he said.[46]

*

In fact, events worked in her favour. Apart from one outsider, Hugh Fraser, impulsively throwing his hat in the ring, Margaret Thatcher was the only challenger. Appointed by Heath to be shadow treasury number two, Thatcher was able to demonstrate her parliamentary skills in 12 Finance Bill Committee debates on the floor of the House, while Airey Neave artfully canvassed 'the knights of the shires', a key group whom Heath, an astonishingly poor campaigner, had largely ignored. Neave also attracted supporters of Whitelaw and Prior to vote for Thatcher by saying, 'Margaret is doing well but not quite well enough.' When the first ballot votes were counted, Thatcher was ahead, with 130 votes to Heath's 119 and Fraser's 16. Heath belatedly resigned, while Thatcher, with the momentum now strongly behind her, proceeded to the second ballot.

Whitelaw, who had for so long been waiting loyally in the wings, at last decided to join the contest (as the rules entitled him to do). Thatcher later claimed that she expected him to win. Whitelaw clearly thought he had a chance, declaring to his supporters, 'Ted's out of the running, I'm going to have a go.'[47] But three other candidates (Howe, Prior and John Peyton) entered the ring, helping to undermine the impact of his candidature. When Whitelaw and Thatcher spoke at the Young Conservatives' conference at Eastbourne, Willie's contribution appeared bumbling besides Thatcher's barnstorming speech. He also allowed himself to be filmed in an apron doing the washing up, an unconvincing spectacle, which was hardly likely to reassure a largely male electorate. By contrast, Thatcher seemed very much in command, 'in love with power, success and with herself'.[48] The result of the second ballot was decisive, with 146 for Thatcher, 79 for Whitelaw, 19 each for Prior and Howe and 11 for Peyton. Margaret Thatcher's triumph shocked the political world. An official at the US Embassy in London reported that the mood of the Conservative Party was 'a curious mixture of relief, excitement, guilt and misgivings'.[49]

However, Thatcher's position was still precarious. She owed her victory to a backbench revolt. Almost all of Heath's Shadow Cabinet had opposed her, while Heath himself retreated into a prolonged sulk. It was her alliance with Whitelaw which was crucial in shoring up her leadership. At their first meeting after the election, Mrs Thatcher immediately offered him the deputy leadership. As she pointed out in her autobiography, he had 'demonstrated his popularity in the leadership election. He was immensely experienced and his presence would be a reassuring guarantee to many on the backbenches that evolution rather than revolution was the order of the day.'[50]

Whitelaw had already decided that, as Thatcher was the legitimately elected leader, it was his duty as the party's senior statesman to work with her, even though, as he frankly admitted in his memoirs, they were very different personalities with contrasting backgrounds and interests and held 'rather dissimilar political positions on some issues'. He also had reservations 'about the capacity of women to stand the immense physical and mental strains of leadership', though he later accepted these fears were founded 'on male chauvinism of the worse order'.[51]

However, during the war, he had been the number two to a commanding officer with a dominant personality, so he had previous experience of subordinating himself to a strong character. His understanding of his role as a loyal deputy was that he was there to warn her, if necessary, about the reaction of colleagues in the Cabinet, in Parliament, and in the constituencies but not to oppose her publicly. He was also there to assist her by persuading doubters, as well as by consoling those whose egos had been bruised by Thatcher's abrasive style. One of her biographers, John Campbell, assessed the significance of Whitelaw's contribution in the following terms: 'His unwavering support over the next thirteen years was indispensable to her survival and her successes.'[52]

In opposition, Whitelaw was indispensible to Thatcher. The fragility of her position forced her to retain most of Heath's colleagues in her Shadow Cabinet, even though it was obvious that they were not fully committed to her or to her ideas. She gave Geoffrey Howe, a fellow monetarist, the shadow chancellorship, though she would have preferred Keith Joseph, whose appointment was blackballed by Whitelaw, who mistrusted his judgement.

185

She also took Willie's advice and made his cousin, Peter Thorneycroft, party chairman, kept on the prominent Heathite, Lord Carrington, as leader of the House of Lords, and reappointed the moderate Jim Prior as shadow employment secretary. Despite differences (above all between the new leader and many of her colleagues), Thatcher's Shadow Cabinet held together, not least because of Whitelaw's remarkable powers of conciliation.

With Willie's assistance, the Conservatives came through the 1975 referendum on UK membership of the European Community without mishap. Thatcher was marginally in favour of staying in the EC, but felt that her defeated rival Edward Heath should be offered the leading role in the pro-EC camp. Heath, however, turned it down and it was Whitelaw who became vice president of the umbrella organisation, Britain in Europe, working closely with the Labour president Roy Jenkins in the successful 'yes' campaign. The result decisively endorsed Britain's membership of the EC.

In January 1976, Thatcher demonstrated her growing trust in Whitelaw by adding the shadow Home Office portfolio to his responsibilities as deputy leader. Willie wrote in his memoirs that becoming home secretary was one of his greatest ambitions. But he also admitted that the prospect was a heavy responsibility, especially as his policies 'would come under severe scrutiny from my friends'.[53] These critics included Thatcher, who, in a television interview in January 1978, deliberately raised the subject of immigration and of public fears of being 'swamped by people of a different culture'. Whitelaw was furious, both at the tone and content of her remarks and because he had not been consulted. He told Roy Jenkins 'how absolutely ghastly life was with that awful woman, how he was thinking of resigning'.[54] However, he did not resign and Thatcher, without a change in Tory policy, had signalled her real views to a receptive electorate.

The 1970s were difficult years for both government and opposition. Labour administrations under Wilson and Callaghan had to wrestle with high inflation, industrial conflict and political instability. The 1976 International Monetary Fund (IMF) crisis (when, after international pressure on the pound, the government was forced to apply to the IMF for a loan) called into question key elements of the postwar consensus, especially high levels of public spending and the maintenance of full employment. The crisis also gave credence to views and notions associated with Thatcher, including support for market forces, reductions in public spending and the role of state, and backing for the increasingly fashionable (but ultimately sterile) doctrine of monetarism.

However, although Thatcher made some notable speeches (for example, her populist address to the 1975 Tory conference), Whitelaw and other senior colleagues persuaded her to accept the compromise statement of party aims, entitled *The Right Approach*, and the document on economic policy, *The Right Approach to the Economy*, which appeared to back some form of incomes policy. The political reality, as both Whitelaw and Thatcher recognised, was that, following the resignation of Wilson, the election of Callaghan as leader of the Labour Party (and, therefore, prime minister) posed a real threat to the electoral prospects of the Tories. It was significant that Callaghan was consistently more popular with the public than Thatcher. Indeed, Labour, assisted by Britain's improved economic performance, staged a strong recovery during 1978 and by the autumn was running neck and neck with the Conservatives in the polls.

However, three events played into Thatcher's hands and led to her decisive victory in May 1979. The first was Callaghan's decision to delay the general election. If he had gone to the country in October 1978, as most Labour MPs expected and indeed preferred, Labour might still not have won the election but it certainly would have been a close-run affair. Indeed, at the time, Whitelaw felt that Labour would have had 'a reasonable chance of re-election in the autumn'. When he heard that there would after all be no election, he rang Thatcher to tell her that 'We have got him now.'[55] The second event was the subsequent breakdown of the government's 5 per cent pay limit which led to the 'winter of discontent' disputes of 1978–9. The rubbish in the streets, the piles of unwashed hospital sheets and the dead left unburied removed at a stroke Labour's most potent electoral card – its claim to be able to manage the unions. Then, on 28 March 1979, following defeats in the two devolution referendums (the Scottish 'yes' vote failed to meet the required threshold of 40 per cent of those entitled to vote and the Welsh voted 'no'), Thatcher tabled a vote of no confidence which the Labour government lost by one vote. Callaghan called the general election for 3 May.

In 1979, Mrs Thatcher, very much aware that she would only be given one chance, fought a cautious election campaign. In no sense could the Conservative manifesto be called 'Thatcherite'. Indeed, her foreword began with a rejection of dogma: 'For me, the heart of politics is not political theory, it is people and how they want to live their lives.'[56] On trade unions, there were three specific reforms – limiting picketing to a worker's place of work, reforming the closed shop and support for strike ballots. It was the collapse of the Labour government's authority during the winter of 1978–9 which gave the Conservatives their decisive victory. Although, by the end of the election, Callaghan finished 19 points ahead of Thatcher in terms of popularity, the Tories won with an overall majority of 43 seats and 70 seats more than Labour. Labour's share of the poll was its lowest since 1931, with many working-class voters, particularly among skilled employees, going over to the Conservatives.

The defeated prime minister, James Callaghan, generously acknowledged, 'for a woman to occupy that office is a tremendous moment in this country's history.'[57] Somewhat inappropriately, Thatcher, standing outside No 10 Downing Street, quoted the prayer supplied for her by her speechwriter, Ronnie Millar, which began with the words: 'When there is discord, may we bring harmony.' She understood that, even though she had won a dramatic election victory, she had to move cautiously. She was determined not to give a job to Heath (she sent him a letter informing him that she was appointing Carrington foreign secretary), but, guided by Whitelaw and the new Chief Whip, her first Cabinet included a majority of Tory 'grandees' and so-called 'wets' – Whitelaw as home secretary, Carrington as foreign secretary with Ian Gilmour as his deputy in the Commons, Pym at defence, with Prior being confirmed as employment secretary and Walker brought back as agriculture secretary. The Thatcherite Nicholas Ridley claimed that it was Willie Whitelaw's Cabinet which Thatcher first appointed.

It was certainly true that, especially in her first term, Whitelaw was the linchpin that held the Cabinet together. One of her shrewdest biographers pointed out that,

> as the acknowledged leader of the paternalist old Tories he could have rallied a majority of the Cabinet against her had he chosen to do so [...] But he saw his job as defusing tension and ensuring that she got her way. In the last resort he would never set his judgement against hers or countenance any sort of faction against her.[58]

In Cabinet, Whitelaw acted as de facto chairman. Thatcher almost always began meetings by the unusual practice of stating her conclusion first and challenging her colleagues to disagree with her. Some of them found her behaviour intimidating, even intolerable. David Howell, her first energy secretary, said:

> Of course there is a deterring effect if one knows that one's going to go not into a discussion where various points of view will be weighed and gradually a view may be achieved, but into a huge argument when tremendous battle lines will be drawn up and everyone who doesn't fall into line will be hit on the head.[59]

Very often, after this sometimes explosive exchange of views, Thatcher would leave Whitelaw to sum up, which he did with skill and good humour, trying to ensure that the Prime Minister got her way or at least was not obviously defeated, while at the same time soothing the ruffled feathers of his fellow Cabinet members. The constitutional historian Peter Hennessy later called him 'that formidable lifebelt for Cabinet collectivism in the considerable form of Lord Whitelaw'.[60]

Although in her first Cabinet Thatcher may have been in a minority, she was not on her own. With Whitelaw's acquiescence, she ensured that the economic posts went to her mostly monetarist supporters. Although irritated by Geoffrey Howe's manner, she sensibly recognised his loyalty and hard work by making him chancellor. Her favourite, Keith Joseph, went to industry. She made John Biffen (more independent minded than monetarist) chief secretary to the Treasury and John Nott, trade secretary. These men, with the assistance (outside the Cabinet) of the able financial secretary Nigel Lawson, formed the key group in charge of the government's economic strategy. Meeting secretly with Thatcher, mostly over breakfast, they plotted its direction.

Geoffrey Howe's first budget (12 June 1979), supported with some misgivings by the Prime Minister, cut the standard rate of income tax from 33 to 30 per cent and reduced the top rate from 83 per cent to 60 per cent. However, these big changes in direct taxation were paid for by a virtual doubling of VAT, which had an immediate impact on prices. The budget was accompanied by public spending cuts, a rise in interest rates and a relaxation of exchange controls, which were abolished a few months later. Not surprisingly, the months that followed saw rising unemployment, increasing inflation and record interest rates, accompanied by widespread criticism of the government's economic strategy.

Thatcher could afford to ignore the carping of Labour politicians, trade unionists and even of business leaders. But the opposition of members of her Cabinet was another matter. Leading the charge was Employment Secretary Jim Prior, who told Thatcher in a bilateral meeting on 16 July that it would be disastrous for industry 'if public expenditure was cut too much'.[61] To combat inflation in November Howe was forced to put up interest rates by 3 per cent to 17 per cent. Prior said he was both 'disappointed and shocked'. Howe replied, in a phrase subsequently often used by Thatcher, 'There is no alternative.' The question, as she told the *New York Times*, was whether the government could achieve enough by the time of the next election 'to show that it – our programme – is working'.[62]

With the possible exception of the Falklands War, the next two years were the most difficult period of Thatcher's premiership. The economic news continued to be bad, with output falling and unemployment soaring (reaching 2.8 million by the end of 1980). Despite this, Howe's second budget took nearly £1 billion out of planned public spending, while introducing the so-called Medium Term Financial Strategy (MTFS), the brainchild of Nigel Lawson which set targets for both monetary growth and reductions in public spending. Thatcher saw the MTFS (which was later abandoned by Lawson because of the difficulty in measuring the growth of money supply) as a symbol of her commitment not to 'bow to demands to reflate'.[63] At the 1980 Tory party conference, she famously said to delegates, 'You turn if you want to. The Lady's not for turning.' In other words, unlike Heath in 1972, Thatcher was not going to do a U-turn.

Howe's third budget (on 10 March 1981) was the toughest of the three. Although the economy was already plunging into recession, the government, mainly by deciding not to index tax thresholds, actually tightened its fiscal stance. Thatcher's chief economic adviser called it 'the biggest fiscal squeeze of peacetime'.[64] A letter to *The Times* by 364 economists predicted: 'Present policies will deepen the depression, erode the industrial base of our economy and threaten its social and political stability.'[65] High interest rates forced up the value of the pound, UK output and employment declined more sharply than in any other major industrial country and 20 per cent of manufacturing capacity was eliminated.

Following the budget, three ministers – Prior, Walker and Gilmour – considered resignation. Even Whitelaw said there was an 'enormous need for hope'. Outside, there were riots in the streets of London, which spread to Manchester and Liverpool. On 23 July, the Cabinet met to discuss Howe's plans for further cuts of £5 million in public expenditure. The critics had a field day. Even Nott and Biffen sided with the wets, only Joseph backing the Treasury team. Whitelaw remarked, 'There comes a moment in politics when you have pushed the tolerance of a society too far. We aren't there, but we aren't far from it',[66] while Hailsham warned that the government was in danger of destroying the Tory party.

The Prime Minister now realised that, if she was to survive, she would have to reshuffle her Cabinet. Whitelaw and Michael Jopling, the chief whip, though worried by the impact of government policies, were more concerned by the challenge to her authority, so dramatically demonstrated by the Cabinet of 23 July. Whitelaw's position was crucial. As one of Thatcher's biographers, John Campbell, noted, 'Now, if ever, was the moment when he might have exerted his influence, without disloyalty, on the side of an easing of policy.'[67] But he remained loyal to Thatcher. Nicholas Ridley, one of the Prime Minister's closest allies, explained his support as follows:

> Willie Whitelaw himself a Tory patrician, but one who had vowed to support Margaret Thatcher, never wavered. He decided that loyalty, and his sixth (political) sense required that his colleagues saw the 1980–1 squeeze through – and he was right. His political instincts convinced him it would come right in the end and his authority prevailed upon his patrician colleagues.[68]

A further explanation was that, given his lack of understanding of economics, Whitelaw almost invariably backed the Chancellor when there was a crisis. Thus it came about that it was with Whitelaw's backing that Thatcher sacked Gilmour, Soames and Carlisle, exiled Prior to Northern Ireland, replacing him at Employment with Norman Tebbit, appointing Lawson to Energy and making Parkinson chairman of the Conservative Party instead of Thorneycroft. The balance of the Cabinet had shifted decisively in Thatcher's favour.

In her memoirs, Thatcher paid tribute to Whitelaw's loyalty over the 1981 Cabinet crisis.[69] She was not always so loyal to him. In his four years in office Willie proved himself to be a competent and, given the party pressures and the circumstances of the time, a humane home secretary. Helped by a generous pay deal for the police (first introduced by the previous Labour government), he was able to increase police numbers by 9,000 by the time he left office. He also set in train a prison-building programme, while at the same time encouraging non-custodial sentences. He handled the 1981 riots with both firmness and sensitivity, giving the police more modern equipment and supporting policies proposed by the Scarman Inquiry (which he had himself set up) to improve police–community relations.

However, at the 1981 party conference, Whitelaw and Thatcher fell out over capital punishment. During the Home Office debate, Thatcher outrageously applauded a delegate who called for a three-line whip in the Commons on the death penalty, even though she was sitting next to Whitelaw on the platform and was well aware that parliamentary debates on hanging were always decided by a free vote. She also knew that Whitelaw had voted against restoring the death penalty in the most recent debate which had resulted in a decisive majority of 119 against restoration. Whitelaw was furious, the more so as the conference then proceeded to reject the government's law and order policies. After a fierce argument between Thatcher and Whitelaw behind the scenes, Willie offered to resign but she refused to accept his resignation. In his memoirs, Whitelaw concluded, 'In the end we carried on happily as if nothing had happened.'[70] Whitelaw's assessment was not entirely accurate. As Thatcher's memoirs indicated, she had marked Willie's card and after the 1983 election, when she was in a much stronger political position, she moved him from the Home Office.[71]

At the end of 1981, Tory fortunes were at their lowest. In November, Shirley Williams overturned a Tory majority of 18,000 to capture the Lancashire seat of Crosby in a by-election for the Social Democratic Party (SDP). December's national Gallup poll gave over 50 per cent to the SDP and Liberal Alliance, with 23.5 per cent to Labour and 23 per cent to the Tories. With an approval rating of only 25 per cent, Thatcher was the most unpopular prime minister since polling began.

However, even before the Falklands War, the Conservatives were in a stronger position than it seemed. With the SDP breakaway, the distraction of the struggle for the deputy leader's position between Healey and Benn and the weakness of the Foot leadership, the Labour Party was simply not in a fit state to exploit the government's unpopularity. And, though the rise of the SDP seemed, for the first time, to offer in alliance with the Liberals a credible third force, it also split the electoral opposition which, in a first-past-the-post system, was likely to work to the Tories' advantage.

There were also signs that the economy was beginning to recover. Although unemployment reached 3 million in January 1982, output had begun to rise, inflation continued to fall, and, by the time of the budget, interest rates had already come down by three points. In terms of public opinion, the Tories, Labour and the Alliance parties were roughly level pegging at between 30 and 33 per cent each. By the spring of 1982, the government had regained some ground, chiefly at the expense of the Alliance parties, though Roy Jenkins' victory at the Glasgow Hillhead by-election in March 1982 (a week before the Argentine invasion of the Falklands) demonstrated that the SDP had not yet lost its momentum.

But the Falklands War changed the political situation decisively in favour of the government and Thatcher. As Campbell rightly comments, 'The Falklands was a war that should not have happened.'[72] Politically and diplomatically it arose from a sequence of miscalculations, not least by the Thatcher government and its decision to cut defence spending. However, following the sending of a task force, the success of British troops 8,000 miles away in the South Atlantic and the determination and courage of Thatcher's war leadership transformed her 'from a bossy nanny into the breast-plated embodiment of Britannia'.[73] Only six months after she had been the most unpopular prime minister ever, her personal approval rating soared to 52 per cent and the Conservatives had built up an unassailable lead over Labour and the Alliance parties.

The Falklands conflict strengthened the partnership between Thatcher and Whitelaw. Willie was one of five members of Thatcher's War Cabinet, in her words, as 'my deputy and trusted advisor'.[74] The others were the Prime Minster herself , John Nott (defence secretary), Cecil Parkinson (party chairman) and Francis Pym (the new foreign secretary). Following a bitterly hostile meeting of Conservative backbenchers, the experienced foreign secretary, Lord Carrington, had decided, against Thatcher's and Whitelaw's advice, to resign. Thatcher then felt forced to appoint Pym partly because, in the weak position she found herself following the Argentine invasion of the Falklands, he was talked about as her possible successor. Thatcher did not get on with Pym, so Whitelaw, though he was not heading a department (such as Defence or the Foreign Office) closely involved in the war, was crucially important to Thatcher not only for his political nous but also for his wartime experience. She was always prepared to listen to Whitelaw when he questioned the naval and military commanders. Above all, the presence of Whitelaw in the War Cabinet showed that he was the person to whom she turned when there were tough decisions to be taken and when she needed a shoulder to cry on. For his part, Whitelaw was deeply impressed by Thatcher's leadership. As he wrote in his memoirs, 'No one who worked with her through this time could possibly deny that she emerged with flying colours.'[75]

At a critical moment, Whitelaw prevented Thatcher from resigning over the peace plan of the US secretary of state, Alexander Haig. Though Thatcher was determined to secure, by force of arms, the full recovery of British sovereignty over the Falklands, she had to keep world and, above all, American opinion on side. Hence the need for skilful diplomacy as the British task force sailed southwards towards the Falklands. On 26 April, Pym returned to London from the United States with Haig's latest proposals, including the idea of an interim authority for the Falklands on which not only the islanders but also the Argentinians would be represented.

Before the meeting of the War Cabinet, Thatcher told Whitelaw that she could not support the Haig plan. Once again, he backed her judgement. She wrote in her memoirs that, had the War Cabinet accepted the plan as Pym proposed, she would have resigned.[76] However, the War Cabinet agreed with John Nott's suggestion that the plan should be put first to Argentina without British comment. In the event, the Argentinians rejected the Haig proposals and a political crisis was averted. A few days later, the US government came out on Britain's side, promising material and intelligence support, and on 14 June, the Falklands were retaken after a fierce battle by the British task force.[77]

Thatcher unashamedly cashed in on the British victory in the South Atlantic. If Whitelaw with his military background was proud of the exploits of the British armed forces, especially of the Scots Guards at Tumbledown, he may also have felt that such a blatant exploitation of war for political advantage was in dubious taste. This was Mrs Thatcher speaking on 3 July to a Conservative rally in Cheltenham: 'We have ceased to be a nation in retreat. We have instead a new-found confidence – born in the economic battles at home and tested and found 8,000 miles away [...] Britain found herself again in the south Atlantic and will not look back from the victory she has won.' Linking her leadership with military success in the Falklands, she told an interviewer, 'I think people like decisiveness, I think they like strong leadership.'[78] She was right.

At the 1983 election, Thatcher and the Conservatives won a 'landslide 'victory, with a majority of 144, though the Tory share of the vote actually declined slightly compared to 1979. Thatcher owed her triumph not only to the Falklands but also to the disastrous showing of the Labour Party and to the almost equal division of the non-Conservative vote between Labour and the SDP–Liberal Alliance.

Thatcher's second term was the high point of 'Thatcherism'. 'Privatisation', which had begun on a relatively small scale in the first term, took off, becoming 'the jewel in the crown' of the government's legislative programme.[79] By February 1987, 14 major public sector companies had been privatised, 600,000 public sector employees had been transferred to the private sector and individual share ownership expanded from under 3 million in 1979 to more than 8 million in 1987. The explosion of share ownership proved to be short lived as new investors sold their shares, but in his book on *The Thatcher Revolution*, Peter Jenkins persuasively argued that privatisation had an important symbolic impact: 'The sales of British Gas and British Telecom were highly publicized events which served as powerful earnests of the idea that Thatcherism stood for owning things while socialism did not.'[80] The sale of council houses to their tenants at discount prices also proved a popular innovation. By the time Thatcher left office, 1.5 million houses had been sold, bringing £28 billion to the Treasury, as well as a substantial increase in home ownership.

During the second term, the spread of home and share ownership was accompanied by increased prosperity, especially in the South and the Midlands. The combination of economic growth (from 1983 onwards), substantial increases in earnings (real earnings increased by at least a fifth between 1979 and 1987) and politically astute – if arguably sometimes economically dubious – tax cuts was enough to convince many working- and lower middle-class voters that things were really getting better. Thatcherite speeches in favour of enterprise (of which the 'Big Bang' of deregulation in the City was an outstanding example), of incentives and of wealth creation provided a rhetorical underpinning for the government's policies. There was little doubt of the appeal of 'Thatcherism' to the aspiring, the ambitious and the upwardly mobile. But Thatcher had far less to say to the unemployed, the poor or the sick – or to the northern half of the British Isles. In contrast to the Toryism of Macmillan, Butler or Whitelaw, Thatcherism could not, by any stretch of the imagination, be called a 'One Nation' political doctrine.

Following the 1983 election victory, Thatcher's personal position was, for the first time, secure. With newly acquired confidence, she reshuffled her Cabinet, bringing in fresh allies. She sacked Pym and replaced him as foreign secretary by Howe. She made the clever (she called him 'brilliant') Nigel Lawson chancellor of the Exchequer and moved Whitelaw from the Home Office, putting Leon Brittan in his place. As compensation, she appointed Willie Lord President of the Council, leader of the House of Lords, and a hereditary peer.

In her memoirs, Margaret Thatcher commented on the Whitelaw sideways move: 'Willie had become, quite simply indispensable to me in Cabinet. When it really mattered I knew he would be by my side and because of his background, personality and position in the party he would sometimes sway colleagues when I could not.'[81] She went on to say that Whitelaw had not had 'an easy time as Home Secretary'. It was partly, she wrote, because home secretaries never had an easy time. She quoted the saying, 'they have a unique combination of responsibility without power.'[82] However, she admitted that the main reason for moving Whitelaw was because 'we did not share the same instincts on Home Office matters.'[83] Willie was very upset at having to leave the Home Office[84] and was also uneasy at being parachuted into the Lords to replace a popular and competent existing leader, Baroness Young. But, like the 'good soldier' that he was, he accepted the situation.

Whitelaw proved to be an outstanding success as leader of the Lords. Guided by the Tory chief whip, Lord Denham, he quickly learnt that, for all its sometimes arcane procedures, the Lords played a crucial role in the legislative process, above all as a revising chamber. The Prime Minister may have judged Whitelaw in part by his ability to get government business through the Lords but by the time he retired Whitelaw admitted without shame he had presided over more defeats than any of his predecessors. But, as he remarked:

> there is the possibility that even the hardest line people would accept that occasionally the government might be wrong. I would resist if the Commons tried to ride roughshod over the Lords, a group of people who want to see legislation as good as possible. It would be dangerous arrogance.[85]

If, in retrospect, the years from 1983 to 1987 were the apogee of Thatcherism, the period was also marked by a series of crises which the government had to surmount. In 1984, there was the year-long miners' strike which became a fight to the death between the Tory government and the militant miners' leader, Arthur Scargill. There were also bitter battles with local government, as well as disputes with the teachers' unions. In 1986, there was the row over the future of the Westland helicopter company which led to the resignation of two Cabinet ministers and nearly brought the downfall of the Prime Minster. If, in the end, the government easily won the 1987 election, it should not be forgotten that, for more than half the parliament, the Tories trailed Labour in the public opinion polls and were, at times, even in third place behind the Alliance.

In these dramas, Whitelaw played his part as Thatcher's deputy but, despite being given responsibility for the presentation of government policy, was less prominent than he had been in her first term. Willie was not a direct participant in the miners' dispute but, like Thatcher, he was convinced that Scargill had to be defeated. It was a tribute to his tenure of the Home Office that there were enough well-equipped and well-trained police to deal with disorder on the picket line. But if Whitelaw agreed with the Prime Minister that Scargill's sometimes unconstitutional and violent methods had to be overcome, he also realised, as Thatcher did not, that the lengthy strike led to 'unhappy strife and bitterness within communities and between families',[86] as well as to hardship and suffering in mining villages.[87]

Whitelaw also became concerned about the political consequences of the government's attack on local government; more than 50 separate Acts of Parliament between 1979 and 1989 substantially reduced the power of local government, including statutory rate capping. In 1986, the government also abolished the Greater London Council and the metropolitan county councils. The former prime minister, Edward Heath, warned that to get rid of democratically elected councils was to invite reprisals if Labour was returned to power. Whitelaw agreed with the point but was unable to stop Thatcher from proceeding.

Then there was the issue of the poll tax. Before the 1983 election, a committee on local government finance chaired by Whitelaw had concluded there was no satisfactory alternative to the rates. However, early in 1985, Whitelaw came back from a visit to Scotland, much shaken by the local reaction to the revaluation of Scottish rates, which threatened a steep rise in rateable values, especially in middle-class areas. He and the Scottish secretary, George Younger, persuaded Thatcher, who was initially a sceptic, that 'something must be done'. It was pressure from Tories in Scotland that indirectly led to the disastrous poll tax, a fixed charge on individuals, unrelated to ability to pay. The chancellor, Nigel Lawson, put forward a paper, describing the proposed flat-rate charge as 'completely unworkable and politically catastrophic'.[88] Whitelaw, despite his earlier view that there was no alternative to the rates, failed to support Lawson and the poll tax was included in the Tory manifesto. The tax had not yet been introduced in England and Wales when Whitelaw stood down in January 1988 but he cannot be excluded from blame. His biographers described the poll tax fiasco as 'an example of Willie inadvertently setting a ball rolling, and then shrinking away as he watched it gather momentum'.[89]

The Westland crisis was more about a clash between the two biggest egos in the Cabinet – that of Defence Secretary Michael Heseltine and the Prime Minister herself – than about the relatively trivial matter of a small helicopter firm. Heseltine and Thatcher did not get on: Thatcher distrusted his ambition, while Heseltine hated the way she ran her Cabinet. Westland brought this clash of personalities out into the open, with Heseltine advocating that the company should be taken over by a European consortium and Thatcher wanting a merger with the American firm Sikorsky. When she prevented him going to Cabinet on the issue and insisted that he should clear any further statement with the Cabinet secretary, Heseltine literally walked out of the room and out of office.

The crisis took another and even more dangerous turn over the unprecedented leaking of a law officer's letter to Michael Heseltine. After an official inquiry, the secretary of state for trade and industry, Leon Britton, was forced to resign and the Prime Minister, whom most MPs suspected of having authorised the leak, only escaped by the skin of her teeth. As she left Downing Street for the crucial opposition emergency debate in the Commons on the afternoon of 27 January 1986, she herself said that she might not be prime minister by 6 o'clock that evening. However, a powerful speech by Thatcher and a weak one by Neil Kinnock, the leader of the opposition, enabled her to survive. The next day, Whitelaw privately pronounced his leader to be 'just' in the clear.[90] However, the combination of high-handedness, manipulation and lack of candour which the Westland crisis had revealed was a prelude to a slump both in Thatcher's personal ratings and in the fortunes of her party.

Writing about Westland in his memoirs, Whitelaw accepted that he was 'a bad judge of the whole affair, because for once in my life I was in no way a conciliator but an absolutely committed supporter of one side of the argument'. He had become, he admitted, increasingly bored by what he regarded as 'an unnecessary and potentially damaging controversy' by a minister (Heseltine) who had become 'obsessed with his own proposals'.[91] Indeed, at a private meeting with the Prime Minister on 18 December 1985, he and the Chief Whip had argued that Heseltine should be sent an ultimatum but at that stage she was not yet willing to confront the Defence Secretary directly. However, in a televised interview after his retirement, Whitelaw openly conceded that Heseltine should have been given the opportunity to put his case to Cabinet and implicitly admitted that it was Thatcher's refusal to allow collective discussion which led to Heseltine's dramatic resignation.

Despite the fall in Thatcher's popularity at the beginning of 1986, by the autumn the Tories had begun to stage a political recovery, driven by a surge in consumption. In the 18 months before the June 1987 election, real GDP grew at a rate of 4 per cent a year and credit and consumption rose sharply. It was the Lawson 'boom' and the feeling of prosperity it engendered which turned the tide for Mrs Thatcher. In the 1987 election, the Conservatives won 42.3 per cent of the vote and a massive overall majority of 101 seats. Despite a new leadership, some modifications in policy (though not in defence) and an energetic campaign (superior to that of the Tories), Labour still finished 11 percentage points behind the Tories.

Thatcher's third term began on a note of unabashed triumphalism. Making her leader's speech to the 1987 conference, she rejoiced in her third successive victory. Rejecting any idea of consolidation, she promised that 'the third election was only a staging post on a much longer journey.' Thatcherite ideas and Thatcherite policies, she crowed, now dominated British politics and, quoting the example of Lord Liverpool, hinted that she would be prime minister for at least 15 years. Her new Cabinet was now made up not so much of Thatcherites but of ambitious pragmatists like Kenneth Baker, Douglas Hurd, Kenneth Clarke, John Major and John MacGregor, chosen to do her bidding. The party chairman, Norman Tebbit, had resigned to care for his wife, who had been severely injured in the 1984 Brighton bomb incident, and Thatcher had sacked the leader of the House, John Biffen, for suggesting – accurately as it turned out – that her premiership might not last throughout the entire parliament. Her deputy, Willie Whitelaw, remained on as her faithful elder statesman.

Even after the 1987 election Whitelaw continued to be influential. The return of Cecil Parkinson to the Cabinet as secretary of state for energy apparently received Willie's support, as demonstrated by his warm embrace of Thatcher's favourite at the 1987 party conference. A few weeks later, Whitelaw and the chief whip, John Wakeham, vetoed the plan to make another Thatcher favourite, Lord Young, party chairman, in addition to being secretary of state for industry. Whitelaw was also involved in the sacking of Michael Havers as Lord Chancellor. Tongue in cheek, a *Guardian* journalist suggested that Whitelaw was modelling himself on the character from the Hollywood film *The Terminator*: 'Suddenly, harmless peers who encounter the lumbering figure of the Lord President in the corridors of power flatten themselves against the wall in genuine alarm. For there is real blood on those vast, ham-like hands, and two illustrious political scalps now dangle from his belt.'[92]

However, on 14 December, Whitelaw suffered a transient ischemic attack (a mini-stroke) at a carol service at St Margaret's Westminster. Although he rapidly recovered, his doctor told him that only retirement from office could stave off a much more serious attack. Thatcher was anxious that Willie should stay on, even contacting his doctor to try and persuade him to reconsider his professional advice. However, Whitelaw wisely decided to put his life and family first, and on 10 January 1988 announced that he would be leaving the administration.

*   *   *

There was general agreement that Willie's resignation represented a major loss to the government. *The Times'* editorial noted that, 'There is now no-one in Cabinet who could reasonably affect the title of elder statesman.' The *Telegraph*'s assessment was that his departure was 'the sharpest loss the Prime Minister has suffered while in office'.[93] In her memoirs, Thatcher wrote that he was 'an irreplaceable deputy Prime Minister'.[94] Her biographer, John Campbell, judged that 'his reassuring and defusing presence was hugely important to the survival and success of

Mrs Thatcher's governments. His departure left the government without its sheet anchor in the increasingly heavy seas of the next three years.'[95]

Whitelaw's contribution was at different levels. He was the government's most effective chairman. From 1982 until he retired, he was chairman of the Star Chamber, the ad hoc Cabinet subcommittee set up to adjudicate unresolved issues between the Treasury and spending. The former chancellor, Nigel Lawson, wrote in his memoirs that Whitelaw was an excellent chairman:

Quite apart from his great personal authority and political skill, he held to a small number of constitutional doctrines, one of which was that, while each individual issue had to be decided on its merits, overall the cause of good government required that the Treasury did not suffer many defeats.[96]

A less senior Cabinet minister, Malcolm Rifkind, described Willie in action:

On one occasion, I was in a minority of one in a Cabinet committee discussion. At the end, I asked for my dissent to be recorded. This would have meant that the problem would have gone to full Cabinet, with the possibility of a crisis clearly underlined. Whitelaw swung into action; I was made an offer that met my bottom line, and the crisis was averted. It was a classic example of both his authority and the soundness of his political instincts.[97]

Another Cabinet minister, Norman Fowler, attested to his exceptional skill in steering a committee on AIDS (which until Whitelaw's appointment as chairman in 1986 had made little progress) to a successful conclusion; Fowler recalled that his chairmanship 'was absolutely essential in saving many lives in this country'.[98]

Ministers were also convinced that Whitelaw played a crucial role in keeping Thatcher on an even keel. These were the comments of two of her most senior colleagues. Nigel Lawson wrote,

Only someone who served at the heart of the Thatcher government can fully appreciate the key role that Willie played. It was not simply that he was a wise statesman of immense experience and acute political instinct, unfailingly loyal and devoid of personal ambition, to whom Margaret could always turn. He also resolved many of the tensions that arise between Cabinet colleagues in any government before they even reached Margaret. And when she was involved, it was he alone who could sometimes, although inevitably not always, prevail upon her to avoid needless confrontations or eschew follies.[99]

Geoffrey Howe, Lawson's predecessor, wrote,

Particularly in my Treasury years, Margaret and I were often the joint beneficiaries of his support. But increasingly, as the years went by, it was his cautionary voice that steered us away from reckless proximity to the rocks. We did not always agree, and his view did not always prevail. But time and time against he provided that mixture of ballast and yeast which secured second thoughts – and often ensured that they were fruitful.[100]

Nicholas Ridley, a Cabinet minister who was close to Thatcher, wrote that Whitelaw had:

almost supernatural political antennae. He knew exactly when to warn Margaret Thatcher that a situation was approaching breaking point. He knew even not to do it until it was necessary [...] He never wavered and he was even prepared to accept the consequences of the 1981 monetary squeeze in supporting her although in his heart of hearts I suspect he was uneasy.[101]

Some of Thatcher's ministers go so far as to trace her downfall to Whitelaw's resignation. Even after his resignation, Willie told Thatcher (and Nigel Lawson as well) that, if she wished it, he would continue to give advice, but she did not take up his offer. Howe explained the underlying problem: 'Margaret's most important weakness – the flipside of her strength – was the extent to which her colleagues were driven in the end to choose between submission or defection [...] "I must prevail" was the phrase that finally broke Nigel Lawson's "bond of loyalty and affection".'[102] It was much the same attitude which led to the revolt of the Cabinet and her downfall. If Whitelaw had still been there, would he have been able to defuse the volcanic personality clashes which undermined her government? His biographers doubted this on the grounds that the conflicts had, by this time, become too bitter for compromise.

What is clear is that Whitelaw had a unique mix of authority and judgement which, on occasions, provided a necessary foil to Thatcher's supercharged personality. After he retired, he agreed (but only in private conversation) that he could have perhaps done more to stop Thatcher going over the top – as, for example, over the extent of the 1981 fiscal squeeze, over Westland and over the poll tax. But his colleagues were surely correct when they said that the combination of Thatcher and Whitelaw, of initiator and facilitator, was more effective than Thatcher alone.[103] The troubled last three years of her premiership demonstrated the truth of that assessment only too clearly.

6

NEW LABOUR

Blair and Brown

Most recent discussions of the Blair–Brown relationship have focused on its problems, above all on the rows between the two principals and their respective entourages. But, as this chapter seeks to show, the partnership between the two men was a highly successful combination which not only created and sustained the New Labour project, but also gave the party the longest period of power in its history. It is time that the achievements of Blair and Brown were subject to objective examination[1] and not seen solely through the dark spectacles of Iraq, or against the backdrop of world recession, or as a sideshow to the melodrama of the TB-GBs, as civil servants used to call them.

Tony Blair and Gordon Brown had complementary gifts. Blair was the initiator. He was stylish and charismatic, with a winning smile and charm. By far and away the best communicator of modern British politics, he was a master not only of parliamentary debate and of party conference but, above all, of television. Partly because he was an outsider without deep roots in the Labour Party, he had the ability to appeal beyond its heartlands to the aspirational voters of the Midlands and the south. As prime minister, he was good at focusing on the main issues confronting him – and taking decisions about them. His persuasiveness and persistence enabled him to become a highly effective negotiator, as his outstanding contribution in Northern Ireland demonstrated. Recently, he has been demonised by his critics on both right and left but they have tended to forget just what an impressive politician he was in his prime.

Brown also fancied himself as an initiator, but he was more effective as a facilitator. He was the policy expert of New Labour. He devoured ideas and policies as others devoured food. He was clever, hardworking and obsessive about politics. In small gatherings, particularly of policy experts and intellectuals, he was stimulating and incisive, and he could make eloquent set speeches in Parliament or at party conferences. But, unlike Blair, he was not a natural communicator, and on television he could appear wooden, even robotic.

Brown was an outstanding chancellor of the Exchequer, at least until the end of the second term, introducing a number of creative policy initiatives, including transferring control over interest rates from the Treasury to the Bank of England and introducing the Working Families Tax Credit to help the working poor. Until the global crash of 2008, the British economy expanded steadily for a decade, with national output growing a third, and inflation being kept under firm control.

For three general elections – 1997, 2001 and 2005 – the Blair–Brown duo was unbeatable. As Andrew Rawnsley put it, 'They were the rock on which New Labour was built and the rock on which it so often threatened to break apart. When they were working together, their complementary skills created a synergy which made the government pretty much unstoppable.'[2] The two men needed each other. Blair needed Brown's economic competence; Brown needed Blair's popular appeal. In combination, they carried all before them. While it lasted, it was a mighty partnership.

James Gordon Brown was born in Govan, Glasgow on 20 February 1951; Anthony Charles Lynton Blair was born in Edinburgh on 6 May 1953. As children of the 1950s, both were brought up not only in the welfare state created by the 1945 Labour government but also in the increased affluence associated with Macmillan and Butler. Brown and Blair shared a middle-class upbringing. Gordon's father, Dr John Brown, was a highly respected minister in the Church of Scotland, while Tony's father was a lecturer in law who was also a barrister.

However, Tony Blair's background was different from that of Gordon Brown, Whereas Brown was very much a Scot, rooted in the Scottish Church, education and later in Scottish politics – especially the Labour Party and its history – Blair's upbringing was far more rootless and diverse. As he told the *Observer* in 1994, 'I never felt myself anchored in a parliamentary setting or class.'[3]

In part, this was because of the unconventional background of his father, Leo Blair. Leo, who was the illegitimate child of two English actors, Charles Parsons (whose stage name was Jimmy Lynton) and Celia Ridgway, was fostered out to the Blairs – Glasgow shipyard rigger James and his Communist wife Mary. Leo grew up on Clydeside as a young Communist. During the war, he served his country in the Royal Signals and by the time he was demobilised he described himself as a Conservative, attributing his conversion to the 'great change from living in a tenement to life in the Officers' mess'.[4] After studying for a law degree at Edinburgh University, Leo took up a lectureship in administrative law at the University of Adelaide in Australia, returning home with his family (including Tony) to Durham University, where he had been appointed lecturer in law. He was highly ambitious, reading for the law as well as becoming chairman of the local Conservative Association. He drove himself to the limit, admitting that his ambition was 'boundless – I wanted to be Prime Minister'.[5]

It was on 4 July 1964 that Tony's mother, Hazel, broke the news to him that his father had had a severe stroke during the night. According to Tony, the day of his father's stroke was when his childhood ended. Yet, though his father's illness was clearly a key event in his life, it was perhaps an exaggeration to say that Tony Blair's political ambition began at the age of 11, when his father Leo's ended.[6] Later developments, particularly his time at Oxford and his marriage to Cherie, were more important.

In 1966, Tony Blair joined his elder brother Bill at Fettes, a public school in Edinburgh. Tony did not enjoy Fettes. After a promising beginning (including winning an exhibition), at the start of his second year he tried to run away from school. Part of the problem was his dislike of boarding school but, as he became a rebellious adolescent, it was also a rejection of the conservative Fettes ethos – the petty rules, the fagging and the beatings. Tony's school career was saved from complete disaster by Eric Anderson, a young master who returned to Fettes after a spell at Gordonstoun to set up a new house, which was to be run without beating or fagging and which Blair immediately volunteered to join. Anderson intelligently succeeded in channelling some of Blair's energies into acting. Tony's greatest triumph was playing the part of Captain Stanhope in R.C. Sheriff's *Journey's End.*

Unfortunately, in Blair's last year, Anderson left to become headmaster of Abingdon School. His successor as housemaster was far less sympathetic to Tony and, instead of making him a prefect, beat Blair and two friends for 'persistent defiance'. Only the intervention of Lord Mackenzie-Stuart, Scottish law lord and school governor, prevented him from being expelled. If, for Tony, Fettes was largely a negative experience, he also took a few positives from the school. The first was discovering that, through acting, he could hold the attention of an audience. The second was learning to think and speak for himself. The third was getting good enough A-level grades to be accepted for St John's College, Oxford.

On the face of it, the years between leaving Fettes and coming down from Oxford (from July 1971 to June 1975) seemed to be ones in which nothing much happened in Blair's life. In his 'gap' year, he tried to launch a career as a rock band promoter. At Oxford, he got a good second in law (though afterwards he wished he had read history) and, in his third year, became the lead singer in a rock group of former public school boys called Ugly Rumours. The group did not last long, playing only half a dozen gigs in its brief career, but Tony the showman was born. A contemporary recalled that he had 'an aura about him even then; people noticed him; he stood out [… he] was already deploying the sort of trendiness and charm – which have been in evidence ever since.'[7]

More significant were the beliefs and values that he acquired while he was at Oxford. As often happens with students, a group of friends, including Tony, used to meet in college to discuss ideas. The most influential figure was Peter Thomson, a priest in the Anglican Church of Australia. Thomson introduced Blair to the ideas of a Scottish philosopher, John Macmurray, who argued that individuals can only be understood in terms of their relationship to others. Tony was very excited by Macmurray's thinking because it brought together the Christian concept of duty with the values of left-of-centre politics and thus provided him with a working set of beliefs both to underpin his life and to give a rationale for social action.

Charles Falconer, an acquaintance from Scotland who became a close friend and flatmate of Blair's after he came to London and later one of his Cabinet ministers, described Tony's intellectual progress as follows: 'During Oxford and immediately after he became utterly immersed in a sort of Christian spiritual approach for the solutions of social problems [...] He concluded the only way forward was by political action within the confines of conventional politics.'[8] At the end of his second year, Blair was confirmed in the Church of England at the Chapel of St John's College and, after coming down from Oxford, he not only started reading for the bar but joined the Labour Party.

Gordon Brown's path into the Labour Party was more orthodox. Gordon's early life was shaped by the influence of his father, John Brown, and his father's calling as a Church of Scotland minister. According to Brown, his father made a great impression on him: 'First, for speaking without notes in front of so many people in that vast church [St Brycedale's, Kirkcaldy ...] But mostly, I have learned a great deal from what my father managed to do for other people. He taught me to treat everyone equally.'[9]

In Scotland, especially for a son of the manse, education was paramount. Gordon was an exceptionally precocious pupil, being rapidly promoted up his primary school and going at the age of 10 to Kirkcaldy School, when he was put in the so-called 'E' stream, an experimental scheme of fast-track development. At 14, he passed eight O levels, at 15 he got five straight As in his Highers (the Scottish equivalent of A levels) and at 16 he passed the Edinburgh University entrance exam, being placed first in history in the bursary competition. As a teenager, Gordon was also a natural leader, excelling at games and setting the pace socially. As one of his classmates remembered, 'Gordon was always the quickest to come out with a funny line and would soon have the rest of us doubled over in laughter.'[10]

It was during a rugby match (between the Kirkcaldy School XV and the Old Boys) that Brown received a kick in the head that led to him becoming blind in one eye. After ignoring the injury for some months, he had a lengthy operation at Edinburgh Royal Infirmary to reattach a detached retina, but it came too late to save the sight of the left eye and, over the next 18 months, he had to have two further operations to save his right eye. He was forced to miss the whole of his first university term and was forbidden to read. A less ambitious person might have allowed the accident to affect the course of his life, but Gordon became more and not less determined. He was awarded a general arts degree at the age of 19 and, in 1972, aged 21, he graduated with first-class honours in history with, according to one of his tutors, the best collection of papers the department had ever seen.[11]

At Edinburgh University, he also began his ascent to political stardom by becoming a celebrated long-haired student activist at a time when student unrest was common across Europe. In his second year, he became editor of the student magazine, *The Student*, masterminding a scoop which revealed that, despite a denial by the principal, the university was investing in South African companies with links with apartheid. His second triumph was being elected university rector. In contrast to his predecessors (mostly celebrity figures from the media), Brown took the rectorship seriously, pursuing student issues and trying to open up the university to the wider community. A dispute about the rector's relationship with the university court, including the right to chair the court's meeting, was settled in Brown's favour.

Although his father was not a member of the Labour Party, it was almost inevitable that Gordon should join the party. From an early age, Gordon and his elder brother were encouraged to take an interest in politics. At university, Brown joined the Labour Party and was elected chairman of the Labour Club. At the 1970 general election and twice in 1974, Gordon and his friends helped Robin Cook (later foreign secretary) in his bid to be elected MP for Edinburgh North, an ambition which he achieved in February 1974.

Brown had his own ambitions and, over the next decade, concentrated on developing his career. In Scotland, the main issue was devolution and, outside Parliament, Gordon became its leading advocate. In 1976, he was elected to the executive of the Scottish Labour Party and two years later he was chosen to chair its Devolution Committee, working closely with his fellow Scot, John Smith, the minister responsible for the legislation. Already, he was something of an obsessive, committed above all to Labour politics and Scottish devolution. The journalist Neal Ascherson called him 'the outstanding Scot of his generation'.[12]

At the 1979 election Brown stood as the Labour candidate for Edinburgh South, a Tory-held marginal, but was defeated by 2,460 votes and had to wait four more years to become an MP. For employment, he turned to media, joining Scottish Television as a programme producer. It was an appropriate training for a future top politician. Arguably, it was also a good time to be out of Parliament, as the Labour Party descended into civil war. On the Scottish Labour Party executive, Brown spoke up for the Foot–Healey leadership, emerging as a pragmatic loyalist with contacts across the Scottish Labour Party. Brought up by his father as an egalitarian, he was in politics not to be a romantic rebel (like his hero James Maxton, about whom he wrote a biography), but, by winning power both for himself and his party, to make a real difference.

His chance came at the eleventh hour when, on 16 May 1983, with the support of the Transport and General Workers' Union, he won the Labour nomination for the newly created 'safe' seat of Dunfermline in the heart of the former Fife coalfields, near his hometown of Kirkcaldy. On 9 June, amid the crushing defeat of Michael Foot's Labour Party by Margaret Thatcher, Brown romped home with 51.5 per cent of the vote.

With a rare combination of luck, skill and charm, Tony Blair, a newcomer to Labour politics, also made it to Westminster at the same time as Gordon Brown. After he came down from Oxford, Blair's first priority had been to advance as a barrister. Through a chance meeting at a party, he got an introduction to Alexander 'Derry' Irvine, a brilliant barrister at a well-known chambers. Irvine was bowled over by Tony's enthusiasm and took him on as a pupil.

Irvine, who had himself stood for Parliament in 1970 as a Labour candidate and was a close friend of John Smith, a former Cabinet minister and a rising figure in the party, supported Blair in his ambition to try for Parliament. For a prospective middle-class politician with Blair's outlook, it was a difficult time to be looking for a Labour seat, as the constituencies were increasingly dominated by the left-wing ideas of Tony Benn and his adherents. However, in spring 1982, encouraged by Derry Irvine, John Smith and Tom Pendry (Labour MP and friend of the father of Blair's lawyer wife, Cherie), Blair put his name forward to be the Labour candidate for the Beaconsfield by-election and won the nomination. Although Tony lost his deposit in this safe Tory seat, he made a highly favourable impression on the party's leading politicians and convinced both them and himself that his future lay at Westminster. But the question of how to get there remained.

Then, a year later, when the 1983 general election campaign had already begun, and against all the odds, Blair was chosen for the newly created 'safe' seat of Sedgefield in County Durham. Although Tony had gained the support of the Transport and General Workers' Union, there were few union delegates to the constituency party. So, if Blair was to gain the Sedgefield nomination, he had to win the backing of the ordinary branch members. In a whirlwind campaign and helped by five local activists, he proceeded to win their support. At the selection conference, he spoke with fire and vigour and managed to win over a number of delegates initially committed to other candidates, triumphing on the fifth ballot. At the June general election, he was elected to Parliament with a majority of 8,281, a remarkable achievement for such an outsider.

It was a defeated and depressed Parliamentary Labour Party which assembled at Westminster after Thatcher's landslide victory. The two new MPs, Brown and Blair, were almost immediately involved in a Labour leadership election. Brown confirmed his already considerable reputation and his left-of-centre credentials by being invited to join the campaign committee of Neil Kinnock, the eloquent left-wing shadow education secretary from Wales. Blair, like an undergraduate in freshers' week, went to all the leadership candidates' campaign meetings – Kinnock, Roy Hattersley, Peter Shore and Eric Heffer. In the end, backing the winner, he voted for Kinnock as leader and for Hattersley as deputy leader – the so-called 'dream' ticket which won over two-thirds of Labour's electoral college at the 1983 Brighton party conference and was to guide the affairs of the Labour Party over the next two years.

The two new boys, Brown and Blair, quickly formed a close friendship, sharing a small windowless room off the main committee corridor of the Commons – little more than a cupboard with two desks. At this stage, Brown was very much the senior partner. As chairman of the Scottish Labour Party, he was already a leading figure in Scotland. He was the author and editor of several published books. And, as a former television reporter and editor, he knew his way round the media. According to Charles Falconer, Blair was 'mammothly dazzled by Brown's power. I don't think he ever thought at that stage that he would be leader of the party.'[13]

But if Brown was the dominant figure in the relationship, it was a genuine friendship. Gordon may have had the knowledge, the experience and the historical perspective, but Tony brought something to the partnership as well. He knew influential people in London outside politics whom Brown had never met. He also had charm and freshness. At Westminster, at an exceptional low point for Labour, Brown and Blair began to be talked about.

Both young men made accomplished maiden speeches, Brown quoting unpublished statistics which showed, he claimed, the real extent of unemployment and poverty in his constituency; Blair, also focusing on unemployment, concluded with a striking peroration in which he discussed his political beliefs. There was the emphasis on values, especially cooperation and fellowship, which he had learnt at St John's College, Oxford, as well as perhaps a hint in his last sentence of the 'one nation, big tent' thinking which was to become such a feature of New Labour under Blair.

John Smith, in his role as shadow employment secretary, chose the two new MPs to serve on a Commons Standing Committee set up to examine the Conservative government's latest trade union bill. The junior member of the government's frontbench team, Alan Clark, better diarist than minister, wrote: 'Labour has a very tough team. Little John Smith, rotund, bespectacled Edinburgh lawyer [...] And two bright boys called Brown and Blair.'[14] It was only a matter of time before the two 'bright boys' were promoted to the opposition front bench. In November 1984, Blair was the first to be appointed, becoming a shadow Treasury spokesman under Roy Hattersley (who ironically later became one of the most outspoken critics of Blair as leader of the party). Brown, who at the time of Blair's promotion had turned down a position as a Scottish spokesman, was appointed to the front bench a year later, working on regional policy under Smith, who had become shadow secretary of state for trade and industry. Brown proved himself an energetic campaigner and, for the first time, was able to raise his profile outside Scotland.

At the 1987 election, thanks to the leader Neil Kinnock and the new director of communications, Peter Mandelson, Labour fought a glitzy campaign. But its unilateralist defence policy cost the party over a million votes, while the Tories outscored Labour on the economy by a margin of two to one. The Tories, with 42.3 per cent of the vote, won a majority of 101 seats. As relatively junior spokesmen, Brown and Blair played only minor parts in the campaign. However, Labour's 1987 defeat opened up the road to the top for these two able and ambitious men, bearing out the dictum that it is often better to enter Parliament at the nadir of one's party's fortunes than as part of a triumphant landslide.[15]

Following the 1987 election defeat, Brown and Blair succeeded in getting on the soft-left 'Tribune slate' of recommended candidates for the Shadow Cabinet elections, which gave them a better chance of success. It was Brown who was elected to the Shadow Cabinet at his first attempt, though Blair followed a year later. The record of the two young men as opposition spokesmen proved to be outstanding. Brown, who was appointed shadow chief secretary, had to step in when his boss, John

Smith, the shadow chancellor who had succeeded Roy Hattersley after the election, suffered a serious heart attack. In reply to Nigel Lawson's autumn statement that year, Brown had a genuine parliamentary triumph, so much so that he won first place in the 1988 Shadow Cabinet elections. In 1988–9, Kinnock appointed Blair shadow energy secretary to lead the opposition to electricity privatisation. He was so successful in this role that in 1989 he was promoted to shadow employment secretary.

It was Blair's performance as shadow employment secretary that provided the real breakthrough in his rise to the top. A month after his appointment, he spoke in favour of the latest draft of the European Social Charter which gave positive rights to employees, including the right to join a union. However, as a Tory MP showed, there was a conflict between Labour's support for the Social Charter and the unions' backing for the closed shop – the arrangement whereby all employees in a plant or a firm were forced to join a union. Working in close cooperation with Peter Mandelson, Blair informed top trade union leaders that he proposed to abandon Labour's traditional support for the closed shop. So, when Norman Fowler, the Conservative employment secretary, brought forward a bill to abolish the closed shop, he found that his shadow's boldness had enabled Labour to escape from the dilemma on which he had hoped to impale it.

Labour went into the 1992 election thinking it had at least a chance of winning. But, despite Kinnock's best efforts to change the party, it still lost, finishing 7 percentage points behind the Tories, with the results in the southern part of the country being especially disheartening.[16] On the morning after Labour's election defeat, Blair, who, like Brown, had expected Labour to lose, went on television to say that the party had failed to win not because it had changed too much but because it had not changed enough. His initiative, coming at a moment when most of Labour's leaders were still in a state of shock, showed courage and a sense of timing – crucial attributes in a potential leader.

Kinnock's resignation, which quickly followed Labour's election defeat, opened up fresh political opportunities for Brown and Blair. Over the weekend after the election, the two modernisers held a series of meetings to decide on their tactics for the Labour leadership election. It was later claimed by one of his allies that Blair felt that Brown had bottled out of entering the leadership contest.[17] In fact it was entirely understandable that, in the circumstances of 1992, Brown should have decided not to challenge his friend and mentor John Smith for the leadership, who was, in any case, odds-on favourite.

The real issue was the deputy leadership and whether Blair should run for it. Smith had already ruled Brown out as his deputy on the grounds that two Scots in leadership positions would be unacceptable to voters. Blair, with his youthful charisma and southern middle-class connections, would have added a crucial balance to the Smith leadership.[18] But Smith had already decided to back Margaret Beckett, who was not only a woman but represented a Midlands seat and was supported by the biggest union, the TGWU. In these circumstances the modernisers were undecided about whether Blair should stand: Brown was unenthusiastic about a Blair candidature, possibly fearing that Blair might get ahead of him in the race for the succession to John Smith. In the end, Blair deferred to Brown, as Brown deferred to Smith. However, Blair's frustrating experience in the days after the 1992 defeat had the effect of making him all the more determined to put himself forward if and when the opportunity occurred in the future, whatever his friend Gordon Brown might say. In this sense, what happened in 1992 was crucial to Blair's rise to the leadership.

In his 22 months as leader, John Smith established his authority over his party, command over the Commons and the respect and trust of the British voters. By the time of his death, his reassuring and self-confident performance had put Labour on the road to victory.

Yet for the modernisers, Smith's brief reign as leader was a frustrating period. Smith was cautious about party modernisation because, for understandable tactical reasons, he wanted the media to concentrate on the government's difficulties, not on Labour's. Brown and Blair, joined by Mandelson – who was now MP for Hartlepool – may have been critical of their leader's approach, but they underestimated his success in getting his proposals for one member, one vote for the selection of parliamentary candidates and the election of the leader through the 1993 party conference. The acceptance of the principle of one member, one vote took power away from trade union leaders and, in doing so, helped Blair win the leadership in 1994.

It was during John Smith's period as leader that Tony Blair emerged as the favourite for succession. Smith had recognised Gordon Brown's outstanding ability and pre-eminence in the party by making him shadow chancellor. Brown was determined to use his new post to establish Labour as a party that voters could trust on tax and spending. That meant ditching the economic policy on which Labour had fought the 1992 election and enforcing a strict control over spending commitments on the Shadow Cabinet. Some of his closest friends argued that his tough attitude, which he had adopted for the sake of the party, lost him the leadership. Yet, if he had taken a softer line, he would have been rightly criticised for not doing his job properly. A more valid criticism was that, during this period, his television appearances became somewhat monotonous and predictable. However, the main reason that Brown did not become leader in 1994 was not so much because of the inadequacy of his own television performances but because of the flair and presentational brilliance of his friend and close colleague, Tony Blair.

Blair had been appointed shadow home secretary in place of Roy Hattersley, who had resigned with Neil Kinnock. Since the liberalising reforms of Roy Jenkins in the 1960s, Conservative critics had tried to portray the Labour Party as 'soft on crime'. By skilful positioning, Blair sought to combine a liberal attitude on issues such as abortion, gay rights, racial equality and the death penalty with a tough approach to crime and family responsibility. In a Radio 4 interview on 10 January 1993, Blair said, 'I think it's important that we are tough on crime and tough on the causes of crime too', a formula suggested to him by Brown. Tony's stance on crime and the fresh language in which it was expressed caught the attention of the media across the political spectrum. At the 1993 party conference, he proclaimed his success by saying, 'We are the party of law and order.' Philip Stephens of the *Financial Times* noted that political commentators increasingly referred to Blair as the party's foremost moderniser and the next Labour leader.

When John Smith tragically died of a massive heart attack on the morning of 12 May 1994, it immediately became clear that Blair was the hot favourite to succeed him. Blair, on his return from a campaign trip to Scotland, was met at Heathrow by his wife, Cherie, who had been very disappointed that her husband had not run in 1992 and was determined that he should run this time. Blair did not need convincing. The only question was whether Brown would also decide to put his hat in the ring.

At their first meeting, which took place in the home of Blair's brother Bill, Brown made it clear that he had every intention of standing. He also reminded Blair that they had an informal pact not to run against each other and that, when they had last discussed the matter in 1992, they had agreed that Brown, as the senior partner, had first claim. Blair replied that things had moved on since then and that he, Blair, was now the clear favourite. Over the next 19 days, there were further meetings and frequent telephone conversations between the two to try and resolve the issue.

The reality was that all the pressure was on Brown. He might have had some support from the trade unions and possibly in the constituency section of the electoral college. But the media and public opinion polls carried the powerful (but, for Brown, unpalatable) message that Blair was far more likely to win the election for Labour. As the opinion polls showed, Blair had the 'modernising vote' virtually sewn up. If Brown was going to mount a challenge, then it would have to be as a more traditionalist candidate. But on 28 May, Margaret Beckett hinted that she was preparing to run. It was likely that she would get the nomination of the big unions such as the TGWU and the GMB, making it virtually impossible for Brown to assemble a winning coalition. Though his campaign team were still urging him to stand, Brown came reluctantly to the conclusion that the best course was to secure a deal from Blair.

Allegedly, the deal was that Brown would allow Blair a clear run at the leadership, in return for which Brown would get what amounted to a 'super chancellorship' in government and the succession to the leadership when Blair stood down. These terms were popularly believed to have been agreed over a meal at the then-fashionable Granita restaurant (now defunct) in Islington, though, as the political biographer John Campbell put it, 'Like an international summit meeting, the Granita dinner was only the formalisation of an agreement tortuously negotiated over the previous days.'[19]

Nobody knows exactly what was agreed at the Granita restaurant as there were no minutes taken. On the face of it, a candidate who is withdrawing from a contest has few cards in their hands. However, Blair was desperately anxious to have Brown on his side. Both Blair and Mandelson, who was now advising Blair, feared that, if slighted, Brown would be a dangerous enemy. They also greatly respected Gordon's ability. In Blair's case, there was an element of guilt too; though it was now no longer operative because things had moved on, there *had* been a pact in 1992 by which Blair had agreed to let Brown have first shot at the leadership. For all these reasons, Blair was prepared to offer Brown generous terms.

The Granita agreement gave Brown an unprecedented role in government if Labour won the general election. As Mandelson foresaw, it amounted almost to a 'dual premiership', giving Brown control over much of domestic policy. In opposition, such a deal may not have seemed so important. In government, Blair would come to regret the extent of the concessions which he had made to Brown, whether out of respect, fear or guilt, or a mixture of all three.

There was a future issue which was also discussed – and that was the question of the succession. The Brown camp later claimed it was Blair who raised the issue, promising to stand down as leader and back Brown after 10 years. The supporters of Blair denied that he made any such precise commitment. Indeed, it is not a commitment that is in the power of anyone, not even a prime minister, to make. Tony, who instinctively understood that Brown needed to be given hope, might well have said, 'Look, Gordon, I am not going to be leader for ever – and, when I stand down, I will back you to succeed me.' In his February 2010 television interview with Piers Morgan, Brown seemed to confirm this version.

However, in practice, he behaved as though he expected Blair to step down sometime during his second term.

Accepting the predominant position of Blair was a bitter blow for Brown, who continued to believe that he was better qualified to be prime minister. There is a persuasive argument that it would have been better for all concerned if Brown had stood for the leadership as it would have produced a definite result – almost certainly a decisive Blair victory over Brown – and therefore put Blair in a stronger position when he became prime minister.

But, in the circumstances of the 1994 leadership election, Blair felt that the danger of an open conflict between the two modernising standard-bearers would weaken the modernising cause and open up the possibility, however remote, that it would let in a more traditional candidate, such as Margaret Beckett or John Prescott.

The Granita deal had the merit of ensuring Blair a clear run at the leadership, while at the same time giving Brown an exceptional role both in opposition and government, as well as hope for the succession. So, for some years, the bargain, by providing a basis for the continuing partnership between Blair and Brown, worked to the benefit not only of the two men but also of the Labour Party in opposition and in government. But the fact that the partnership was now governed more by mutual self-interest than by their former close friendship and that, from the outset, there were differences in the two men's interpretation of the Granita deal, meant that, in the longer term, the relationship between Blair and Brown became more unstable and open to challenge.

Blair won an overwhelming victory in all sections of the electoral college, including the unions. His own flair and ambition, the triumph of one member, one vote, and above all Labour's desperation for power brought Blair to the leadership. The new Labour leader inherited a strong legacy from John Smith. Far more than in 1992, the party was ready for Tony Blair and Gordon Brown. They were also fortunate to be facing a Tory party still demoralised by 'Black Wednesday', when sterling was driven out of the European Exchange Rate Mechanism, deeply divided by Europe and increasingly out of touch with the electorate. However, Blair was convinced that, if Labour was to establish political dominance stretching beyond just one election, then, like Margaret Thatcher in the 1980s, it would have to win the battle of ideas.

In 1997, at the start of the election campaign, he wrote a short memorandum, outlining the main themes which he later incorporated into his campaign manifesto. He stressed that he joined Labour not because of background but through beliefs and that values were at the heart of his politics. Drawing on what he had learnt at Oxford, he argued that individuals prospered best within a strong and cohesive society 'where opportunity and obligation go hand in hand'.[20] Although Blair saw the need for new policy directions, especially on the economy, welfare, the constitution and Europe, his major contribution – and his special skill – was in providing a new framework or narrative within which he could reinvigorate and reposition his party.

In the run-up to the 1994 party conference, Blair considered the case for a revision of Clause IV of the party constitution as a symbol of change.[21] The clause, which had been written by Sidney Webb over 70 years before, committing the party 'to secure for the workers by hand or by brain the full fruits of their industry [...] upon the basis of common ownership of the means of production, distribution and exchange' was clearly out of date. But Blair's immediate predecessors as leaders, Smith and Kinnock, did not believe that a revision was worth the trouble that it could create. Screwing up his courage, Blair now decided that revising Clause IV would provide the ideal opportunity to demonstrate that, under his leadership, Labour really had changed.

In his leader's speech to the Labour conference, in which he called for a 'new politics – without dogma and without swapping our prejudices for theirs', Blair concluded by calling for a clear and up-to-date statement of the party's aims and objectives to be debated by the party and, if agreed, to become part of the constitution. The speech was given a standing ovation. George Robertson, later to be general secretary of NATO, described what happened next: 'As the applause died, you could hear the sound of pennies dropping all around the hall.'[22] Two days later, a resolution reaffirming Clause IV was narrowly carried – a reminder that the new Labour leader had a fight on his hands.

Blair, however, took personal charge of a campaign to persuade party members to back revision. Visiting 22 towns and cities, he held a series of meetings at which the party saw the Labour leader at his most persuasive. On 29 April 1995, a new clause was approved by 65 per cent of the vote. Critics argued the clause, which was expressed primarily in terms of values, was so general that it could be supported by a wide swathe of progressive opinion, but that was precisely the point. Blair was determined that the party should be in a position to attract new support, well beyond its core vote. The adoption of a revised Clause IV, with its 'one-nation' message was a key turning point for New Labour. Encouraged by Mandelson, Blair now called the party New Labour.

From the revision of Clause IV until the general election, Blair, with a characteristic mixture of radicalism and caution, prepared the party for the coming contest. Roy Jenkins characterised Blair's behaviour thus: 'Tony is like a man who is carrying a precious vase across a crowded and slippery ballroom. He is desperate above all that the vase should not fall and be smashed.'[23]

Brown had been badly bruised by missing out on the leadership. Robert Peston, who wrote a sympathetic account of Brown's chancellorship and was given full access to Brown and his entourage, said that, after 1994, a change came over his personality. According to Peston, he became more sombre, less relaxed and more introspective. Blair found Brown difficult to manage, especially as the Shadow Chancellor had fallen out with Mandelson over who should do what in the coming election campaign.

However, the partnership between the two men survived. Even if there was no longer the trust (at least on Brown's side), they still needed each other. If Brown did not play a prominent part in the campaign to change Clause IV, he was always on hand to give advice on tactics. Blair required Brown's economic advice, while Brown needed Blair's support in the Shadow Cabinet. Above all, they both needed an election victory.

The two were bound together by hoops of steel – and, for many years, would continue to be so.

As the election drew nearer, Blair's campaign team summed up New Labour's approach: 'reassure (the party really had changed), remind (about the Tory record) and reward (with what Labour could offer)'.[24] As for what New Labour could offer, Blair and Brown, afraid of being accused by the Tories of excessive spending and of raising taxes, were extremely cautious. They came up with the idea of a pledge card, giving specific and achievable commitments – smaller classes for five-, six- and seven-year-olds, paid for by abolishing the assisted-places scheme; fast-track punishment for persistent young offenders; cutting NHS waiting lists by an extra 100,000 patients by releasing £100 million saved from NHS red tape; getting 250,000 under-25-year-olds into work, using money from a windfall levy on the privatised utilities; tough rules for government spending and borrowing; low inflation and interest rates. For the media and politicians, these pledges may have seemed small beer but for voters they were persuasive because they connected to people's lives, were relatively small and were costed. And these symbolic pledges were linked to a popular new Labour leader, whose photograph was on the other side of the pledge card.

Blair took a number of other initiatives to strengthen Labour's electoral chances. He opened contacts with the Liberal Democrats about cooperation or even coalition, to provide a way into government if Labour failed to win an overall majority. He formed an especially warm relationship with Roy Jenkins. Jenkins told the Liberal leader, Paddy Ashdown, 'I think Tony treats me as a sort of father-figure in politics. He comes to me a lot for advice, particularly about how to form a government.'[25] Blair put out feelers to business; while the trade unions were firmly told they should expect 'fairness not favours', the Labour leader sought the backing of well-known business figures such as Alan Sugar and Richard Branson. However, the most blatant example of 'supping with the devil' was Blair's wooing of the media magnate Rupert Murdoch, including flying to Australia to address the News Corp 'Leadership Conference'. Blair was rewarded when the *Sun*, which had attacked Kinnock in 1992, came out for Blair.

Brown made his own contribution to Labour's victory. Meeting with his special group of advisers (including Ed Balls) at the well-appointed London flat of the millionaire Labour MP Geoffrey Robinson, Brown carefully prepared Labour's economic approach. In a much-publicised speech, he made it clear that an incoming Blair government would neither increase the basic rate of income tax nor put up the top rate. In a move which would cause trouble in the future, he also pledged not to spend more than the Tory chancellor, Kenneth Clarke, had already set aside for the first two years of the next government. Even the *Daily Mail* was impressed by the prudence of the Shadow Chancellor: 'What can no longer be denied is that, on the Tories' favourite battleground of tax, he is proving an ever more formidable adversary.'[26] Slowly but surely, Brown was building Labour's reputation for economic competence and fiscal credibility.

In March 1997, the Conservative prime minister, John Major, after putting off polling day as long as possible, finally called an election for 1 May. He gambled on a long six-week campaign in which the Conservatives would have time to put Blair and Brown under pressure. In the event, it was Tory weaknesses on sleaze and Europe which were exposed.

In New Labour, the Tories faced a formidable fighting force. Tony Blair, the popular young leader, scarcely put a foot wrong throughout the campaign. Gordon Brown, working from the Millbank media centre, chaired both the strategy meetings and morning press conferences very effectively. Peter Mandelson ran the highly professional team at Millbank, with its rebuttal unit, key seats section and a video recording centre. The modernisers were able to present the party as having learnt from its past mistakes and now capable of providing a credible alternative government.

As election day approached, Labour began to scent victory, though, remembering 1992, the party refrained from triumphalism. At 10 p.m. on election day the exit polls predicted a massive swing to Labour. The results confirmed these polls. By 3.10 a.m. on 2 May, Labour had won an overall majority which proved to be a landslide of 178 seats – some gained in surprising places such as Hastings, Hove and Wimbledon.

Mandelson, commenting on Labour's victory, said, 'There was no reason left not to trust Labour [...] we had removed the target. Without New Labour, the Conservatives could have won again.'[27] This was a pardonable exaggeration: John Smith would certainly have beaten the Tories. But, by running as 'the safe alternative', New Labour probably made the victory more decisive. The question now was what the modernisers would do with the power they had won.

Blair's new team was remarkable for its inexperience. None of the top ministers had held office; arguably, it was the most inexperienced administration since the first Labour government in 1924. From the outset, it was clear that the dominant personalities in the Cabinet were Blair and Brown. In opposition, they had been used to running things together. In government, they saw no reason to change their approach. As the respected commentator Peter Riddell (later director of the Institute of Government) remarked: 'Their style was bilateral not collective [...] Their normal method of operation was by pre-emption, selective briefing and bouncing colleagues.'[28] Initially at least, Cabinets were no more than reporting sessions. The real decisions were taken by Blair and Brown, though usually in consultation with the relevant departmental minister.

In the first term (and for at least some of the second term) the partnership between Blair and Brown worked well. As Mandelson had warned might happen, it amounted almost to a 'dual premiership', with two centres of power. But the combination was remarkably effective:

The pulse that beats between Blair and Brown is their government's supply of nervous energy [... It] was their bonded, concentrated power at the centre of their government that allowed an administration of more or less completely inexperienced ministers to manage their first term in a way that produced the second big majority.[29]

The government's first decision, announced on 6 May 1997, a few days after the election, and arguably the most important economic one taken in Labour's first term, was the transfer of operational control over interest rates from the Treasury to the Bank of England. This bold move, which has stood the test of time, created a more predictable and transparent framework and helped create the economic and monetary stability which characterised most of Labour's period in power and was a major factor in its electoral success.

There were two notable features about the decision on bank independence. First, this was a policy devised by Brown and his advisers before the 1997 election. Brown had consulted Blair, who had agreed in principle but, in line with his understanding with his colleague, was content to leave the implementation to Brown. Second, the decision was taken by Brown and Blair alone. It had not been openly endorsed in Labour's election manifesto, which said only, 'we will reform the Bank of England to ensure that decision-making on monetary policy is more effective, open and accountable and free from short-term financial manipulation.' It was not even discussed in Cabinet.

On entering 10 Downing Street on the day after the 1997 election, Tony Blair had said, 'We have been elected as New Labour and we will govern as New Labour.' Speaking in the debate on the Queen's Speech of the new parliament, the new Prime Minister gave a minimalist explanation of his government's intentions. 'The British people do not have false expectations. They simply want a government with clear leadership.'[30] After so long out of power, the modernisers wanted to show that, above all, Labour was capable of providing competent government. They were also determined to win a second term. Hence their stress on economic stability, improved public services, especially education and health, and tackling crime and anti-social behaviour. And hence Blair's emphasis on the 'one nation, big tent' approach.

Tony Blair proved himself to be a dynamic prime minister. Although he had played down talk of a Roosevelt-style 'first hundred days', there was a feeling of excitement, even euphoria, at the change of government, especially one elected with such a huge majority. Blair moved quickly. On 16 May, he flew to Northern Ireland to show his commitment to the peace talks (between Sinn Féin and the Ulster Unionists) which had stalled in the final months of the Major government. In October, Blair met Gerry Adams, leader of Sinn Féin, the first time a British prime minister had met the Sinn Féin leader. He also developed close relations with David Trimble, the Ulster Unionist leader. Then, on 7 April 1998, Blair took a calculated gamble and flew to Belfast to join the negotiations, saying that he felt 'the hand of history' on his shoulder.

There followed days and nights of intense negotiations, in which Blair and the Irish prime minister, Bertie Ahern, were fully involved, with US President Bill Clinton available at the end of a telephone. After a last-minute wobble by the Ulster Unionists, which Blair settled by a personal letter of assurance, an agreement (which included a power-sharing executive, a Northern Ireland Assembly, a North–South ministerial council and a British–Irish council) was finally signed. It was then endorsed in a Northern Ireland referendum, while in the south, an overwhelming majority voted to renounce the Republic's claim to sovereignty. Although there was a long way to go before peace would be fully secured and democratic institutions in Northern Ireland fully assured, the Good Friday Agreement was a genuinely historic achievement of which Blair and the New Labour government were entitled to feel proud.

The Labour election manifesto had contained a number of major commitments on constitutional matters, including a Scottish Parliament with tax-varying powers, a Welsh Assembly and a strategic authority for London. Blair was fortunate to inherit from John Smith a well-prepared 'home-rule' programme which, with the big Labour majority, could now be far more easily implemented. The Labour leader's sensible contribution was to insist on referendums in both Scotland and Wales (with separate questions in Scotland on the principle and on tax-varying powers) in order to prevent the devolution legislation being obstructed by a Tory-dominated House of Lords and to entrench the change.

The Scottish referendum, with Brown playing a leading role in the campaign, was won by large majorities. The 'yes' vote in Wales was also carried, though by the narrowest of margins (0.6 per cent), reflecting the greater divisions and doubts in that country. However, in Wales and in London (which voted in a referendum for a mayor and an assembly) Blair's sure touch deserted him. He tried mistakenly, and in the end unsuccessfully, to prevent the most popular figure in the principality, Rhodri Morgan, from becoming first secretary, while in London, both Blair and Brown were implacably opposed – because of his past record as a left-winger – to the candidature of Ken Livingstone for mayor. Livingstone then ran as an independent, comfortably winning the election.

One of the main priorities of the new government was to end Britain's isolation in Europe. Blair was arguably the most pro-European prime minister since Edward Heath. He had voted 'yes' in the 1975 EU referendum, he took his holidays in France and Italy and his command of French was good enough to speak French to MPs in the French National Assembly. His ambition, he said, was to reconcile the British to membership of the European Union and for the UK to play a cooperative part in its working.

In December 1998, with President Chirac, Blair launched a joint Anglo-French initiative in European defence. The UK also helped the Lisbon agenda of economic reform to make the EU more flexible and innovative. However, the decision not to join the single currency (which was effectively ruled out by Brown's five economic tests in October 1997) inevitably hampered Labour's efforts to take a leading part in the EU. Blair and an unenthusiastic Brown joined the two Tory 'big beasts', Michael Heseltine and Ken Clarke, and the Liberal leader, Charles Kennedy, at the launch of 'Britain in Europe', a cross-party organisation set up to explain the case for British membership. But Blair and Brown were reluctant to do any serious campaigning, lest they aroused the hostility of the Murdoch press. In the end, despite Blair's constructive EU initiatives, he was not prepared to take any risks over Europe, in case it jeopardised Labour's prospects of winning a second term.

Blair was riding high. He had proved himself an impressive prime minister, with the ability – especially over Northern Ireland, intervention in the Kosovo crisis and his understanding of the national reaction to

Princess Diana's death – to rise to the occasion. Without developing any side or pomposity, he was rapidly acquiring real authority, able to dominate the political scene both at home and abroad.

As the economy increasingly flourished with low inflation and steady growth, Brown also grew in confidence and stature. Following on from the transfer of operational control over interest rates from the Treasury to the Bank of England, the Chancellor took a number of other bold initiatives. The centrepiece of his first budget was the windfall tax, levied in two tranches on the private utilities, which raised £5.2 billion, the majority of which was used to fund the Welfare to Work programme to reduce long-term and youth unemployment. In his second budget, Brown introduced the Working Families' Tax Credit (WFTC), the purpose of which was to guarantee a minimum income for working families with children and to tackle the unemployment and poverty traps facing low-paid families. This reform was underpinned by the introduction of a national minimum wage.

In July 1998, the Chancellor published a new three-year Comprehensive Spending Review (CSR) which had the merit of enabling departments to plan ahead. The CSR was accompanied by the adoption of two fiscal rules: first, over the so-called economic cycle, the government would only borrow to invest; and second, it would keep public debt at 'a stable and prudent level' – at around 40 per cent of GDP. The CSR continued the Chancellor's cautious fiscal approach, allowing current spending to rise by only 2.5 per cent a year in line with the Treasury's estimate of trend growth.

At the same time, the Chancellor announced what appeared to be large increases in spending on education and health. The Treasury Select Committee 'rumbled' Brown's wheeze, ticking him off for 'triple accounting' and recommending that, in future, totals should be expressed in terms of annual increases rather than a misleading cumulative total. The financial journalist Robert Peston commented: 'Brown and Balls were endeavouring to have their cake and eat it: they wanted to be generous in the eyes of the Labour Party and mean in the eyes of the City.'[31] It was a posture which proved impossible to maintain.

230

Throughout the first term, the relationship between Blair and Brown was manageable, though it had its ups and downs. One of his Cabinet colleagues described Blair's efforts to control his Chancellor who, despite his towering stature, was moody and insecure: 'He mediates, he negotiates, he diffuses, he cajoles, he rails, he shouts, he hugs, he flatters.'[32] The publication of a biography of Brown by Paul Routledge in January 1998, which revealed that Brown still appeared to believe that Blair had let him down over the 1994 leadership and (erroneously) that, if he, Brown, had run, he could have won, led to the two men's 'spin machines' briefing against each other. A 'senior source' inside Downing Street told Andrew Rawnsley of the *Observer* that it was time for Brown to get a grip on his 'psychological flaws'.[33]

Brown was understandably enraged. Blair was apologetic about the way the row had escalated but pointed out that Brown had brought it on himself by encouraging Routledge's book. Publicly, Blair praised his Chancellor: 'He is my Lloyd George. Gordon has the intellectual fire power of eighteen Ken Clarkes.'[34] He may have forgotten that it was Lloyd George who pushed Asquith, the prime minister, from office.

Another event which disturbed the Blair–Brown relationship was the resignation from the Cabinet (just before Christmas 1998) of Peter Mandelson, recently appointed secretary of state for industry, over his undeclared loan from Geoffrey Robinson, Brown's paymaster general. As the source of the information seemed to be someone in the Brown camp and as, once again, it was a Paul Routledge book, this time about Mandelson, which provided the vehicle for bringing the information into the public arena, it was not surprising that many saw this as Brown's revenge on Mandelson for taking Blair's side in 1994. Geoffrey Robinson was forced to resign at the same time, while Charlie Whelan, Brown's media spokesman, resigned a few days later. At the end of January 1999, I had a meeting with Gordon Brown at which I pointed out that the events surrounding Mandelson's resignation were damaging to the Chancellor. 'It was damaging to us all,' Brown replied. My diary comment was as follows, 'Hopefully he may have decided to stop being manipulative and rely on the fact that he is an excellent Chancellor to speak for itself.'[35]

New Labour had fought the 1997 election as being the safe alternative to the unpopular Conservative Party. In 2001, it ran on its commitments on health and education expenditure. It was the crisis in the NHS in the winter of 1999–2000 that shaped the direction of the government over the second term and beyond.

When Alan Milburn, a northern colleague of Tony Blair, became health secretary in October 1999, he speedily came to the conclusion that the NHS needed a major investment of money as soon as possible. He persuaded the Prime Minister that they could not afford to wait until the next spending review in July 2000 but the Chancellor resisted on the grounds that, without a strategy for making sure that the money was efficiently spent, it would be wasted. But at the beginning of 2000, Brown's hand was forced by a national influenza outbreak, a succession of horror stories about overcrowded hospitals, cancelled operations, patients being shuttled about the country in search of beds and then by Blair's television interview with Sir David Frost on 16 January.

In his Frost interview, the Prime Minister discarded Brown's claim that the health service had had the biggest cash injection in history and accepted that the NHS would have to be given massive extra resources. His most striking commitment, not cleared with Brown, was to bring health service spending up to the European average over the next five years. The next day's press rightly reported this as a big new pledge, which threw the Chancellor into a fury. With some justice, he accused Blair of going beyond what they had agreed. 'You've stolen my fucking budget,' he shouted at the Prime Minister.[36]

However, in his budget speech two months later, the Chancellor announced to Labour cheers that, from 2000 until 2004, spending on the NHS would grow by 6.1 per cent a year in real inflation-adjusted terms. The year 2000 was a turning point for New Labour. Until then Brown and Blair had followed the Tory line on tax and spend. Now it was clear that the voters were demanding increased spending on public services, especially on health and education – and that the government would ignore this changed public mood at its peril.

*

Labour had been ahead of the opposition in the opinion polls every month and, in by-elections, it held every seat it defended. But the government experienced a difficult year in the year before the election. In September 2000, British road hauliers, supported by militant farmers, blockaded oil refineries and, after panic-buying by the public, the pumps ran dry. Following consultation with the oil companies, Blair went on television to announce that the situation would be back to normal 'within the next twenty-four hours'. But it was only after Blair threatened the oil companies with emergency powers and the Health Secretary went on television to say the blockade was putting people's lives at risk that it was called off. Labour's standing in the polls dropped and the Tories went briefly ahead. But at the 2000 Labour Party conference both Blair and Brown made excellent speeches reasserting the government's authority and, by the end of the year, the Conservatives were trailing by 20 points.

The second crisis, the outbreak of foot and mouth disease, influenced the date of the general election. At the end of March, Blair, focused on dealing with the outbreak, decided to postpone the election from 3 May to 7 June. He was confident about the outcome of the election. In Mandelson's absence – after resigning from office, he also resigned from his election post – Brown was in sole charge of the campaign. He took a cautious approach, focusing on the strength of the economy and investment in health and education. Blair fought a more lively campaign, setting out in key speeches the subjects on which he wished to concentrate, including education, reform of public services and Britain's role in Europe. The result of the election was a second 'historic' landslide with an overall Labour majority of 167 seats. Throughout the campaign, Labour maintained substantial poll leads on issues such as effective leadership, economic competence, party unity and a sense of direction. Labour also had large leads on matters which voters considered important, especially on health and education.

Despite the victory, Blair was disappointed by the turnout, which was only 59 per cent – down 12 per cent from 1997. The level of voting was especially low in the party's 'safe' working-class constituencies, an indication that New Labour had failed to get its message across to its 'core' supporters. Blair was also concerned about the deterioration of his relations with Brown. Yet, though the state of their relationship did not bode well for the future, it was the Blair–Brown partnership which had been mainly instrumental in achieving Labour's landslide. If Brown had managed the economy well, Blair's leadership and charisma had delivered the centre ground. The victory was a joint effort – the result of a partnership which they would find more and more difficult to sustain.

Looking back on the first term, the Prime Minister felt that he had wasted too much of it, partly because of the government's inexperience and partly because his main priority had been to win a second term. While relaxing in the garden of his constituency home on election day in 2001, he assured Alastair Campbell that 'it was all going to be different in the second term, that he was older, wiser, more experienced, would deal with the crap better, would be more focused on the things he needed to focus on.'[37] In fact, the second term, though it undoubtedly had its achievements, was far more fraught and traumatic than the first term. Blair became deeply involved first in the aftermath of 9/11 and then in Iraq. His attention was diverted from his domestic agenda; one of his aides said that, 'getting meetings in his diary for domestic policy was a great struggle after 9/11.'[38] Then there was the growing tension between the Prime Minister and the Chancellor.

One of the first decisions Blair had to make was what to do about Gordon Brown. If he wanted to move Brown, the beginning of the second term was the time to do it. Many of his advisers at No 10, fed up with the rival centre of power at the Treasury, argued for such a step. Blair himself understood only too well the case for trying to persuade Brown to go to the Foreign Office.

In the end, the counter arguments proved more powerful. He knew Brown did not want to leave the Treasury. If he was moved against his wishes, he would probably resign and then make trouble on the back benches. It would, in any case, be difficult to explain to the Labour

Party why he was sacking a Chancellor who had proved such a success and whose record had been a major factor in winning a landslide victory. He also continued to respect his abilities.[39] A combination of fear, guilt, respect and probably residual affection persuaded Blair to stay his hand. It was to be his last real chance to assert his authority over Brown.

Domestically, the key issue for Blair was now public sector reform. The increased spending in health and education was designed to bring expenditure in these areas up to European standards. But, as both he and Brown were well aware, improving public services was not only a question of money; it was also one of management, delivery and reform.[40] It was to the government's credit that, during the second term, results in almost every aspect of public services improved sharply. In the NHS, waiting times were dramatically reduced, while mortality rates dropped speedily and care for patients with cancer and coronary disease improved. Primary-school pupils could now read, write and do mathematics much better than their predecessors a decade ago and they compared well in reading and maths standards with the rest of the world. In the case of crime, the large-volume crimes (vehicle crime and burglary) were much reduced, while the chances of being a victim of crime were the lowest since records began in 1981.

Much of these improvements came about as a result of a top-down intervention – what Blair called 'flogging' the system. The Prime Minister wanted these improvements to be self-sustaining, which is why he turned to another model – that of 'quasi markets'. The idea was, as far as possible, to put the user of the service in the driving seat. That was the point behind the Prime Minister's public services reform agenda – above all foundation hospitals, tuition fees, academies and the five-year plans – and it led to fierce rows with the Chancellor, who adopted a more cautious, less market-oriented approach to public service reform.

In the end, after struggles in Cabinet and, in the case of foundation hospitals and tuition fees, on the floor of the House of Commons, Blair got his way. As he wrote later, 'though Gordon resisted many of the reforms and slowed some of them, he didn't prevent them. By the time

I left, choice and competition were embedded in the NHS; academies were powering ahead; tuition fees were in place; and welfare and pension reforms were formulated, if not introduced.'[41]

If, on the whole, Blair managed to get his way over public sector reform, his political authority was substantially weakened by the Iraq War. With his unabashed confidence in his own judgement (following successful interventions in Sierra Leone and Kosovo), he had brushed aside any potential difficulties arising from intervention in Iraq, the damage it might do to his European policy or to his government's standing at home. He went to war in Iraq in 2003 because he believed it was the right thing to do. As he told the Chilcot Inquiry, despite everything that happened subsequently, he would take the same decision again.

There were substantial costs, not only including the loss of life in Iraq, but also to his own reputation. Despite the findings of the Hutton and Butler reports, which had exonerated the Prime Minister of lying and improper behaviour, a large section of opinion, especially amongst the liberal intelligentsia (many of whom had joined the million-strong demonstration in London against the Iraq War) lost trust in Blair. His personal ratings dropped, and Labour suffered in the public opinion polls and at the local and European elections. After Iraq, Blair's 'big tent' began to look a lot smaller and the long-term electoral prospects of New Labour significantly weaker.

The period from 2003 to the summer of 2004 was the most difficult of Blair's premiership. With Iraq going badly wrong, a Mori poll for the *Financial Times* carried out just before the 2003 conference showed that half the public wanted Blair to resign. As Blair faltered, Brown, who was pressing the Prime Minister to stand down so he could take over, was waiting in the wings. By the spring of 2004, Blair's morale was so low that he came close to quitting. However, over Easter, his friends and supporters persuaded him to stay. His wife, Cherie, told him that, in the words of the song, he needed, 'to pick himself up, dust himself off and start all over again'.[42] Immediately after the 2004 party conference, and while Brown was in Washington for an IMF meeting, Blair announced that he intended to fight the next election and serve a third term. Brown's entourage likened Blair's behaviour to the staging of 'an African coup' while a rival was out of the country.

However, until the election was won, Blair and Brown were still bound to each other. During the campaign, the two men were seen together as much as possible – in one election stunt, they were even photographed together side by side, holding ice creams. Asked about Iraq, Brown, who had remained silent until then, gave his support to Blair, saying, 'I not only trust Tony Blair but I respect Tony Blair for the way he went about that decision.'[43] The partnership had just about survived, even if the old friendship was long gone.

Despite a tough and difficult election campaign, Labour won the 2005 election, with a majority of 66. Post-election analysis found that a quarter of defecting Labour voters cited the Iraq War as a reason, while, with only 36 per cent of the vote, Labour had the lowest share of voters for a party winning a majority of seats since the 1832 Reform Act. New Labour may have won a historic third term but it was now on the wane.

Blair had hoped that winning the 2005 election would strengthen his political position in his last term as prime minister. At the Parliamentary Party meeting after the election, he told his MPs that, for the first time, Labour had just won three successive elections and that, if it remained united, the party could win a fourth term. He promised that there would be a 'stable and orderly transition' and pleaded for 'the time and space to ensure that happened'. But, although he was warmly applauded by a majority, for the first time there were calls for his resignation from disgruntled members, while Brown sat glowering beside him on the platform.

This low point for Blair immediately after the election was, however, succeeded by a brilliant summer period which lasted until the autumn. The crucial event was the 'no' vote in the French referendum on the European constitution, followed by a similar result in the Dutch referendum. This enabled Blair to escape his unwise commitment to hold a UK referendum – which he would almost certainly have lost – and to take the opportunity to set out a new, more pragmatic direction for Europe. In an eloquent presidency speech to the European Parliament on 23 June, he warned MEPs, 'The people are blowing trumpets around the city walls. Are we listening?' As if inspired by his European triumph, Blair then showed outstanding powers of leadership in early July: first, in successfully lobbying delegates in Singapore to win the 2012 Olympic games for London; second at the G8(+5) summit on 7 and 8 July which he chaired in the Scottish Highlands; and third in rallying the nation, following the 7/7 bombings in London. He remained in confident, upbeat form at the party conference.

If the last half of 2005 proved unexpectedly fruitful for the Prime Minister, during 2006 Blair's authority drained rapidly away. In November he had lost the battle for the '90-day' clause for detention without trial for terrorist suspects, while the Education and Inspections Bill, which weakened local authority control, needed Conservative support to get through Parliament. The inquiry into cash for honours, which was only dropped after Blair left office, further damaged his credibility. In the May local elections, Labour finished a poor third. On the following day, Brown went on the Radio 4 *Today* programme to call for renewal of the Labour Party.

In July, Blair's refusal to condemn the Israeli shelling of Lebanese territory caused uproar in the PLP and led to open revolt by the Brownites. As Alistair Darling wrote in his memoirs, 'It would be wrong to claim that there was a plot to get rid of Tony Blair; there was no plot. A plot is secret. This was an open campaign, and as far as the Brown cabal was concerned, you were with them or against them.'[44] Then, in September, Blair, in a *Times* interview, repeated his promise to provide ample time for his successor but without giving a firm date for his departure.

This was the trigger for the so-called 'Corporals' Revolt' of Brownites and disgruntled Blairites which, after the publication of 'open' letters and resignations by a junior minister and parliamentary private secretaries, and two meetings between Blair and Brown, led to Blair announcing publicly that he would step down in the summer of 2007. On 27 June 2007, after a breakthrough in Northern Ireland which led to the establishment of a power-sharing executive, Blair tendered his resignation to the Queen.

To his constituents, he summed up his government's achievements in one sentence: 'There is only one government since 1945 that can say all of the following: more jobs, fewer unemployed, better health and education results, lower crime and economic growth in every quarter.'[45] A second sentence might have mentioned the massive reduction in NHS waiting times, the impressive rise in educational standards and the introduction of the minimum wage, while a third sentence could have described devolution in Scotland and Wales, peace in Northern Ireland and the incorporation of the European Convention on Human Rights into UK law. New Labour left a substantial legacy.

* * *

Brown's government without Blair turned out to be an epilogue to the New Labour era. He was unlucky in that his premiership coincided with the tidal wave of world recession; that Britain was suffering from voter fatigue after Labour's longest ever period of power in history; and, above all, he was no longer one half of one of the most formidable partnerships in modern politics. Brown struggled not only because he was left without the complementary talents of Blair, but also because of the fall-out from his long and damaging struggle for power. Alistair Darling wrote that, 'from a ringside seat, I saw the slowly dripping poison of their relationship damage our government [...] Tony and Gordon dominated the Labour Party for more than ten years and were an overwhelming force for good, but by the end their feud allowed a cancer to grow which, I believe, contributed to our defeat in 2010.'[46] Brown also found it difficult to position himself on the ideological and policy spectrum: he was a founding father of New Labour, yet wanted to distance himself from Blair. But he never defined what he stood for, or how and whether a Brown government would be different from Blairism.

The economic crisis revealed weaknesses in Brown's policies in the last years of his chancellorship. Although it is true that by far the largest part of the deficit was caused by the impact of the world recession on output and tax revenues, he can be criticised for allowing public borrowing to rise too fast on the basis of over-optimistic forecasts of economic growth (though his plans were backed by the Conservatives). His 'light touch' regulation of the City, strongly supported by the Tory opposition, led to an unhealthy expansion of bank assets and left Britain overexposed when the credit crunch came. However, there is also a strong case for saying that Brown's contribution, both over bank recapitalisation in October 2008 and then at the G20 London summit in April 2009, was an essential ingredient in ensuring that the world recession did not become a world depression.

Without Blair's talent for connecting with the voters, Brown floundered and Labour lost the 2010 election. Often charming and relaxed in private, he seemed wooden or angry in public. Philip Gould, Labour's pollster, pointed out,

> As became clear in the 2010 election, having two of them campaign together was better than having only one. I lost count of the number of times that campaign staff – from all camps – would say in 2010: if only we had Tony. Not because they necessarily wanted him back as leader, but because the pairing of Tony and Gordon in an election campaign was so much stronger than one alone.[47]

The partnership of Blair and Brown was at its zenith an incredibly powerful combination of initiator and facilitator which worked impressively in the first term, and in the second term – despite the deterioration in relations between the two men – it produced improvement in almost every aspect of public services. Though Blair had a brilliant Indian summer, the beginning of the third term was dominated by Brown's unremitting drive for power (his desire to become an initiator) until Blair finally resigned in 2007.

Together, Blair and Brown created New Labour, brought it to power and sustained it by winning three successive elections. Their government had significant achievements to its credit. If the two men had been able to continue to combine as effectively as in the first term, New Labour would have achieved more.

7
PEACETIME COALITION
Cameron and Clegg

This chapter is about the first peacetime coalition since the 1930s and the resulting partnership between David Cameron and Nick Clegg. This is not to claim that the formation of the coalition necessarily represents a crucial turning point in the nation's history or that Cameron and Clegg have proved themselves in the same league as other politicians in the book. But, in the context of the underlying arguments of *Odd Couples*, it is of interest to consider the factors which led to the coalition, to analyse the development of the relationship between Cameron and Clegg and to assess its success.

The coalition agreement between Conservative leader Cameron and Liberal Democrat leader Clegg was mainly driven by political arithmetic after the Tories failed to win a majority at the 2010. Although the partnership survived (partly due to their good relationship), inadequate leadership by the two men, who were neither strong initiators nor especially competent facilitators, as well as growing pressure from their respective parties (especially from the Tory Eurosceptics), undermined the coalition's effectiveness.

The government managed to reduce the fiscal deficit (though by far less than it had originally promised in 2010). However, the lack of agreement on medium-term policy meant that the government ran out of steam long before the end of its five-year term. It also came very close to disaster over the referendum on Scottish independence, while Cameron's unwise commitment to hold an 'in/out' referendum on UK membership of the European Union early in the next parliament loomed like a dark cloud of uncertainty over British politics.

On the face of it, Cameron and Clegg (who were born within a few months of each other, Cameron on 9 October 1966 and Clegg on 7 January 1967) were very similar in background. Both had fathers who worked successfully in the City, Ian Cameron as a stockbroker and Nicholas Clegg as a banker with Daiwa Securities. Both men went to leading public schools, Cameron to Eton College and Clegg to Westminster School. Both benefited from an Oxbridge education: Cameron gaining a first in politics, philosophy and economics at Oxford and Clegg a 2:1 in social anthropology at Cambridge. Neither was involved in student politics, though a number of Cameron's contemporaries were convinced that he would end up as prime minister, while the Tory MP Greg Hands claimed that, in his first year, Clegg was a paid-up member of the Cambridge University Conservatives. Both were captains of their college tennis teams.

However, there are also significant differences. David Cameron, whose mother, Mary Mount, came from a long-established Berkshire family, had a conventional upper-class upbringing which shaped both his outlook and his politics. Once he had decided on a political career, there was no question other than that he would be a Tory.

In contrast to Cameron, Clegg grew up in a multilingual, socially concerned environment. His mother was Dutch, and had spent most of the war in a notorious Japanese internment camp in Jakarta. After marrying Clegg's father, whom she met at Cambridge, she combined raising her family with a career as a special needs teacher. Nickje, as he was called at home, spoke both English and Dutch and later added French and German as well as Spanish, the language of his wife, Miriam González Durántez. With this international background, it was scarcely surprising that Clegg became a fervent pro-European, studying first for a master's degree at the College d'Europe at Bruges and then working for the European Commission.

Cameron's rise inside the Conservative Party seemed almost effortless. In 1988, straight from Oxford, he landed a job in charge of research into trade and industry at the Conservative Research Department, well known as a nursery for budding Tory politicians. After two and a half years at Smith Square, where his duties included briefing John Major for Prime Minister's Questions, he was promoted to be special adviser to the chancellor of the Exchequer, Norman Lamont. Surviving Black Wednesday when pressure from currency speculators forced the pound out of the European Exchange Rate Mechanism, and a few months later, the sacking of Lamont, Cameron was then recruited to be aide to the home secretary, Michael Howard. Although loyally supporting Howard's controversial anti-crime agenda, Cameron resigned in the spring of 1994, both to look for a winnable seat and to make enough money to marry Samantha Sheffield, the daughter of Sir Reginald Sheffield, the eighth baronet. For the next seven years, Cameron, who had been recommended for the job by his future mother-in-law, Annabel Astor, worked for the media company Carlton Communications. Though he made no secret of his political ambitions, he proved to be an effective director of corporate affairs, adept both at public relations and at managing the tempestuous chairman of Carlton, Michael Green.

In 1996, Cameron won the nomination for Stafford, in normal times a good prospect for the Tories. But in Labour's landslide victory of 1997, he went down to defeat, finishing over 2,000 votes behind the successful Labour candidate, David Kidney. Cameron had to wait for a safer seat and the following general election to get into the House of Commons. Speaking without notes and displaying a fashionable Euroscepticism, he was selected in 2000 for the affluent Oxfordshire constituency of Witney, formerly represented by Douglas Hurd and later by Shaun Woodward (who had defected to Labour). As his biographers remarked, 'There can be few constituencies in the country better suited to Cameron and luckily for him, he suited Witney.'[1] Despite another overall Labour landslide victory, he was returned with a comfortable majority of just under 8,000.

Nick Clegg found his way to the Liberal Democrats and to Westminster via Brussels. In 1994 he got a job in the external trade directorate of the European Commission, working on aid programmes for countries (formerly part of the Soviet Union) in Central Asia and the Caucasus. Two years later, the trade commissioner, Leon Brittan, brought him into his Cabinet, where he played a part in negotiations over China's application to join the World Trade Organisation.

Brittan tried to persuade Clegg to join the Conservatives but Clegg replied that he was unhappy with the Tories' European policies and that, if he was going to join a party, it would be the Liberal Democrats. As it happened, the Liberal Democrat leader, Paddy Ashdown, was in Brussels in May 1997 for a meeting with Brittan. The Trade Commissioner, who told Ashdown that Clegg was 'the brightest young man I've ever come across', warmly recommended him to the Liberal Democrat leader. The upshot was that Clegg joined the Liberal Democrats and became one of the candidates in the 1999 European elections, at which he was returned as the leading Liberal Democrat MEP for the East Midlands.

Clegg used his time as an MEP not only to play a prominent role in the European Parliament (above all in liberalising communications) but also in preparing for his transition to British politics. After announcing that he was not going to stand for a second term in the European Parliament, he was fortunate to be selected for Sheffield Hallam, where the sitting Liberal Democrat MP was standing down. At the 2005 election, at which the Liberal Democrats won 62 seats (their largest total since 1923), Clegg was comfortably elected to Westminster. Already he was being talked about as a future party leader.

The speed of David Cameron's journey to the top was remarkable, taking only four and a half years from his arrival in 2001 as a new backbencher to becoming leader of the Tory party. His ascent was greatly assisted by the rapid downfall of three successive Conservative leaders – William Hague's resignation after the 2001 Labour landslide, Iain Duncan Smith's humiliation in the 2003 leadership ballot and Michael Howard's exit after the Tory defeat in the 2005 election. In the subsequent leadership election, Cameron ran as the modernising candidate and, following an eloquent and noteless speech at the 2005 Blackpool party conference in which he said that 'modern compassionate Conservatism' was 'right for our times, right for our party and right for our country',[2] he won the contest by more than two to one.

Clegg's rise to his party's leadership was as dramatic as that of Cameron – and even swifter. Like Cameron, the deposing of his two immediate predecessors cleared Clegg's way to the top. Only a few months after the Liberal Democrats' success at the 2005 election, Charles Kennedy announced that he had a drink problem and stood down. His successor, Menzies Campbell, was exceptionally experienced in foreign affairs but was, however, unable to establish his authority over his parliamentary colleagues and, after Brown failed to call an election in the autumn of 2007, Campbell decided to resign. Clegg immediately threw his hat into the ring and narrowly defeated his colleague and former MEP Chris Huhne, by 511 votes out of 41,465.

The years leading up to the 2010 general election were marked by the credit crunch, the expenses scandal and New Labour's decline. Despite his skilful handling of the financial crisis, Brown, who was a stilted communicator on television, proved to be an unpopular prime minister. This gave Cameron an excellent opportunity to project the Tories as capable of restoring the nation's finances and also, in line with 'compassionate conservatism', of safeguarding key parts of public spending, especially the NHS. It was more difficult for Clegg to capture the limelight, especially as it was his deputy Vince Cable (sometimes called the 'sage of Twickenham') who had presciently warned of the dangers of an economic and financial crisis.

However, as the election drew near, the Tory lead in the polls began to narrow. While an ICM/*Guardian* poll showed that two-thirds of voters agreed that it was time for a change, less than 40 per cent of respondents said they would vote for the Tories. In other words, the voters were fed up with Labour but, despite Cameron's best efforts, were still unsure about the Conservatives.[3] Cameron hoped that a combination of Brown's unpopularity, the Tories' superior resources and his own ascendancy in the party leaders' debates would deliver victory for the Tories. But it was Nick

Clegg's performance, especially in the opening debate, which brought the election to life and led to a sudden Liberal Democrat surge in the polls. The Conservative press turned on Clegg, the *Mail on Sunday* setting the tone: 'His wife is Spanish, his mother Dutch, his father half-Russian and his spin doctor German. Is there anything British about the Lib Dem leader?'[4]

In the end, the May 2010 general election produced a hung parliament. The Tories won 301 seats, a net gain of 90 but short of the needed overall majority of 326. Labour went down to a crushing defeat, suffering a net loss of 91 seats, giving it a total of 258 seats. Despite Clegg's debating triumph, the Liberal Democrat vote only increased by 1 per cent and overall they lost five seats, finishing with 57. With its second-worst result since 1918, Labour had clearly lost the election. But the Tories had not won it: Cameron had failed to deliver the victory which the Conservatives expected. Paradoxically, despite losing seats, the Liberal Democrats were in a strong position because they held the balance of power.

During the election, Nick Clegg had made it clear that, in the event of a hung parliament, he would talk to the party with the biggest 'mandate' from the electors (though he refused to say whether this was to be judged in terms of votes or seats or both). On the Friday morning after polling day he announced that, in view of the election results, he would approach the Conservatives first. In the afternoon, Cameron gave another crucial statement in which he made what he called 'a big, open and comprehensive' offer to the Liberal Democrats. Momentum was building up behind a Lib Dem–Conservative coalition. Direct talks between Conservative and Liberal Democrat negotiators began later that afternoon in the Cabinet Office in 70 Whitehall and continued throughout the weekend and on Monday and Tuesday as well. There were parallel talks between Labour and the Lib Dems, but these were a later sideshow which the Lib Dems used to put pressure on the Tories and to convince Labour-leaning Lib Dems that the only viable arrangement was with the Tories. At 7.17 p.m. on Tuesday evening, Brown resigned as prime minister, clearing the way for a Tory–Liberal Democrat coalition government, led by Cameron and with Nick Clegg as deputy prime minister.

The deal was finally sealed at 2.15 p.m. on Wednesday in the Rose Garden at 10 Downing Street, where Cameron and Clegg together unveiled the seven-page coalition agreement to the assembled media. Cameron declared that 'we are not just announcing a new government with new ministers; we are announcing a new politics,'[5] while Clegg promised a 'new kind of government, a radical, reforming government where it needs to be and a source of reassurance and stability at a time of great uncertainty in our country too.'[6] The BBC's Nick Robinson described it as 'not so much a political marriage as a political civil partnership ceremony'.[7]

The main factor behind the coalition was the parliamentary arithmetic. According to George Osborne, Cameron's chief negotiator and soon to be chancellor of the Exchequer, the first rule of politics is that one must be able to count.[8] As the biggest party it would, of course, have been possible for the Tories to form a minority government. But it would probably have been a weak government, unsuited to the difficult economic circumstances and subject to political pressure, especially from the Tory right wing. However, if the Tories and the Liberal Democrats combined, they would command a comfortable majority of 59 seats, providing a stable government. By contrast, a Labour–Liberal Democrat combination of 315 seats would have had only eight more seats than the Tories and would have been 11 short of the necessary 326. A Labour–Liberal Democrat coalition would, therefore, have required the support of other, smaller parties, perhaps sufficient to provide a narrow temporary majority, but not able to function effectively. As Peter Hennessy remarked at the time, such an arrangement would have 'too many moving parts'. [9]

If the parliamentary arithmetic provided the essential background to the formation of the Tory–Lib Dem coalition, an additional factor was the personal chemistry between Cameron and Clegg. Though the two men had had little contact before the election (indeed, shortly after his election as Lib Dem leader, Clegg had refused a dinner invitation from the Camerons), their initial telephone conversation on the afternoon of the post election Friday went well.[10]

Throughout the negotiations, the two men seemed to be on the same wavelength. It was not so much their similar educational backgrounds but rather that they were both ambitious, able, affable young party leaders who had just experienced a disappointing election result but who were now being given another chance, through coalition, of achieving the power they had failed to obtain on their own. In terms of political approach and policies, they were not so far apart either. Cameron was a Tory pragmatist who had promoted himself as a moderniser, while Clegg was sympathetic to the 'Orange Book' tendency inside the Liberal Democrats which strongly believed in giving more emphasis to the market and to choice.

In his book on the formation of the coalition, David Laws, later Liberal Democrat education minister, makes the significant point that, whereas Clegg's immediate predecessors as leaders of the Lib Dems 'were defined to a large degree by their opposition to the Conservatives', Clegg was the first leader 'for decades who felt genuinely equidistant in his attitude to the other two parties'. He was as critical of Labour, especially on civil liberties and its style of government, as he was of the Conservatives on Europe. Thus any partnership with another party would be based on a hard-headed assessment of 'our ability to promote Lib Dem policies in government, rather than a presumption in favour of Labour as the natural partner'.[11]

Clegg's predisposition in favour of a deal with the Tories was enhanced by his uneasy relationship with Gordon Brown, who, as over the expenses scandal, tended to lecture the opposition leaders and who, in his opening telephone conversation with Clegg, scarcely allowed the Lib Dem leader to get a word in edgeways. Clegg was, in any case, always doubtful about the Labour option. On the Saturday morning after the election, he stressed to his Shadow Cabinet the difficulties of doing a deal with Labour. Quite apart from the uncertain parliamentary arithmetic, there was the Brown issue: 'First I think Brown himself is pretty toxic politically. Secondly, Labour has clearly lost, and putting them back in power would not be popular.'[12]

Brown's announcement on the Monday, following talks with Clegg, that he would step down as leader did not solve the problem, as the Lib Dems were uncertain who would now lead Labour. And, though the Labour Cabinet approved Brown's strategy, there was now growing opposition inside the Labour Party to any effort to continue in government. Lord Falconer, the former Lord Chancellor, spoke for many when he told the BBC that Labour was doing itself damage 'in trying to do a deal. The sense that people will bargain on any basis in order to stay in power is unacceptable.'[13] One of the most enthusiastic supporters of a Labour–Lib Dem arrangement, Andrew Adonis, admitted that, 'The party was exhausted, demoralised, almost leaderless, with many ministers and MPs anxious to escape into opposition [...] Thirteen years in government had drained them dry.'[14] Even if the Lib Dem leadership, above all Clegg, had been more sympathetic to a deal with Labour, on Labour's side the will to power was no longer there. A Lib Dem–Conservative coalition may not have been inevitable but, given the election result, it was always by far the most likely option.

Even in democracies such as Germany and Scandinavia, where hung parliaments are the norm, coalition governments are difficult to manage. In 2010, Cameron and Clegg were travelling in uncharted territory. It was not so much 'new politics' as 'unknown politics'. There had, of course, been minority governments, as in 1974 and the winter of 1978–9, and also the Lib–Lab parliamentary arrangement from March 1977 to July 1979. But, though they were well served by party advisers and by the civil service, Cameron and Clegg virtually had to make it up as they went along. The fact that the coalition survived its full term was because of their persistence and determination, most obviously on the part of Clegg but also by Cameron as well. Indeed, some argue, like the editor of the *Spectator*, Fraser Nelson, in the *Daily Telegraph*, that its survival is its only success.[15]

The two men approached coalition from different perspectives. For Cameron, coalition was the lifeboat, which, despite the election result, secured power for the Tories after 13 years in opposition and, assisted by a fixed-term parliament, virtually guaranteed them five years in government, with the Conservative leader as prime minister. Although he gave Clegg the deputy premiership, David Cameron also buttressed his own party's position in the coalition by ensuring that the three main offices of the state – the Treasury, Foreign Office and the Home Office – were safely in Tory hands.

For Clegg, the leader of the weaker third party, coalition was an end in itself, as it provided the only realistic way in which the Lib Dems could ever obtain power. He therefore had an interest in demonstrating not only that his party could secure effective government, but also that it would be a responsible partner in any coalition. Another pressure on Clegg was the disturbance in the global markets created by the financial and economic crisis. As one commentator put it, 'This was no time for uncertainty, delay or political games.'[16]

For these reasons, as well as maybe sheer inexperience, Nick Clegg arguably failed to ensure that Liberal Democratic power was strongly enough entrenched inside government. As Andrew Adonis has pointed out, Clegg's decision to become deputy prime minister without a major department and with constitutional reform as his only portfolio, gave him insufficient leverage.[17] Although he had a weekly meeting with Cameron, and although the so-called 'quad' (Cameron, Osborne, Clegg and Danny Alexander) also met to discuss issues with spending implications, the Deputy Prime Minister did not attend the crucial daily planning meeting where the Prime Minister, Osborne and the Cabinet Secretary met to discuss the government's key tactical and strategic business. Indeed, it has been suggested by Tories that the real deputy prime minister was not Clegg, but Chancellor of the Exchequer George Osborne. In respect of the other Lib Dem Cabinet ministers, the problem was not so much their numbers but Clegg's failure to ensure that enough of them were heads of important departments.[18] This meant that the Tories dominated coalition decisions, often leaving the Lib Dems out in the cold, with only delaying power or the occasional veto on which to fall back.

At the beginning of the coalition, Clegg made a conscious effort to 'throw myself at Rose Garden politics'.[19] He took the view that the Lib Dems had to show that bipartisan government worked by 'owning everything' in the coalition and not just the bits in the coalition government which had come from the Lib Dem manifesto. For example, Clegg gave strong public support to the Chancellor's announcement of £6 billion of public spending cuts in the current year which his party had opposed during the election and to the emergency budget which, amongst other tough measures, increased VAT to 20 per cent. Danny Alexander, who, following the resignation of David Laws over an expenses transgression, became chief secretary to the Treasury, enthusiastically backed Osborne's plan of eradicating the structural deficit by the end of the parliament, which, as it was also supported by Clegg, became the coalition's main priority. However, Clegg's policy of 'owning everything' came under almost immediate strain.

In October 2010, the Browne Report on university tuition fees recommended that the cap on tuition fees be lifted entirely. The government response, announced on 3 November, was to set a limit of £9,000 a year. This presented a major difficulty for the Lib Dems and particularly for Clegg as, during the election, Clegg, Cable (who as business secretary was in charge of higher education) and all Liberal Democrat MPs had signed the National Union of Students' pledge not to vote in favour of higher tuition fees if elected to Parliament. An option for the Lib Dems to abstain was built in to the coalition agreement but Clegg decided that, despite his election pledge, he had to vote for the government's policy on tuition fees. It might have been a brave decision but there was a price to pay. The politician who had caught the popular imagination during the election now became a hate figure, burnt in effigy by student protestors.

If the drama over tuition fees was primarily a Liberal Democrat show, the row over health service reform affected both coalition partners. Cameron had made much of his support for the NHS. As he told the 2006 Tory party conference, 'Tony Blair explained his priorities in these words: education, education, education. I can do it in three letters: NHS.' In addition, the coalition programme for government had specifically promised that the government would 'stop the top-down reorganisations of the NHS that have got in the way of patient care'. Yet Cameron and

Clegg allowed the Conservative health secretary, Andrew Lansley, to come forward with a major reform White Paper, proposing the abolition of key health service institutions (primary care trusts and strategic health authorities) and replacing them with commissioning consortiums of general practitioners, while encouraging competition among providers in a way which critics called 'privatisation by the back door'. The 300-clause Bill was published in January 2011 to almost universal hostility and in March the Liberal Democrat conference made its opposition very clear. With Clegg under pressure to withdraw his support for the Bill, Cameron announced a humiliating pause. It was the only way to save the Bill, which in the end limped its weary way through Parliament, much amended and little loved. It was not the coalition's finest hour.

The fiasco of the alternative vote (AV) was an even greater blow to the coalition, especially for Clegg, but for Cameron as well. For Clegg and the Lib Dems a referendum on AV, enshrined in the coalition agreement, was the game-changer which clinched the coalition with the Tories. AV was not a proportional system but a majoritarian one in which the voters ranked the candidates in order of performance. If on the first ballot no candidate won 50 per cent of the vote, the voters of the candidate with the fewest first preferences were redistributed until there was a majority candidate. The Lib Dems would have preferred proportional representation (PR) but AV was clearly in their interest because the party was the second choice of many voters.

After the debacle over tuition fees, Clegg badly needed a success and, with Cameron's informal agreement not to campaign against AV in his pocket, thought that there was a reasonable chance of winning the referendum. However, when at the turn of the year the polls appeared to suggest a comfortable victory for the 'yes' campaign, Tory MPs panicked and put strong pressure on their leader to become involved. The 'no' campaign used aggressive tactics to turn the polls in its favour, including personal attacks on the Liberal Democrat leader. The result of the referendum, held on 5 May 2011, was a humiliation for Clegg: 67.9 per cent for the 'nos' to only 32.1 per cent for 'yes'.

Clegg's relationship with Cameron survived, but it changed for good, becoming purely transactional. As the coalition's historian wrote, 'Where Clegg had previously seen his governing partner as a reasonable, moderate man with broadly similar instincts to his own, he now regarded him as the acceptable face of a truly appalling party.'[20] For Clegg, Cameron was no longer his 'Rose Garden' friend but somebody with whom he was condemned to do business. Clegg also rightly suspected that Cameron was unable to control the ill-disciplined right wing of his party.

In July 2011, there was a massive Tory revolt when 91 Tory backbenchers, including this time some promising members of the 2010 intake, defied a three-line whip and voted against a second reading of a bill designed to create a mainly elected House of Lords; this was after a committee chaired by Clegg had proposed an 80 per cent elected upper chamber. The rebellion followed the withdrawal of a timetabling motion when it became clear that such a motion would be defeated. A furious Clegg then withdrew the Bill and announced that he was instructing Lib Dem MPs to vote against boundary changes for the 2015 election, a measure which, like the AV referendum and House of Lords reform, was included in the coalition agreement but, unlike the other two, was supported by the Tories, mainly because it would have given them 20 extra seats. This was an act of political revenge, but it also signalled the end of Clegg's attempts to bring about major constitutional reforms.

For Cameron, it was Europe which was the most intractable issue. Unlike the hardline Tory Eurosceptics, the Prime Minister was pragmatic about British membership. To win the leadership, he had been prepared to pull the Conservative Party out of the centre-right European People's Party grouping on the grounds that it was too federalist – a move which, by infuriating his main continental ally, German Chancellor Angela Merkel, was to cost him dear. But in his first conference speech in 2006, he warned his party to 'stop banging on about Europe'. One of the benefits of a coalition with the Lib Dems, as he saw it, was that it gave him some protection against the demands of Eurosceptic backbenchers. The commitments on Europe contained in the coalition programme for government set out both that no further powers would be transferred to Brussels without a referendum, *and* that 'Britain should play a leading role in an enlarged European Union'.

At first, this compromise between Cameron and Clegg enabled Britain to operate as a relatively effective member of the EU – as, for example, over the negotiations of the EU budget and the British contribution to the Irish bailout. However, in October 2011, 81 Tory MPs, defying a three-line whip, supported a motion in favour of an 'in/out' referendum on European membership, an act of rebellion which clearly rattled a nervous Prime Minister. Perhaps partly as a consequence, two months later he vetoed an EU plan to strengthen fiscal coordination between member states, the so-called fiscal compact. On his return from Brussels he was given a hero's welcome by Tory backbenchers but, as Lib Dem critics, including Clegg, pointed out, leaving Britain isolated (with the support of only one other member state) was not an effective way to promote the national interest.

A year later, Cameron made a big speech about Europe which he hoped would put to bed the Tory party's internal row over Europe until after the 2015 general election. Its key commitment, which was opposed by Clegg, was that, if re-elected, he would hold an 'in/out' referendum on the basis of renegotiated terms for the UK. This did not satisfy Cameron's critics, who insisted that, even if a referendum could not be held until after the election, a law authorising such a referendum should be put on the statute book in the 2010–15 parliament. Although Cameron pointed out that, under the terms of the programme for government, the coalition had not agreed to bring forward such legislation, he nevertheless proceeded to give official Tory party backing to a Tory private member's bill setting out the details of an 'in/out' referendum. However, following strong opposition from Lib Dem and Labour peers, the Bill was eventually talked out in the Lords.

After Cameron's failed attempt to block the appointment of Jean-Claude Juncker as president of the European Commission, Charles Grant of the Centre for European Reform (in an open letter to the Prime

Minister) reported that European leaders were now saying that Cameron was more focused on party management, satisfying Conservative Eurosceptics and winning back votes from the UK Independence Party (UKIP) than on keeping Britain in the EU. It was certainly the case that Cameron found it very difficult to handle his Eurosceptic critics, who continued to resent his failure to win the 2010 election and the necessity for a coalition with the Lib Dems and who feared the growing challenge from UKIP. When the coalition was formed, the Conservatives, unlike their coalition partners, had failed to consult their party, so that there was never any feeling of 'ownership'. However, when faced with strong opposition on Europe from his backbenchers, the Prime Minister nearly always gave way, though this never seemed to satisfy his critics, many of whom were determined that, whatever the cost, Britain should leave the EU. The German chancellor, Angela Merkel, was strongly opposed to any attempt of Cameron to restrict the free movement of labour, a basic principle of the EU, in an attempt to reduce immigration.

* * *

The relationship between the Tory leader David Cameron and the Liberal Democrat leader Nick Clegg was a major factor in the formation of the coalition. It also proved strong enough to sustain the government through the ups and downs of a five-year parliament. Both men had compelling reasons for continuing to support the coalition. For Cameron, it provided the means to keep his party in power and him in 10 Downing Street. In addition, it gave parliamentary backing for a number of Conservative policies, as well as a measure of protection against the more extreme demands of Tory Eurosceptics. For Clegg, coalition enabled the weaker third party to obtain a share of power. Paradoxically, the fiasco over tuition fees and his humiliation over the AV referendum strengthened the argument for sticking with the coalition, given that precipitating an early general election would have been politically disastrous for the Liberal Democrats.

As time went on, and the election approached, relations between Cameron and Clegg inevitably became cooler. However, despite their growing number of spats, it is arguable that the two leaders had a closer relationship with each other than they did with their own parties. The Tories, especially the Eurosceptics, tended to blame Cameron for failing to win the 2010 election and for his inability to secure an 'in/out' referendum on UK membership of the EU, while the Lib Dems disliked having to provide a fig leaf for what they saw as Tory policies and suffering successive local by-election and European election defeats. Relations between the two parties deteriorated alarmingly. In January 2013, *The Economist* summed up the situation as follows: 'Although relations between senior politicians remain strong and the coalition seems likely to last until the 2015 election, Tory and Lib Dem MPs have openly come to loathe their supposed allies – and often hold their leaders in contempt for compromising with the other side.'[21]

Despite the influence of the 'Orange Book' tendency on the Lib Dem leadership, an underlying problem with the coalition was that there was an insufficient identity of values and policy, especially over Europe, constitutional issues and welfare, to make a genuinely joint programme viable in the medium term.[22] There were also flaws in the formation and conduct of the coalition which made things worse, especially for the junior partner. Arguably Clegg needed to command a major government department, or at least ensure that the deputy prime minister's office had real clout. There should have been a Lib Dem Cabinet minister in each of the main sectors of government, and there ought to have been a mechanism for policy development to prevent the coalition running out of steam in the last two years of the parliament.

In respect of policies, both parties continued to back the deficit-reduction programme announced in 2010, which they saw as a political as well as an economic priority; however, they were forced to announce that public spending cuts would have to continue after the next election. Clegg argued that the Lib Dems acted as a restraint on the Tories – for example, blocking cuts in inheritance tax and preventing the government focusing on welfare cuts alone. He also pointed to the increase in the personal income tax allowance to £10,000 and the pupil premium for children on free school meals as Lib Dem in origin. But an examination of coalition measures, such as those concerning health and education, cuts in welfare spending, taxation and immigration policy, underlines that the Tories were very much the dominant influence in the coalition.

Cameron and Clegg claimed that they were creating a new kind of government and that they were putting aside party differences because of the economic crisis. In fact, their cooperation was as much the result of electoral necessity and pursuit of power as of patriotism. Compared with the record of other couples discussed in this book, their achievements seemed meagre, especially in the last half of the coalition's life.

It may be that future elections will again throw up a hung parliament which will make another coalition a possibility. If so, lessons must be learnt from the shortcomings and failures of the 2010–15 coalition. What is clear, however, is that coalition is not necessarily a form of government superior to single-party government and that constructive cooperation between individual politicians can take place just as effectively within a party or even across parties as in a coalition.

CONCLUSION

This book has sought to show how pairings have made a crucial contribution to key moments in recent political history. In 1940, Churchill and Attlee, with their contrasting but complementary abilities (with the first an initiator and the second a facilitator), came together to form the wartime coalition which saved the country from catastrophic collapse and stayed in office until the war in Europe was eventually won.

In the creative early years of Attlee's postwar governments, the Labour Cabinet was dominated by two 'big beasts', Bevin and Morrison, both of them examples of 'initiating' politicians. They worked not in partnership but in a special kind of combination devised by Attlee, who, though prime minister, continued to act much in the style of his wartime role as a chairman – facilitator. Allocating the two men different spheres of operation, he put Bevin in charge of foreign affairs, with Morrison as the chief coordinating figure on the home front, an arrangement which proved highly successful. In a sustained burst of creativity, Bevin played a key role in the setting up of the Western Alliance and the implementation of the Marshall Plan, while Morrison ensured that Labour's programme of social welfare and public ownership (mostly backed by the Tories) was speedily put on the statute book.

Macmillan and Butler (the first an initiator, the second a facilitator) were the two most intelligent and forward-looking of postwar Conservative politicians. Although their relationship was partly one of rivalry, they were able to establish a working partnership. Together they launched the revival of the Tories as the party of affluence. The Macmillan governments, with Butler as loyal deputy, led the decolonisation of Africa and forged a new European orientation for British foreign policy. It proved to be one of the most creative combinations in Tory party history.

Nearly 20 years later, another partnership – that of Thatcher and Whitelaw – took the Conservatives – and the country – in a different direction. The two participants were far apart in temperament and approach to politics. Thatcher was an initiator and conviction politician who believed in the market and private enterprise, while Whitelaw, very much a facilitator, acted as conciliator and sheet anchor. Although at heart a 'One Nation' Tory, he saw it as his duty to give Thatcher his loyalty, even when he did not agree with her policies. As Thatcher said, Whitelaw was 'the ballast that helped to keep the government on course'.

It is sometimes forgotten that, for most of their time together, the Blair–Brown double act provided one of the most powerful and creative partnerships in Labour Party history. They had complementary gifts. Blair was a superb communicator, good at taking decisions and able to think 'out of the box'; Brown was New Labour's policy expert and, until the end of the second term, an outstanding chancellor of the Exchequer. Together they won three successive elections and achieved significant economic, social and constitutional reforms.

Although Heath and Wilson, as leaders of competing political parties, were never a partnership, it was they who made the biggest contribution to securing British membership of the European Community, the most far-reaching development in postwar foreign policy and one which still remains controversial today. Heath was the visionary, Wilson the pragmatist: approaching the issue from different perspectives, in the end they came to the same conclusion. Heath took Britain in, Wilson ensured that the country stayed in.

The coalition agreement between the Tory leader, David Cameron, and the Liberal Democrat leader, Nick Clegg, was mainly driven by political arithmetic after the Tories failed to win a majority in the 2010 election. Although the partnership survived, inadequate leadership by the two men, who were neither strong initiators nor especially competent facilitators, as well as growing pressure from their respective parties – especially from the Tory Eurosceptics alarmed by the electoral success of UKIP – undermined the coalition's effectiveness.

As the relationships between Churchill and Attlee, Macmillan and Butler, and Thatcher and Whitelaw all show, successful combinations usually require an alliance between an initiator and facilitator. The retirement of Whitelaw in 1988 had disastrous consequences for Thatcher, leading indirectly to her downfall in 1990; while at a critical moment Macmillan's premiership was weakened when he gave Butler responsibility for liquidating the Central African Federation which required Butler to be out of the country for months on end. The partnership between Blair and Brown was effective until Brown, who wanted to become prime minister, withdrew his backing after 2005. Brown's inability to accept the power relationship between the two men was key to the ultimate failure of New Labour and was in contrast to Whitelaw's unstinting support for Thatcher and Attlee's loyalty to Churchill.

The experience of the 1945 Labour government, the Macmillan governments of the late 1950s and early 1960s, and the administrations of Margaret Thatcher and Tony Blair, underlines the importance of a common agenda (carried through with determination) in the success of a partnership. By comparison, Cameron and Clegg had no medium-term policy agenda, with the possible exception of getting rid of the deficit. That is why the first peacetime coalition since the 1930s ran out of steam and was so vulnerable to party influence and to the pressure of events.

Whether or not there will be coalitions in the future, partnerships either between or within parties require a combination of 'initiating' and 'facilitating' skills, loyalty and trust between partners and a clear long-term agenda. As this book has shown, the key moments of modern British politics have often been shaped by partnerships. Such partnerships will be even more necessary in the years ahead, if we are to achieve effective government and a healthy democracy.

A NOTE ON SOURCES

I have consulted cabinet papers, diaries, biographies and books on the period (1940–2015) covered by *Odd Couples*. For the later part of the period, I have supplemented these sources with a number of interviews and conversations, as mentioned in the Preface.

For the chapter on Churchill and Attlee, Churchill's memoirs and the wartime volumes of Martin Gilbert's official life of Churchill are indispensable. I also found the one-volume lives by Roy Jenkins and Geoffrey Best, as well as Max Hasting's book on Churchill as war lord, extremely valuable. For Attlee, there is Kenneth Harris' biography and the recent life by Nicklaus Thomas-Symonds, while Robert Crowcroft's analysis of Attlee's influence on the domestic front during the war is very perceptive. Francis Beckett's short life is especially good on Attlee the man.

Bevin and Morrison have been well served. Alan Bullock's three-volume biography of Ernest Bevin is rightly described by Attlee as 'as a massive work about a massive man', while Francis Williams' attractive portrait of Bevin helps bring him to life. Bernard Donoughue and G.W. Jones' biography, based on a wide range of interviews, gives a comprehensive study of Morrison. The author's *The Tortoise and the Hare* describes the relationship between Attlee and his cabinet. Kenneth O. Morgan's *Labour in Power*, Peter Hennessy's *Never Again* and David Kynaston's *Austerity Britain* provide an authoritative background.

Like Churchill before him, Macmillan told his own story in his six-volume memoirs. In his preface to his elegant one-volume biography, Butler wrote that he preferred a single book 'which is not too heavy for anyone to hold up and doze over in bed'. There are two excellent recent biographies of Macmillan, by D.R. Thorpe and by Charles Williams, as well as Alistair Horne's earlier massive two-volume work. Anthony Howard wrote a sympathetic biography of Butler 30 years ago. Hennessy's *Having it so Good* provides a colourful background history.

Wilson's accounts of his years in government are records rather than histories. Heath's autobiography is more revealing, if unforgiving to his enemies. Philip Zeigler has written valuable biographies of both Heath and Wilson, while Ben Pimlott's life of Wilson has become a classic. It should be supplemented by Bernard Donoughue's excellent diary of Wilson's final term. Stephen Wall's official history of Britain and the European Community is essential reading.

Thatcher's memoirs are an exercise in self-justification. However, a number of ministerial accounts of the Thatcher years, especially those of Heseltine, Howe and Lawson, provide a balance. Whitelaw's autobiography brings out the authentic flavour of the man; there is also a lively authorised biography by Garnett and Aitken. There are some good biographies of Thatcher, including ones by John Campbell, Hugo Young and Peter Jenkins, while one of her ministers, Gillian Shephard, has written a sympathetic portrait. The first volume of Charles Moore's authorised life is outstanding.

New Labour politicians have been extremely prolific. Blair's memoir is highly readable while Brown has produced a treatise on the crash. The third man, Peter Mandleson, described what it was like at the heart of New Labour. Two senior cabinet ministers, Alistair Darling and Jack Straw, have published revealing autobiographies, and Robin Cook explained why he resigned from the government over Iraq. Blair's chief of staff, Jonathan Powell, has written a modern Machiavelli; Alastair Campbell has provided an insight into life at No 10. Chris Mullin's three volumes of diaries give an entertaining view of a junior minister's life, while the later half of the author's diaries deals with the relationship between Blair and Brown. There are also some informative accounts by able journalists, including books by Andrew Rawnsley, James Naughtie, John Rentoul, Robert Peston, Philip Stephens, Steve Richards and Peter Riddell.

The history of the peacetime coalition has not yet been written. Meanwhile, Matthew D'Ancona has written a lively insider's story; there are also valuable accounts of the formation of the coalition by David Laws and Andrew Adonis as well as Vernon Bogdanor's *The Coalition and the Constitution*. There are also useful biographies, including Elliot and Hanning on Cameron, Janan Ganesh on George Osborne and Chris Bowers on Nick Clegg.

I found four general books helpful: Archie Brown's *The Myth of the Strong Leader,* John Campbell's *Pistols at Dawn*, David Marquand's *Britain since 1918* and Robert Skidelsky's *Britain since 1900*. Other sources are to be found in the end notes.

NOTES

1. Their Finest Hours: Churchill and Attlee

1 Frank Field (ed.), *Attlee's Great Contemporaries* (London: Continuum, 2009), p. 157.
2 Peter Hennessy, *The Prime Minister: The Office and its Holders since 1945* (London: Allen Lane, 2000), p. 148.
3 Kenneth Harris, *Attlee* (London: Weidenfeld and Nicolson, 1982), p. 179.
4 Giles Radice, *The Tortoise and the Hares* (London: Politico's, 2008).
5 See Winston Churchill, *My Early Life* (London: Butterworth, 1930) for an entertaining description of his exploits.
6 Randolph Churchill and Martin Gilbert, *Biography of Churchill, Companion Volume 1* (London: Heinemann, 1966–86) p. 751.
7 Roy Jenkins, *Churchill* (London: Macmillan, 2001), p. 447.
8 Robert Rhodes James, *Churchill: A Study in Failure* (London: Penguin, 1970).
9 C.R. Attlee, *As it Happened* (London: Odhams Press, 1956), p. 9.
10 Harris, *Attlee*, p. 15.
11 Attlee, *As it Happened*, p. 26.
12 Roy Jenkins, *Mr Attlee: An Interim Biography* (London: William Heinemann, 1948), p. 44.
13 Harris, *Attlee*, p. 64.
14 Hugh Dalton, *The Political Diary of Hugh Dalton*, ed. Ben Pimlott (London: Jonathan Cape, 1986), pp. 312–13.
15 Hansard, HC Deb., 7 May 1940, vol. 36, col. 1093.
16 Ibid., col. 1094.
17 Ibid., col. 1150.
18 Harold Nicolson, *Diaries and Letters 1939–45* (London: Collins, 1967), p. 79.
19 Hugh Dalton, *The Fateful Years: Memoirs 1931–1945* (London: Frederick Muller, 1957), p. 306.
20 Winston Churchill, *The Second World War, Vol. 1: The Gathering Storm* (London: Cassell, 1949), pp. 595–6.
21 David Dilks (ed.), *Diaries of Sir Alexander Cadogan 1938–1945* (London: Cassell, 1971), p. 280.
22 Francis Williams, *A Prime Minister Remembers* (London: Heinemann, 1961), pp. 32–3.

23 War Cabinet no. 119 of 1940, quoted in Martin Gilbert, *Finest Hour* (London: Heinemann, 1989), p. 312.

24 Churchill, *The Gathering Storm*, p. 600.

25 Attlee, *As it Happened*, p. 132.

26 Churchill, *The Gathering Storm*, p. 600.

27 Alan Bullock, *The Life and Times of Ernest Bevin, Vol. 1: Trades Union Leader 1881–1940* (London: Heinemann, 1960), p. 652.

28 Report of the Annual Conference of the Labour Party 1940, pp. 123–4.

29 Hansard, HC Deb., 13 May 1940, vol. 360, col. 1502.

30 The National Archives, Public Record Office (TNA, PRO) CAB 65/13, confidential annexe to War Cabinet minutes, 26 May 1940, 9 a.m.

31 TNA, PRO, CAB, 65/13, confidential annexe to War Cabinet minutes, 27 May 1948, 4.30 p.m.

32 Halifax's diary, 27 May 1940, quoted in John Lukacs, *Five Days in London, May 1940* (New Haven, CT, and London: Yale University Press, 1999), p. 155.

33 TNA, PRO, CAB 65/13, confidential annexe to War Cabinet minutes, 28 May 1940, 4 p.m.

34 TNA, PRO, CAB 65/13, confidential annexe to War Cabinet minutes, 28 May 1940, 7 p.m.

35 Lukas, *Five Days in London*, p. 2.

36 Chief of Staff paper 168 of 1940, 27 May 1948, Cabinet Papers, 80/11, quoted in Martin Gilbert, *Finest Hour*, p. 408.

37 Hansard, HC Deb., 20 August 1940, vol. 364, col. 1167.

38 Clement Attlee, in *Churchill by his Contemporaries* (London: Hodder and Stoughton, 1965), p. 16.

39 Geoffrey Best, *Churchill: A Study in Greatness* (London: Penguin, 2002), p. 188.

40 Winston Churchill, *The Second World War, Vol. 3: The Grand Alliance* (London: Cassell, 1950), p. 3.

41 Quoted in Dalton, *The Fateful Years*, p. 358.

42 Paul Addison, *The Road to 1945: British Politics and the Second World War* (London: Quartet, 1977), chs 4 and 5.

43 Quoted in Michael Foot, *Aneurin Bevan: A Biography, Vol. 1: 1897–1945* (London: MacGibbon and Lee, 1962), p. 498.

44 See Hugh Dalton, *The Second World War Diary of Hugh Dalton, 1940–45*, ed. Ben Pimlott (London: Jonathan Cape, 1986), pp. 500–1.

45 Nicolson, *Diaries and Letters 1939–1945*, p. 276.

46 Unpublished diary of R.M. Barrington-Ward, 8 March 1942.

47 Robert Crowcroft, *Attlee's War* (London: I.B.Tauris, 2011).

48 Ibid., p. 231.

49 See J.M. Lee, *The Churchill Coalition 1940–1945* (London: Batsford, 1980), p. 84.

50 Quoted in Jenkins, *Mr Attlee*, pp. 229–30.

51 See Attlee's essay in *Churchill by his Contemporaries*.

52 Best, *Churchill*, p. 304.

53 Dalton, *Second World War Diary*, p. 142.

54 Quoted in Ben Pimlott, *Hugh Dalton* (London: Jonathan Cape, 1985), p. 48.

55 James Chuter Ede, *Labour and Wartime Coalition: From the Diaries of James Chuter Ede, 1941–45* (London: Historians' Press, 1987), 18 February 1942.

56 Hansard, HC Deb., 2 July 1942, vol 381, col. 528.

57 Martin Gilbert, *Road to Victory: Winston S. Churchill 1941–1945* (London: Heinemann, 1986), p. 154.

58 *Churchill by his Contemporaries*, p. 32.

59 Quoted in Harris, *Attlee*, pp. 220–1.

60 Crowcroft, *Attlee's War*, p. 145; for the official circulated record of the War Cabinet meeting of 12 and 15 February, see TNA, PRO, CAB 65/33, 28th and 29th conclusions; for the longhand record of the meetings contained in the Cabinet Secretary's notebook, TNA, PRO, CAB 195/2, pp. 76–81.

61 Dalton, *Second World War Diary*, p. 557.

62 Addison, *The Road to 1945*, pp. 227–8.

63 Crowcroft, *Attlee's War*, p. 145.

64 TNA, PRO, CAB 65/40, WM (43) 190, confidential annexe to War Cabinet minutes, 14 October 1943, also Churchill interview, 22 October 1943, cited in W.P. Crozier: *Off the Record: Political Interviews, 1933–43*, ed. A.J.P. Taylor (London: Hutchinson, 1973).

65 TNA, Prime Minister's Office Files (PREM) 4/88/1, unsent note by Churchill to Attlee, 20 November 1944.

66 Harris, *Attlee*, pp. 242–3; for full letter; also John Colville, *The Fringes of Power: Downing Street Diaries 1939–1955* (London: Phoenix, 2005), p. 526.

67 TNA, PREM 4/65/4, Churchill to Eden, 12 May 1945, quoted in Addison, *The Road to 1945*, p. 257.

68 Winston Churchill, *The Second World War, Vol. 6: Triumph and Tragedy* (London: Cassell, 1953), p. 512.

69 Dalton, *The Fateful Years*, p. 459.

70 Quoted in Bernard Donoughue and G.W. Jones, *Herbert Morrison* (London: Weidenfeld and Nicolson, 1973), p. 332.

71 Isaac Kramnick and Barry Sherman Harold Laski, *A Life on the Left* (London: Hamish Hamilton, 1993), pp. 480–1.

72 Ibid., p. 481.

73 Quote in Giles Radice (ed.), *What Needs to Change: New Visions for Britain* (London: HarperCollins, 1996), p. 253.

74 Quoted in Addison, *The Road to 1945*, p. 265.

75 Jenkins, *Churchill*, p. 704.

76 R.B. McCallum and A. Readman *The British General Election of 1945* (London: Macmillan, 1999), p. 175.

77 Attlee, in *Churchill by his Contemporaries*, p. 21.

2. New Jerusalem: Bevin and Morrison

1 Bernard Donoughue and G.W. Jones, *Herbert Morrison* (London: Weidenfeld and Nicolson, 1973), p. 346.
2 Ibid., p. 346.
3 Ibid., p. 415.
4 Ibid., p. 345.
5 Francis Williams, *Ernest Bevin: Portrait of a Great Englishman* (London: Hutchinson, 1952), p. 41.
6 Alan Bullock, *The Life and Times of Ernest Bevin* (London: Heinemann, 1960), vol. 1, p. 365.
7 Lord Morrison of Lambeth, *Herbert Morrison: An Autobiography* (London, Odhams Press, 1960), p. 19.
8 Donoughue and Jones, *Herbert Morrison*, p. 7.
9 Ibid., p. 12.
10 Morrison, *Autobiography*, p. 52.
11 Ibid., p. 53.
12 Donoughue and Jones, *Herbert Morrison*, p. 28.
13 Margaret Cole (ed.), *Beatrice Webb's Diaries 1924–1932* (London: Langarans Green, 1956), 23 January 1930.
14 Frank Field (ed.), *Attlee's Great Contemporaries* (London: Continuum, 2009), p. 128.
15 Williams, *Ernest Bevin*, p. 187.
16 Hansard, HC Deb., 28 March 1924, vol. 57, col. 1742.
17 Archives of the British Labour Party, Cardiff University, Labour Party Conference Report 1932, pp. 214–16.
18 Donoughue and Jones, *Herbert Morrison*, p. 235.
19 Williams, *Ernest Bevin*, p. 231.
20 Robert Crowcroft, *Attlee's War* (London: I.B.Tauris, 2011), p. 161.
21 Trinity College, Cambridge, Butler Papers, G15 p. 37 notes by Butler, 25 May 1943.
22 Bullock, *Ernest Bevin*, vol. 2, p. 117.
23 Kenneth Harris, *Attlee* (London: Weidenfeld and Nicolson, 1982), p. 224.
24 Bodleian Library, Attlee Papers, Morrison to Attlee, 24 July 1945.
25 Francis Williams, *A Prime Minister Remembers* (London: Heinemann, 1961), p. 4.
26 Hugh Dalton, *The Fateful Years: Memoirs 1931–1945* (London: Fredrick Muller, 1957), p. 468.
27 Bullock, *Ernest Bevin*, vol. 2, p. 394.
28 Dalton, *The Fateful Years*, p. 469.
29 Ibid., p. 470.
30 Ibid., p. 479.
31 Bullock, *Ernest Bevin*, vol. 3, p. 55.

32 John Maynard Keynes, *The Collected Writings of John Maynard Keynes, Vol. 24: Our Overseas Financial Prospects*, ed. Donald Moggridge (London: Macmillan, 1979), pp. 398–411.

33 TNA, PRO, CAB, 195/3, note by Sir Norman Brook, Cabinet Secretary, of Cabinet meeting, 6 November 1945, 4.30 p.m., p. 325.

34 Hansard, HL Deb., 18 December 1945, vol. 138, col. 783.

35 Edmund Dell, *The Chancellors* (London: HarperCollins, 1996), p. 61.

36 Donoughe and Jones, *Herbert Morrison*, p. 357.

37 Ibid., p. 376.

38 Quoted in ibid., p. 371.

39 Bullock, *Ernest Bevin*, vol. 3, p. 133.

40 Williams, *Ernest Bevin*, p. 256.

41 Bullock, *Ernest Bevin*, vol. 3, pp. 362–3.

42 Donoughue and Jones, *Herbert Morison*, p. 402.

43 Hugh Dalton, *The Political Diary of Hugh Dalton*, ed. Ben Pimlott (London: Jonathan Cape, 1986), p. 405.

44 Hugh Dalton, *High Tide and After: Memoirs 1945–1960* (London: Frederick Muller, 1962), p. 230.

45 Henry Pelling, *A Short History of the Labour Party* (London: Macmillan, 1961), p. 125.

46 Dalton, *High Tide and After*, p. 245.

47 Harris, *Attlee*, p. 349.

48 Dalton, *High Tide and After*, p. 245.

49 Harris, *Attlee*, p. 350.

50 Donoughue and Jones, *Herbert Morrison*, p. 425.

51 Kenneth O. Morgan, *Labour in Power 1945–51* (Oxford: Clarendon Press, 1984), p. 275.

52 David Watt, 'Withdrawal from Greece', in Michael Sissons and Philip French (eds), *Age of Austerity* (London: Hodder and Stoughton, 1963), p. 105.

53 Bullock, *Ernest Bevin*, vol. 3, p. 404.

54 Hansard, HC Deb., 22 January 1948, vol. 446, cols 383–409.

55 'Western Union', *The Times*, 23 January 1948.

56 Marshall to British Ambassador, 12 March 1948, in *Foreign Relations of the United States, 1972–5* (Washington, DC: Office of the Historian of the US Department of State).

57 Bullock, *Ernest Bevin*, vol. 3, p. 672.

58 Williams, *Bevin*, p. 268.

59 TNA, PRO, CAB 128/16, 54 conclusions, 29 August 1949.

60 Edwin Plowden, *An Industrialist in the Treasury: The Post-War Years* (London: André Deutsch, 1989), pp. 61–2.

61 Ibid., p. 64.

62 Donoughue and Jones, *Herbert Morrison*, p. 443.

63 Ibid., p. 446.
64 Ibid., p. 442.
65 Ibid., p. 451.
66 Ibid., p. 452.
67 Ibid., pp. 453–4.
68 Plowden, *An Industrialist in the Treasury*, p. 93.
69 Dean Achesen, *Present at the Creation: My Years in the State Department* (London: Hamish Hamilton, 1970), p. 478.
70 Ibid., p. 384.
71 Bullock, *Ernest Bevin*, vol. 3, p. 856.
72 Donoughue and Jones, *Herbert Morrison*, p. 466.
73 Bullock, *Ernest Bevin*, p. 834.
74 Harris, *Attlee*, p. 472.
75 Donoughe and Jones, *Herbert Morrison*, p. 505.
76 Ibid., p. 490.
77 Morgan, *Labour in Power*, p. 503.

3. Never Had it so Good: Macmillan and Butler

1 D.R. Thorpe, *Supermac* (London: Chatto and Windus, 2010), p. 15.
2 Ibid., p. 28.
3 'Macmillan, (Maurice) Harold', *Dictionary of National Biography* (Oxford: Oxford University Press, 2004–14).
4 Thorpe, *Supermac*, p. 51.
5 Ibid., p. 58.
6 Harold Macmillan, *Winds of Change* (London: Macmillan, 1966), p. 110.
7 Alistair Horne, *Macmillan* (London: Macmillan, 1988), vol. 1, p. 57.
8 Thorpe, *Supermac*, p. 76.
9 Macmillan, *Winds of Change*, p. 155.
10 R.A. Butler, *The Art of the Possible* (London: Hamish Hamilton, 1971), pp. 5–6.
11 Ibid., p. 9.
12 Ibid., p. 16.
13 Anthony Howard, *Rab: The Life of R.A. Butler* (London: Cape, 1987), p. 30.
14 Butler, *The Art of the Possible*, p. 30.
15 Thorpe, *Supermac*, p. 101.
16 *The Times*, 27 May and 28 May 1930.
17 Roy Jenkins, *Churchill* (London: Macmillan, 2001), p. 457.
18 Hansard, HC Deb., 5 June 1935, vol. 302, col. 1911.
19 Howard, *Rab*, p. 64.
20 Butler, *The Art of the Possible*, p. 61.
21 Hansard, HC Deb., 5 October 1938, vol. 339, cols 453–4.

22 Thorpe, *Supermac*, p. 136.

23 Butler, *The Art of Possible*, p. 77.

24 Howard, *Rab*, p. 87.

25 Harold Nicolson, *Diaries 1930–39* (London: Collins, 1966), 11 April 1939.

26 Horne, *Macmillan*, vol. 1, p. 126.

27 Harold Macmillan, *The Macmillan Diaries, Vol. 1: The Cabinet Years, 1950–57* (London: Macmillan, 2003), 13 October 1954.

28 Butler, *The Art of the Possible*, p. 85.

29 Howard, *Rab*, pp. 97–8.

30 Butler, *The Art of the Possible*, p. 82.

31 Harold Macmillan, *The Blast of War, 1939–1945* (London: Macmillan, 1967), p. 161.

32 *Sunday Telegraph*, 9 February 1964.

33 Hansard, HC Deb., 8 December 1944, vol. 406, col. 908.

34 Thorpe, *Supermac*, p. 202.

35 Nikolai Tolstoy, *The Minister and the Massacres* (London: Hutchinson, 1986).

36 Anthony Cowgill et al., *The Repatriations from Austria in 1945: Report from an Inquiry* (London: Sinclair-Stevenson, 1990).

37 Harold Macmillan, *War Diaries* (London: Macmillan, 1984), p. 757.

38 Charles Williams, *Harold Macmillan* (London: Weidenfeld and Nicolson, 2009), p. 174.

39 Butler, *The Art of the Possible*, p. 87.

40 Ibid., p. 90.

41 Butler, *The Art of the Possible*, p. 92.

42 Howard, *Rab*, p. 129.

43 Butler, *The Art of the Possible*, p. 120.

44 D.R. Thorpe, *The Uncrowned Prime Ministers* (London: Parkhouse, 1980), pp. 181–2.

45 Butler, *The Art of the Possible*, p. 132.

46 Ibid., p. 144.

47 Horne, *Macmillan*, vol. 1, p. 297.

48 Ibid., p. 290.

49 Howard, *Rab*, p. 158.

50 Thorpe, *Supermac*, p. 284.

51 Howard, *Rab*, p. 158.

52 Williams, *Harold Macmillan*, p. 188.

53 Butler, *The Art of the Possible*, p. 149.

54 Reginald Maudling, *Memoirs* (London: Sidgewick and Jackson, 1978), pp. 45–6.

55 Butler, *The Art of the Possible*, p. 154.

56 Horne, *Macmillan*, vol. 1, p. 332.

57 Butler, *The Art of the Possible*, p. 157.

58 J.C.R. Dow, *The Management of the British Economy 1945–60* (Cambridge: Cambridge University Press, 1964), p. 77.

59 *The Economist*, 13 February 1954, p. 440.

60 Macmillan, *The Macmillan Diaries, Vol. 1*, 4 July 1953.

61 Thorpe, *Supermac*, p. 283.

62 Horne, *Macmillan*, vol. 1, p. 34.

63 Butler, *Art of the Possible*, p. 173.

64 Thorpe, *Supermac*, p. 299.

65 Macmillan, *The Macmillan Diaries, Vol. 1*, 9 January 1955.

66 Howard, *Rab*, p. 213.

67 Macmillan, *The Macmillan Diaries, Vol. 1*, 28 March 1956.

68 Hansard, HC Deb., 27 October 1955, vol. 545, col. 408.

69 Butler, *The Art of the Possible*, p. 180.

70 TNA, PREM 5/228, Harold Macmillan to Sir Anthony Eden, 24 October 1955.

71 Edward Heath, *The Course of My Life* (London: Hodder and Stoughton, 1998), p. 175.

72 Macmillan, *The Macmillan Diaries, Vol. 1*, 1 August 1956.

73 Ibid., 3 August 1956.

74 Horne, *Macmillan*, vol. 1, p. 439.

75 Williams, *Harold Macmillan*, p. 265.

76 Horne, *Macmillian*, vol. 1, p. 442.

77 TNA, Cabinet Minutes (CM) 56 80 conclusions, 6 November 1956.

78 TNA, CM 54th conclusions, 27 July 1956.

79 Butler, *The Art of the Possible*, p. 192.

80 'Butler, Richard Austen', *Dictionary of National Biography*.

81 Maudling, *Memoirs*, p. 64.

82 Butler, *The Art of the Possible*, p. 194.

83 Ibid., p. 194.

84 Heath, *The Course of my Life*, p. 179.

85 Butler, *The Art of the Possible*, p. 196.

86 Horne, *Macmillan*, vol. 1, p. 447.

87 Thorpe, *Supermac*, p. 365.

88 Macmillan, *The Macmillan Diaries, Vol. 1*, 3 February 1957.

89 Howard, *Rab*, pp. 249–50.

90 Ibid., p. 250.

91 Thorpe, *Supermac*, p. 373.

92 Horne, *Macmillan*, vol. 2, p. 27.

93 Thorpe, *Supermac*, p. 399.

94 Harold Macmillan, *The Macmillan Diaries, Vol. 2: Prime Minister and Beyond, 1957–66* (London: Macmillan 2009), 7 January 1958.

95 Thorpe, *Supermac*, p. 430.

96 Harold Wilson, *A Prime Minister on Prime Ministers* (London: Weidenfeld and Nicolson, 1977), p. 315.

97 Macmillan, *The Macmillan Diaries, Vol. 2*, 1 September 1959.

98 Horne, *MacMillan*, vol. 2, pp. 151–2.

99 Macmillan, *The Macmillan Diaries, Vol. 2*, 9 October 1959.
100 Extract from Roy Jenkins, *Portraits and Miniatures* (London: Macmillan, 1993).
101 Macmillan, *The Macmillan Diaries, Vol. 2*, 18 October 1959.
102 Howard, *Rab*, p. 269.
103 Butler, *The Art of the Possible*, p. 199.
104 Ibid., p. 197.
105 Ibid., pp. 202–3.
106 Howard, *Rab*, p. 266.
107 Butler, *The Art of the Possible*, p. 200.
108 Howard, *Rab*, p. 286.
109 Ibid.
110 Peter Hennessy, *Having it so Good: Britain in the Fifties* (London: Penguin, 2006), pp. 577–97.
111 Robert Shepherd, *Iain Macleod* (London: Hutchinson, 1994), p. 162.
112 Horne, *Macmillan*, vol. 2, p. 188.
113 Anthony Sampson, *Macmillan: A Study in Ambiguity* (London: Allen Lane, 1967), p. 188.
114 Hennessy, *Having it so Good*, p. 597.
115 Michael Chorlton, *The Price of Victory* (London: BBC Books, 1983), p. 237.
116 Hennessy, *Having it so Good*, p. 615.
117 Sampson, *Macmillan*, p. 212.
118 Macmillan, *The Macmillan Diaries, Vol. 2*, 30 July 1962.
119 Ibid., 21 August 1962.
120 Howard, *Rab*, p. 285.
121 Butler, *The Art of the Possible*, pp. 208–30.
122 Harold Macmillan, *At the End of the Day* (London: Macmillan, 1973), p. 92.
123 Butler, *The Art of the Possible*, p. 232.
124 Horne, *Macmillan*, vol. 2, p. 439.
125 Macmillan, *The Macmillan Diaries, Vol. 2*, 28 January 1963.
126 Butler, *The Art of the Possible*, p. 199.
127 Ibid., p. 231.
128 Howard, *Rab*, p. 290.
129 Dennis Walters, *Not Always with the Pack* (London: Constable, 1989), p. 111.
130 Howard, *Rab*, p. 305.
131 Macmillan, *The Macmillan Diaries, Vol. 2*, 4 October 1963.
132 Howard, *Rab*, p. 313.
133 Macmillan, *The Macmillan Diaries, Vol. 2*, 14 October 1963.
134 Thorpe, *Supermac*, p. 624.
135 Butler, *The Art of the Possible*, p. 248.
136 Williams, *Harold Macmillan*, p. 451.
137 Thorpe, *Supermac*, p. 613.
138 Horne, *Macmillan*, vol. 2, p. 384

4. Into Europe: Wilson and Heath

1 Philip Ziegler, *Edward Heath* (London: Harper Press, 2010), p. 161.
2 Roy Jenkins, *Life at the Centre* (London: Macmillan, 1991), p. 416.
3 Stephen Wall, *Britain and the European Community* (London: Routledge, 2013), p. 2.
4 Bernard Donoughue, *The Heat of the Kitchen* (London: Politico's, 2003).
5 Edward Heath, *The Course of my Life* (London: Hodder and Stoughton, 1998), p. 4.
6 Ben Pimlott, *Harold Wilson* (London: HarperCollins, 1992), p. 66.
7 Heath, *The Course of my Life*, p. 68.
8 Ibid., p. 71.
9 Philip Ziegler, *Wilson: The Authorized Life* (London: Weidenfeld and Nicolson, 1993), p. 28.
10 Ziegler, *Edward Heath*, p. 40.
11 Pimlott, *Harold Wilson*, pp. 78–9.
12 Heath, *The Course of my Life*, p. 97.
13 Ibid., p. 96.
14 Ibid., p. 106.
15 Pimlott, *Harold Wilson*, p. 93.
16 Ibid., p. 93.
17 Roy Jenkins, 'Harold Wilson', *Dictional of National Biography* (Oxford: Oxford University Press, 2004).
18 Pimlott, *Harold Wilson*, p. 186.
19 Harold Macmillan, *Riding the Storm: 1956–59* (London: Macmillan, 1971), p. 48.
20 Jenkins, 'Harold Wilson'.
21 Hansard, HC Deb., 26 June 1950, vol. 476, cols 959–64.
22 Ziegler, *Edward Heath*, p. 88.
23 Heath, *The Course of my Life*, p. 169.
24 Douglas Hurd, 'Heath, Sir Edward Richard George', *Dictionary of National Biography*.
25 Ibid.
26 Ziegler, *Edward Heath*, p. 109.
27 Ibid., p. 121.
28 Heath, *The Course of my Life*, pp. 228–9.
29 Wall, *Britain and the European Community*, p. 8.
30 Heath, *The Course of my Life*, pp. 234–5.
31 Hansard, HC Deb., 3 August 1961, vol. 645, cols 1651–714.
32 Richard Crossman, *Diaries of a Cabinet Minister* (London: Hamish Hamilton, 1975), vol. 1, pp. 292–3.
33 Ziegler, *Edward Heath*, p. 163.
34 James Griffiths, *Pages from Memory* (London: Dent, 1964), pp. 186–7.

35 James Callaghan, *Time and Chance* (London: Politico's, 2006), p. 192.

36 Pimlott, *Harold Wilson*, p. 400.

37 *The Times*, 19 March 1966.

38 Peter Paterson, *Tired and Emotional: The Life of Lord George Brown* (London: Chatto and Windus, 1993), p. 192.

39 Ibid., p. 214.

40 Pimlott, *Harold Wilson*, p. 435.

41 Harold Wilson, *Labour Government 1964–70* (London: Weidenfeld and Nicolson, 1971), p. 384.

42 Wall, *Britain and the European Community*, pp. 150–1.

43 Ibid., p. 163.

44 Hansard, HC Deb., 2 May 1967, vol. 746, cols 310–32.

45 Wall, *Britain and the European Community*, pp. 216–17.

46 Ibid., p. 158.

47 Ibid., p. 330.

48 Hansard, HC Deb., 10 February 1970, vol. 795, cols 1080–97.

49 David Butler and Michael Pinto-Duschinski, *The British General Election of 1970* (London: Macmillan, 1971), p. 347.

50 Heath, *The Course of my Life*, pp. 358–60.

51 Ibid., p. 372.

52 Jenkins, *Life at the Centre*, p. 316.

53 Pimlott, *Harold Wilson*, p 581.

54 Wall, *Britain and the European Community*, p. 415.

55 Jenkins, *Life at the Centre*, p. 320.

56 Denis Healey, *The Time of my Life* (London: Politico's, 2006), p. 360.

57 Jenkins, *Life at the Centre*, p. 332.

58 Tony Benn, *The Benn Diaries* (London: Hutchinson, 1995), 11 November 1970, p. 316.

59 Pimlott, *Harold Wilson*, p. 592.

60 Jenkins, *Life at the Centre*, p. 365.

61 Roy Hattersley, *Who Goes Home?* (London: Abacus, 1995), p. 152.

62 Hansard, HC Deb., 3 April 1974, vol. 871, col. 1260.

63 Hugo Young, *This Blessed Plot* (London: Macmillan, 1999), p. 289.

64 Gallup poll quoted in D. Butler and U.W. Kitzinger, *The 1975 Referendum* (London: Macmillan 1976), p. 253.

65 Jenkins, *Life at the Centre*, p. 424.

66 Pimlott, *Harold Wilson*, p. 659.

67 Quoted in Wall, *Britain and the European Community*, p. 589.

68 *Guardian*, 14 March 1975.

5. Thatcher's Revolution: Thatcher and Whitelaw

1 Ronald Millar, *A View from the Wings* (London: Weidenfeld and Nicolson, 1993), p. 319.
2 Margaret Thatcher, *The Downing Street Years* (London: HarperCollins, 1993), p. 27.
3 Nigel Lawson, *The View from No. 11* (London: Bantam, 1992), p. 709.
4 M. Garnett and I. Aitken, *Splendid! Splendid!* (London: Cape, 2002), p. 219.
5 Thatcher, *The Downing Street Years*, p. 27.
6 William Whitelaw, *The Whitelaw Memoirs* (London: Headline, 1990), p. 3.
7 Garnett and Aitken, *Splendid! Splendid!*, p. 17.
8 Whitelaw, *The Whitelaw Memoirs*, p. 21.
9 Ibid.
10 Ibid., p. 43.
11 Garnett and Aitken, *Splendid! Splendid!*, p. 37.
12 Whitelaw, *The Whitelaw Memoirs*, p. 46.
13 Ibid., p. 49.
14 Charles Moore, *Margaret Thatcher, Vol. 1* (London: Allen Lane, 2013), p. 35.
15 Ibid., p. 41.
16 John Campbell, *The Iron Lady* (London: Vintage Books, 2012), pp. 12–13.
17 Gillian Shephard, *The Real Iron Lady* (London: Biteback, 2013), p. 133.
18 Campbell, *The Iron Lady*, p. 19.
19 Moore, *Margaret Thatcher*, p. 77.
20 Margaret Thatcher, *The Path to Power* (London: HarperCollins, 1995), p. 66.
21 Moore, *Margaret Thatcher*, p. 135.
22 Garnett and Aitken, *Splendid! Splendid!*, p. 51.
23 Moore, *Margaret Thatcher*, p. 151.
24 Richard Crossman, *Diaries of a Cabinet Minister* (London: Hamish Hamilton, 1975), vol. 3, 26 October 1969.
25 Moore, *Margaret Thatcher*, p. 179.
26 Philip Ziegler, *Edward Heath* (London: Harper Press, 2010), p. 178.
27 Garnett and Aitken, *Splendid! Spendid!*, p. 116.
28 Whitelaw, *The Whitelaw Memoirs*, p. 118.
29 Garnett and Aitken, *Splendid! Splendid!*, p. 162.
30 Whitelaw, *The Whitelaw Memoirs*, p. 153.
31 Ibid., p. 168.
32 Ibid., p. 169.
33 Ziegler, *Edward Heath*, p. 435.
34 Moore, *Margaret Thatcher*, p. 214.
35 Ibid., p. 227.
36 Campbell, *The Iron Lady*, p. 16.
37 Philip Whitehead *The Writing on the Wall* (London: Michael Joseph, 1985), p. 330.
38 Whitelaw, *The Whitelaw Memoirs*, p. 177.

39 Garnett and Aitken, *Splendid! Splendid!*, p. 198.

40 Moore, *Margaret Thatcher*, p. 265.

41 Campbell, *The Iron Lady*, p. 74.

42 Jim Prior, *A Balance of Power* (London: Hamish Hamilton, 1986).

43 Whitelaw, *The Whitelaw Memoirs*, p. 183.

44 Garnett and Aitken, *Splendid! Splendid!*, p. 204.

45 Moore, *Margaret Thatcher*, p. 276.

46 Ibid., p. 275.

47 Garnett and Aitken, *Splendid! Splendid!*, p. 205.

48 Barbara Castle, *The Castle Diaries 1974–76* (London: Weidenfeld and Nicolson, 1980), p. 303.

49 Moore, *Margaret Thatcher*, p. 296.

50 Margaret Thatcher, *The Autobiography* (London: HarperPress, 2013), p. 176.

51 Whitelaw, *The Whitelaw Memoirs*, p. 189.

52 Campbell, *The Iron Lady*, p. 78.

53 Whitelaw, *The Whitelaw Memoirs*, p. 195.

54 Garnett and Aitken, *Splendid! Splendid!*, p. 231.

55 Whitelaw, *The Whitelaw Memoirs*, p. 201.

56 Moore, *Margaret Thatcher*, p. 404.

57 Campbell, *The Iron Lady*, p. 114.

58 Ibid., p. 121.

59 Peter Hennessy, *The Prime Minister: The Office and its Holders since 1945* (London: Allen Lane, 2000), p. 405.

60 Ibid., p. 430.

61 Moore, *Margaret Thatcher*, p. 474.

62 Ibid., pp. 480–1.

63 Thatcher, *The Downing Street Years*, p. 97.

64 Jenkins, *Mrs Thatcher's Revolution* (London: Cape, 1987), p. 99.

65 Moore, *Margaret Thatcher*, pp. 631–2.

66 Ibid., p. 638.

67 Campbell, *The Iron Lady*, p. 180.

68 Nicholas Ridley, *My Style of Government* (London: Hutchinson, 1991), p. 175.

69 Thatcher, *The Downing Street Years*, p. 149.

70 Whitelaw, *The Whitelaw Memoirs*, p. 259.

71 Thatcher, *The Downing Street Years*, p. 307.

72 Campbell, *The Iron Lady*, p. 203.

73 Ibid., p. 191.

74 Thatcher, *The Downing Street Years*, p. 188.

75 Whitelaw, *The Whitelaw Memoirs*, p. 275.

76 Thatcher, *The Downing Street Years*, p. 208.

77 Max Hastings and Simon Jenkins, *The Battle for the Falklands* (London: Michael Joseph, 1983).

78 Jenkins, *Mrs Thatcher's Revolution*, pp. 164–5.

79 Peter Riddell, *The Thatcher Decade* (Oxford: Blackwell, 1991).

80 Peter Jenkins *The Thatcher Revolution*, p. 370.

81 Thatcher, *The Downing Street Years*, p. 307.

82 Ibid., p. 307.

83 Ibid.

84 Author's interview with Lord Jopling.

85 Garnett and Aitken, *Splendid! Splendid!* p. 306.

86 Whitelaw, *The Whitelaw Memoirs*, p. 333.

87 Giles Radice, *Diaries 1980–2001* (London: Weidenfeld and Nicolson, 2004).

88 Lawson, *The View from No. 11*, p. 574.

89 Garnett and Aitken, *Splendid! Splendid!*, p. 309.

90 Hugo Young, *One of Us* (London: Macmillan, 1989), p. 455.

91 Whitelaw, *The Whitelaw Memoirs*, p. 335.

92 Garnett and Aitken, *Splendid! Splendid!*, p. 321.

93 Ibid., p. 326.

94 Thatcher, *The Downing Street Years*, p. 27.

95 Campbell, *The Iron Lady*, p. 473.

96 Lawson, *The View from No. 11*, p. 290.

97 *New Statesman*, 1 October 2002.

98 Garnett and Aitken, *Splendid! Splendid!*, p. 323.

99 Lawson, *The View from No. 11*, p. 709.

100 Geoffrey Howe, *Conflict of Loyalty* (London: Methuen, 2007), p. 548.

101 Ridley, *My Style of Government*, p. 24.

102 Howe, *Conflict of Loyalty*, p. 251.

103 Five of her former Cabinet ministers made this point in interviews with the author.

6. New Labour: Blair and Brown

1 The excellent works of Polly Toynbee and David Walker have gone some way to do this in *Did Things Get Better? An Audit of Labour's Successes* (London: Penguin, 2001); *Better or Worse? Has Labour Delivered* (London: Bloomsbury, 2005) and *The Verdict: Did Labour Change Britain?* (London: Granta, 2011).

2 Andrew Rawnsley, *The End of the Party* (London: Penguin, 2010), pp. 55–6.

3 *Observer*, 2 October 1994, quoted in John Rentoul, *Tony Blair: Prime Minister* (London: Faber, 2001), p. 13.

4 Ibid., p. 8.

5 Ibid., p. 4.

6 Rentoul, *Tony Blair*, p. 3.

7 James Naughtie, *The Rivals* (London: Fourth Estate, 2001), p. 17.

8 Anthony Seldon, *Blair* (London: Free Press, 2004), pp. 49–50.

9 *The Times*, 15 May 1993.
10 Paul Routledge, *Gordon Brown* (London: Simon & Schuster, 1998), pp. 39–40.
11 Ibid., p. 54.
12 Routledge, *Gordon Brown*, p. 76.
13 Rentoul, *Blair*, p. 118.
14 Alan Clark, *Diaries* (London: Weidenfeld and Nicolson, 1993), 8 December 1983.
15 John Campbell, *Pistols at Dawn* (London: Cape, 2009), p. 352.
16 See Giles Radice's Fabian pamphlet, *Southern Discomfort* (1992).
17 Rentoul, *Blair*, p. 180.
18 Giles Radice, *Diaries 1980–2001* (London: Weidenfeld and Nicolson, 2004), 12 April 1992.
19 Campbell, *Pistols at Dawn*, p. 363.
20 Philip Gould, *The Unfinished Revolution* (London: Little, Brown, 1998), pp. 202–3.
21 Radice, *Diaries*, 27 July 1994.
22 Alastair Campbell, *The Blair Years* (London: Arrow, 2007), 4 October 1994.
23 Radice, *Diaries*, 23 July 1996.
24 Seldon, *Blair*, p. 237.
25 Paddy Ashdown, *The Ashdown Diaries* (London: Allen Lane, 2001), p. 346.
26 Quoted in William Keegan, *The Prudence of Mr Gordon Brown* (Chichester: Wiley, 2003), pp. 148–9.
27 Author's interview with Peter Mandelson.
28 Peter Riddell, *The Unfulfilled Prime Minister* (London: Politico's, 2005), p. 42.
29 Naughtie, *The Rivals*, pp. 282–3.
30 Hansard, HC Deb., 14 May 1997, vol. 294, col. 70.
31 Robert Peston, *Brown's Britain* (London: Short Books, 2005), p. 169.
32 Andrew Rawnsley, *Servants of the People* (London: Penguin, 2000), p. 145.
33 Ibid., p. 150.
34 Rentoul, *Blair*, p. 384.
35 Radice, *Diaries*, 27 January 1999.
36 Rawnsley, *Servants of the People*, p. 339–40.
37 Campbell, *The Blair Years*, 7 June 2001.
38 Anthony Seldon, *Blair Unbound* (London: Simon & Schuster, 2007), p. 47.
39 Tony Blair, *A Journey* (London: Hutchinson, 2010), pp. 498–500.
40 Michael Barber, *Instruction to Deliver* (London: Methuen, 2008).
41 Blair, *A Journey*, p. 499.
42 Cherie Blair, *Speaking for Myself* (London: Little, Brown, 2008), p. 370.
43 *Sunday Times*, 1 May 2005.
44 Alistair Darling, *Back from the Brink* (London: Atlantic Books, 2011), p. 322.
45 Giles Radice, *Trio* (London: I.B.Tauris, 2010), p. 201.
46 Darling, *Back from the Brink*, pp. 321–3.
47 Gould, *The Unfinished Revolution*, p. 479.

7 *Peacetime Coaltion: Cameron and Clegg*

1 Francis Elliot and James Hanning, *Cameron* (London: Fourth Estate, 2012), p. 203.
2 Ibid., p. 294.
3 Philip Kavanagh and Denis Cowley, *The British General Election of 2010* (Houndmills: Palgrave Macmillan, 2010), p. 131.
4 Chris Bowers, *Nick Clegg* (London: Biteback, 2011), p. 21.
5 Matthew D'Ancona, *In it Together* (London: Viking, 2013), p. 33.
6 'David Cameron and Nick Clegg Pledge "United Coalition"', *BBC News*, 12 May 2010. Available at http://news.bbc.co.uk/1/hi/8676607.stm (accessed 23 October 2014).
7 Kavanagh and Cowley, *The British General Election of 2010*, p. 226.
8 Janen Ganesh, *George Osborne: The Austerity Chancellor* (London: Biteback, 2012), p. 251.
9 Kavanagh and Cowley, *The British General Election of 2010*, p. 224.
10 Elliot and Hanning, *Cameron*, p. 396.
11 David Laws, *22 Days in May* (London: Biteback, 2010), pp. 269–70.
12 Ibid., p. 74.
13 Kavanagh and Cowley, *The British General Election of 2010*, p. 218.
14 Andrew Adonis, *5 Days in May* (London: Biteback, 2013), p. 141.
15 Fraser Nelson, 'The Tories Said Coalition Wouldn't Work – and they Were Dead Right', *Telegraph*, 14 May 2014. Available at www.telegraph.co.uk/news/general-election-2015/10833847/The-Tories-said-coalition-wouldnt-work-and-they-were-dead-right.html (accessed 23 October 2014).
16 D'Ancona, *In it Together*, p. 38.
17 Adonis, *5 Days in May*, p. 166.
18 Ibid., pp. 168–71.
19 D'Ancona, *In it Together*, p. 59.
20 Ibid., p. 85.
21 'Divided they Fall', *The Economist*, 5 January 2013.
22 Adonis, *5 Days in May*, p. 174.

INDEX

Index